THEY BUILT THE CAPITOL

The United States Capitol, seen from the northeast. Photograph by the author

THEY BUILT THE CAPITOL

IHNA THAYER FRARY 1873—

(Select Bibliographies Reprint Series)

BOOKS FOR LIBRARIES PRESS

FREEPORT, NEW YORK

1969, 194

First Published 1940
Reprinted 1969

" Reprint of the 1940 edition"

STANDARD BOOK NUMBER:
8369-5089-5

LIBRARY OF CONGRESS CATALOG CARD NUMBER:
76-99660

PRINTED IN THE UNITED STATES OF AMERICA

PREFACE

THE GENESIS of the story told in these pages takes us back a considerable number of years to a brief stop-over in the City of Washington. I had been there before, and on various occasions had plodded through the Capitol, but only as a casual sightseer. This time, however, the stay though brief was dignified by a serious desire to make photographic records of the stately building that houses our nation's lawmakers.

I wandered innocently into the sacred precincts of the Capitol grounds, set up tripod and camera, and took the picture that is reproduced herein as the frontispiece. No sooner had the shutter given out its cheery little "click" than the law claimed me for its own, the claimant being a definitely large and impressive policeman. From his rather pointed remarks I gathered the general idea that a camera, as a camera, is regarded even by governmental authorities as a reasonably harmless item of impedimenta but— when used in conjunction with a tripod, it becomes sinister.

The combination seems to develop potentialities which, for subtle reasons not evident to my simple mind, bode no good when pointed at the Capitol of the United States. Hence my personally conducted tour, under police direction, to the office of the Architect of the Capitol.

The official objective of this trek was to equip me with a photographer's permit that should serve as a mascot against the evil eye of the camera. As the permit-issuer was out, a lengthy wait ensued which afforded opportunity to form an agreeable acquaintance with Charles E. Fairman, the veteran official in charge of the art of the Capitol.

Eventually, when the permit had been achieved, I emerged from the lower recesses of the building bearing not only the required certificate but, with what proved to be much more important in my life, a copy of Hazelton's *The National Capitol, Its Architecture, Art, and History.*

The unexpected acquisition of this handbook led my first steps into the fascinating field of Capitol history. The next acquisition was Glenn Brown's large, two volume, *History of the United States Capitol* which was retrieved from an enticingly musty and out-of-the-way old book shop.

Then came Mr. Fairman's own, *Art and Artists of the Capitol,* followed by a varied assortment of volumes from which were gleaned more or less important contributions to Capitol lore.

A visit to the Library of Congress was rewarded by a private view of original drawings for the Capitol, generously displayed by Dr. Leicester B. Holland, in whose Division of Fine Arts these precious documents are preserved. This was followed by a similar treat at the Maryland Historical Society in Baltimore, where I was thrilled to find the rejected drawings that were submitted in the original competition of 1792.

Growing interest in the Capitol itself quite naturally developed a desire for closer acquaintance with the men involved in the three-quarter-of-a-century building operation. *The Journal of Latrobe* edited by J. H. B. Latrobe, the lives of Robert Mills by H. M. Pierce Gallagher, and of Charles Bulfinch by Charles A. Place, came one after another into my library and, with the excellent biographies that are to be found in the *Dictionary of American Biography,* especially those by Fiske Kimball, made possible a fairly well rounded study of the men in question.

An inexhaustible source of data, and a referee in disputes, has been provided by an ever thoughtful government in the *Documentary History of the Construction and Development of the United States Capitol Building.* Into this ponderous tome of over thirteen hundred pages has been distilled the essence of legislation and reports pertaining to the Capitol, from more than a century's accumulation of governmental documents.

Overwhelming riches in source material are of course always available in the Division of Manuscripts, Library of Congress; while an opportunity to browse through and copy from a book of original letters from Latrobe to Lenthal (owned by Lenthal's great-grandson, Hamilton Abert) brought fresh light on intimate details pertaining to the work of construction. Articles in various magazines illuminated many an otherwise obscure passage in the story.

Still closer contact with these early wielders of the T-square, compasses and trowel was established by endless journeyings to places where their professional services had been invoked. With cameras always at hand, these visits yielded pictorial records of work by the Capitol builders from places as remote as Maine to the north, and New Orleans to the south.

Unexpected treasures turned up in unsuspected places; as for instance the original drawings of Latrobe for the old courthouse at Hagerstown, Maryland, which looked calmly down over my shoulder from their frames on the wall, while I stood all unwittingly asking the clerk whether information were available regarding the long lost building.

Documentary evidence of great value was also unearthed in various places of pilgrimage, among them being the Library of the University of South Carolina, at Columbia, which possesses a rare collection of publications by and about Robert Mills.

Especial thanks for statistical data and courtesies extended are due David Lynn, who now carries on the traditions and responsibilities of the Architect of the Capitol, an office first held by Dr. Thornton, and continued for a century and a half in the hands of such men as Latrobe, Bulfinch, and Walter. These thanks should be shared by Charles E. Fairman.

I am most deeply grateful to William M. Millikeu, Director, and to the Trustees of The Cleveland Museum of Art for their cooperation in adjusting my position on the museum staff to a part-time basis, thus affording me opportunity for research and writing.

At the Cleveland Public Library, where invaluable assistance was received from Miss Ruth Wilcox, the casual remark was made that a great-granddaughter of the French architect, Hallet, was a member of the library staff. An interview was arranged immediately and as a result the great-granddaughter, Miss Elima Adelaide Foster, copied from the Hallet family records data that have been unknown apparently to previous biographers.

Such experiences and discoveries tend to clothe the dry bones of stark history with warmth and color; and the attempt has been made here to assemble the fruits of research in such form as to add human interest to the facts regarding those who gave us our imposing Capitol. It is hoped at the same time that the great structure itself will be invested with an atmosphere replete with personalities, that will add the spark of life to the part which it plays in our nation's history.

I. T. FRARY.

The Cleveland Museum of Art,
Cleveland, Ohio.

CONTENTS

●

PLATES

INTRODUCTION

MILLIONS OF TOURISTS, visiting the City of Washington, thrill at the classic beauty, and historic significance of the Capitol. They troop through its corridors, visit sessions of Congress, and recall with awe the famous personages who have labored, fought, and made history here; but how many of these admiring millions give thought to the men in whose brains was conceived the design, and whose technical skill made possible the creation of this vast structure? They stand reverently on spots that have been hallowed by historic events, but it seldom occurs to them to wonder whose genius made possible such spots to hallow.

These millions of pilgrims may find their spinal columns all aquiver with thoughts of the great men who have moulded our nation's history in this building but, curiously enough, they experience scarcely a quiver at the thought (if they have any such thoughts) of those less heralded men who thought out and placed on paper the plans from which the fabric was built; the men who sought out stone and marble among the hills and valleys, transported it here, determined the forms into which it was to be cut, and supervised its placing in the walls.

The hypnotic spell of vocal cords and brass bands arouses tingling emotions, but creative genius, even as inspired as that which was responsible for the Capitol, is apt to be unrewarded by more than a ripple of merited recognition. Yet from the lives of these men may be distilled stories as intriguing and rich in romance as can be concocted in the imagination of the novelist.

The great pile of stone and marble on Capitol Hill was practically three-quarters of a century in building. During that period many men noted in our nation's history were concerned with its creation. Washington, Jefferson, Madison, and Jefferson Davis were among those who assumed immediate responsibility for creation, but we seldom link their names with it excepting as we consider it the theatre of their political activities. Yet to their sympathetic coöperation is due very largely the existence of the building in its present form.

They directed and controlled the selection of its designers and its design. They checked the vagaries of temperamental architects and superintendents who, had they been left to carry out their own wills, and their regrettable desires to "get even" with rivals, might very possibly have ruined the superb picture that the Capitol presents today.

Among those directly responsible for the design and its execution were Thornton, Latrobe, Bulfinch, and Walter, while Hallet, Hadfield, Hoban, Lenthal, Mills, and other master builders supplied the engineering and constructive skill required to transmute drawings and specifications into enduring and beautiful masonry.

The great structure sits so serenely on its hill that it seems always to have been there. If the mind of the casual visitor chances to wander back to its beginnings, he probably has but hazy ideas as to how and by whom it was brought into being. In view of their achievements he vaguely regards them as supermen.

Titans and geniuses these men doubtless were but as we read their story we can but learn that they were not devoid of frailties, and that the creation of even this masterpiece was in the hands of humans, not of demigods.

I

THE OLD CAPITOL

THE IMMORTALS MAKE PLANS

THE CITY OF WASHINGTON is somewhat unique in having been located and planned with the deliberate intent of making it the capital of a great nation. It was not the outgrowth of an earlier settlement; its streets, parks, squares, and avenues were drawn out on paper while the area on which the future city was to rise was still practically a wilderness, partly swamp land and partly upland covered with forest.

The location beside the Potomac, at the head of tidewater, was determined by a curious blending of unselfish patriotism and politically inspired selfishness. Some of the greatest characters in American history had a part in choosing the site, and their decision was dictated by a more or less sincere endeavor to reconcile sectional jealousies that threatened to dissolve the union of states.

News that location of the future capital was under consideration, produced the inevitable scramble for position on the part of contestants who coveted the capital city for their own, several of the sovereign states manifesting more than casual interest in acquiring the prize.

The contest began with the seat of government temporarily established at New York. That city was quite definitely agreeable to the idea of retaining governmental headquarters in her midst. Philadelphia, which had witnessed the birth of the infant republic, yearned to take it back under her protecting wings; and Annapolis offered as inducements her new State House, together with houses for representatives of the several states.

The problem of selecting and establishing a capital for the young nation was not a new one. It had been discussed even before the Constitution was adopted. Congress, in 1784 had appointed a commission to choose a site on the Delaware, and make contracts for the erection of buildings suitable for the needs of the President, Congress, and other governmental departments.

The commission charged with this responsibility had established a precedent that has been followed faithfully since then by innumerable commissions and committees—it did nothing. This sum total of achievement left for the framers of the Constitution final action in the matter, and they, in the 8th Section and 1st Article of that document, provided that "Congress shall have power to exercise exclusive legislation in all cases whatsoever, over such district (not exceeding ten miles square) as may, by cession of particular States, and the acceptance of Congress, become the seat of government of the United States."

The State of Maryland, which had not succeeded in coaxing Congress to settle down on the little hill at Annapolis, now followed up its desire for national honors and, on December 23, 1788, formally offered to provide a "District of ten miles square in this state, for the seat of government of the United States." Not to be outdone by her neighbor on the east, Virginia made a similar gesture through an act passed a year later, on December 3, 1789.

Meanwhile the Pennsylvanians had, apparently, been quite definitely alert and active for, on September 27, 1789, both houses of Congress voted to locate the Capital at Germantown. Unfortunately, for the aspirations of that city, and its neighbor Philadelphia, there was a joker somewhere in the bill which had to be extracted before the measure could take effect, and as Congress adjourned before it could be referred back to the Senate, the opposition managed to secure its defeat at the next session.

Baltimore and Wilmington had fighting chances to secure the coveted prize, and when it became evident that the site was to be somewhere along the banks of the Potomac a proposal was made in the Senate that it be located "within thirty miles of Hancock Town." This suggestion was doubtless based on the idea of having it far enough above the head of navigation to prevent attack by hostile powers.

George Washington had long entertained dreams of a capital located not too far from his beloved Mount Vernon and, during his first term as President (on July 16, 1790), signed a Senate bill establishing the future seat of government beside the Potomac, the exact location to be determined later. By the terms of this bill the President was empowered to appoint three commissioners who, under his direction, were to survey and acquire the necessary land and provide the buildings required for governmental use; all to be complete and ready for occupancy on or before the first Monday in December, 1800.

This program had not sailed the seas of politics without encountering storms; too many sections of the country had their eyes on the rich plum. Many political snarls had to be untangled, and in those days politics were politics (!) and the average citizen took his politics very, very seriously.

The agriculturalists of the South were suspicious of the money-changers of the North; and the astute financiers of the northern cities had little in common with the easy going southern planters who were content to raise endless crops of tobacco, and spend the proceeds on fine houses, fast horses, and leisurely living. There was little spirit of generous give and take at best between the two sections, and just now the possible acquisition of a national capital was something much more suggestive of taking than giving.

Finally the question was settled by a bit of polite "log rolling" which verged closely on the unsavory, and for which Thomas Jefferson became somewhat apologetic years later in the pages of his *Anas*.

Now it happened that the great financial wizard, Alexander Hamilton, as Secretary of the Treasury, was nursing as a pet project the plan to have the national government assume some $20,000,000.00 of unpaid debts that had been incurred by the several states during the Revolutionary War. As some of the states, especially those of the South, had already met their obligations, they could see no really good reason why they should pay the other fellows' debts. Argument pro and con was heated, and Congress was becoming involved in a serious deadlock, while North and South were ever more militantly arrayed against each other.

Hamilton, though sensing danger, was unwilling to drop Assumption, and in his keen mind worked out a solution. He recognized the popularity and power of Thomas Jefferson, who had just returned from his four years of diplomatic life at the court of France. There he had added "fresh laurels" to those which he had been acquiring continuously since he wrote the *Declaration of Independence*.

President Washington had invited Jefferson to be his Secretary of State and, in spite of a desire to retire to Monticello and spend his life there as a gentleman-farmer in the manner of all well bred Virginians, the gentleman from Monticello accepted the invitation of the gentleman from Mount Vernon. Both Washington and Jefferson were devotedly attached to their country estates and the agrarian life; giving up both for public careers only at great sacrifice to themselves.

Soon after Jefferson's arrival in New York (1789) Hamilton contrived to meet him on the street near the President's home. He engaged him in conversation and explained the difficulties involved in bringing together North and South and inducing them to agree on a reasonable solution of the two problems, debt assumption and capital location. Hamilton feared that the newly formed and as yet loosely knit nation might be wrecked on these two rocks of disagreement, for the little craft was far from being seaworthy. The individual states were jealous of their rights as states, and little sense of national patriotism had been developed.

So, argued Hamilton, if the South can be made to throw a few of its votes to the cause of Assumption, and the North be induced to reciprocate by giving the national Capital to the South, everyone will be satisfied, and the nation preserved from possible disintegration. With little to hold North and South together, and New England even then indulging in unpleasantly pointed talk of seceding from the South, the danger in Hamilton's estimation was acute. Would Jefferson help save the nation?

The two walked "backwards and forwards before the President's door for half an hour." (The quotation is from Jefferson's *Anas.)* "He painted pathetically the temper into which the legislature had been wrought; the disgust of those who were called the creditor states; the danger of the secession of their members, and the separation of the states. He observed that the members of the administration ought to act in concert; . . . that the President was the centre on which all administrative questions ultimately rested, and that all of us should rally around him; . . . I told him that I was really a stranger to the whole subject; that not having yet informed myself of the system of finances adopted, I knew not how far this was a necessary sequence, that undoubtedly, if its rejection endangered a dissolution of our Union at this incipient stage, I should deem that the most unfortunate of all consequences, to avert which all partial and temporary evils should be yielded."

The outcome of this conversation was an invitation to a little group of men to dine with Thomas Jefferson, Secretary of State of the United States.

It must have been a good dinner, and there may have been some excellent wine to follow! At any rate, Congress adopted Hamilton's plan for assumption of the state debts; the national government was located at Philadelphia for ten years (from 1790 to 1800) as a possible sop to Pennsylvania pride; and the Capital of the United States was then established permanently on the Maryland side of the Potomac River.

This deal has been looked upon askance ever since, and Jefferson, to excuse his participation, wrote that "The discussion took place. I could take no part in it but an exhortatory one, because I was a stranger to the circumstances which should govern it." Rather pathetically he said, "To this I was most ignorantly and innocently made to hold the candle."

Whatever may be thought of the means, the ends achieved were, (1st) the acquisition of the Capital city by the South and (2nd) enrichment of the "stock jobbing herd," as Jefferson termed the beneficiaries of the Hamiltonian scheme of debt assumption.

With these problems settled, President Washington proceeded to appoint as commissioners, to locate and build the proposed city, Thomas Johnson and Daniel Carroll of Maryland, and David Stuart of Virginia. The President was probably more familiar with this area than were the commissioners themselves, for most of his life had been spent in the vicinity, and he had made the first survey of the Potomac, above tidewater, with a party of friends in a canoe hollowed out of a large poplar tree.

On March 3, 1791, an amendment was added to the bill which established the Federal City. This permitted the District to extend across the Potomac, taking in the town of Alexandria and a part of Hunting Creek, which cuts through Washington's estate, but restricted public buildings to the Maryland side of the Potomac. This area in Virginia was later on ceded back to that state.

L'ENFANT ON THE SCENE

Having decided on a site near Georgetown, the commissioners went about the task of securing possession of the land from its owners. One of these, with a plantation known as the Widow's Mite, containing six hundred and fifty acres, refused pointblank to sell. Public interest finally compelled him to yield, and on March 30, 1791, the nineteen proprietors signed an agreement to convey their lands "in trust to the President of the United States, or Commissioners, or to such person or persons as he shall appoint." The site now occupied by the Capitol was an estate known as Cern Abby Manor, owned by Daniel Carroll.

With the land in their possession, the next move was to secure an engineer competent to plan the city. For this position President Washington chose Pierre Charles L'Enfant, who had made application previously for the position.

L'Enfant rode over the ground on horseback with the President and commissioners, afterward transmitting to them, on March 26, 1791, a written report on his observations. He speaks enthusiastically, in rather Frenchified English, of the site for the capital of a "mighty empire," stating that the "country . . . present a most eligible position for the first settlement of a great city and . . . many of the most desirable position offer for to erect the publiques edifices thereon. . . . Then the attractive local will lay all Round . . . within the which a city the capital of an extensive empire may be delineated."

Jefferson assisted L'Enfant (at the latter's request) by supplying him with maps of various European cities, which he had carefully collected during his service as Minister to France, but the Frenchman followed his individual bent and developed the plan largely in conformity with the grandiose scheme of Versailles, in which regularly laid out streets are intersected by radiating avenues.

L'Enfant was the unfortunate victim of temperament which

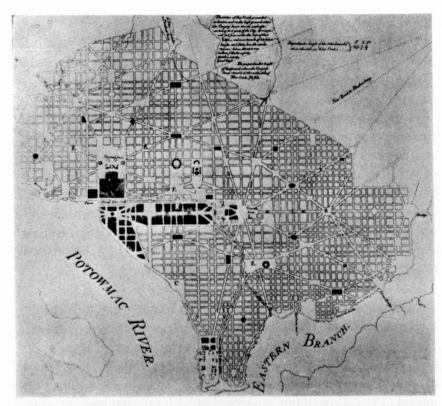

PLATE 1. Map of the City of Washington, 1791. By Pierre Charles L'Enfant.
Reproduced from Brown's "History of the United States Capitol"

involved him constantly in bickerings with those about him. He
calmly demolished a house that Mr. Carroll of Duddington was
erecting where the engineer proposed to open a street. An in-
junction served in due process of law meant nothing to him, and
he proceeded without hesitation to complete the work of demoli-
tion.

He also refused to turn over his plans for public inspection,
when ordered to do so by the commissioners, arguing that by
doing this he would enable unscrupulous speculators to avail
themselves of the information and "immediately leap upon the
best land in his vistas and architectural squares, and raise huddles
of shanties which would permanently embarrass the city."
L'Enfant was probably correct in this assumption, for land sharks
had already made themselves felt. Unfortunately for the engineer,
he had not the authority to determine policies. His independence

[7]

and defiance of authority finally became unendurable, and on March 14, 1792, he was informed by the commissioners that "We have been notified that we are no longer to consider you as engaged in the business of the federal city."

The temperamental Frenchman failed to take this let-down with meekness and humility. Instead, he left his office in a high huff, and with him went sundry documents and drawings, the absence of which might have handicapped seriously the work of planning had it not been for the efficiency of Andrew Ellicott, who retained in his mind and surveys quite perfect records of the plan and work. L'Enfant was offered five hundred guineas for his past services but, with characteristic pride, or stubbornness, he refused to accept it.

*   *   *   *

Pierre Charles L'Enfant was a tragic example of the failure that a genius can make of life if that genius is not tempered with tact. There is no question as to the ability of this young French engineer, but his inability to adjust himself to existing conditions, and to "play the game" with others, offset very largely the success that should have followed one possessed of such unusual endowments.

He was born August 2, 1754, of excellent parentage, his father, Pierre L'Enfant, having been a "painter in ordinary to the King" and one of those assigned to the famous Gobelins factory. Some of his work is to be seen today at Versailles.

When twenty-three years of age the young engineer came to this country as a volunteer to fight, at his own expense, for its freedom from British domination. He reached here a month ahead of Lafayette, spent the winter of 1777 at Valley Forge, and on February 18, 1778, was commissioned captain of engineers.

He saw service during the Revolution from the northern frontier to the Carolinas, was wounded at Savannah, and held for some time as a prisoner by the British, following the capture of Charleston.

His artistic ability was recognized and requisitioned in various ways, such as drawing a portrait of Washington at the request of Lafayette; designing a pavilion for the celebration at Philadelphia, July 15, 1782, of the birth of the French Dauphin; and designing the ensignia and diploma of the Society of the Cincinnati. He also designed the reredos of St. Paul's Church, New York; and remodeled the old Jacobean City Hall into Federal Hall, for the use of Congress when it met in that city. On this job he was permitted to spend with a lavish hand for it was hoped that the beautifully appointed building would prove a lure to keep the seat of government at New York.

Here we begin to find evidence of the temperament that kept L'Enfant continually in difficulties, and eventually wrecked his career. The offer of a handsome testimonial and ten acres of land in the vicinity of Provost Lane, as a reward for his services in remodeling the Hall, was indignantly refused by him, as he considered the amount inadequate. Some years later when low in finances he made a request for a settlement in cash, and was tendered $750.00 which he also refused.

In spite of his vagaries, L'Enfant was summoned by the President to lay out the projected Federal City on the Potomac, for Washington had come to know him well during his service in the Revolution, and recognized his ability.

Even when it became necessary to discharge him because of insubordination toward those in charge of the city, this confidence remained largely unshaken, not only in the mind of Washington, but of such astute business men as Alexander Hamilton and Robert Morris.

These two employed L'Enfant in 1792 to lay out the industrial city of Paterson, New Jersey, at the falls of the Passaic, and Morris further commissioned him to design a residence at Philadelphia. In both undertakings his imagination, as usual, ran away with his judgment, and he was dropped by the industrial group, to whom he refused to relinquish certain drawings. The Morris mansion developed into such a huge and fantastically expensive undertaking that it became one of the causes of bankruptcy for the owner, and the never-completed structure was long known as "Morris' Folly." It was torn down in 1801.

Another house, built by him for Morris' partner, John Nicholson, was said to have cost $50,000.00, a rather tidy sum for those days.

In spite of the various fiascos in which L'Enfant was involved, his ability as an engineer was recognized, and in 1794 he was given temporary employment by the government strengthening the fortifications of Fort Mifflin, on an island in the Delaware River. Again, in 1812, he was offered a position as professor of civil and military engineering at West Point, which he quite characteristically disdained to accept.

During the ensuing war with England he was employed for a time at Fort Washington, where work designed by him may still be seen, but again he got into some kind of trouble.

Apparently incapable of adjusting himself and his teeming imagination to the practical requirements of life, L'Enfant's later life was spent without employment and in poverty. He has been described as being almost daily in the Rotunda of the Capitol, a tall, gaunt figure in a blue military coat, buttoned up to the throat, wearing a black stock, but without evidence of a shirt underneath. His hair was plastered down smooth, and on his head was a tall, bell-crowned beaver hat. He usually carried under his arm a roll of papers, relating to supposed claims against the government, and in his right hand swung a large silver headed cane.

Fortunately for him he had indulgent friends in the Digges family of Maryland, who humored his idiosyncrasies and gave him the protection of their homes, in his declining years.

One of these friends described him as "quiet, harmless, and unoffending as usual," as "picking up fossils and periwinkles," and as "working hard with his instruments eight or ten hours every day" on just what plans it would be interesting for us to know today.

L'Enfant died June 14, 1825, at Green Hill, the estate of William Dudley Digges in Prince Georges County, where he had laid out the gardens. His estate was appraised at $46.00 and he was buried in the garden in an unmarked grave.

More than three-quarters of a century later, on April 28, 1909, his remains were transferred to Arlington, and laid to rest in a tomb on which his map of the city of Washington is engraved, and from which a magnificent view is had of the great city which he planned.

The original L'Enfant plan was somewhat modified by himself and by his successor, Andrew Ellicott. Since their time it has been mutilated by successive generations of scheming speculators and ignorant politicians; yet today the genius of its creator is evidenced by the broad avenues, numerous parks, circles, and splendid vistas that excite the admiration of visitors and facilitate communication throughout the city.

Some of the most striking features of the plan have been lost, perhaps forever. Conspicuous among these losses is that due to the injudicious, perhaps we had better say stupid, location of the Treasury Building on one side of the White House, and the State, War and Navy Building on the other, which completely cut off the splendid vista along Pennsylvania Avenue from the Capitol to the White House and beyond. The Library of Congress in a similar manner destroys the vista along Pennsylvania Avenue to the southeast, while other buildings that should have been tied into the grand scheme were shunted off into obscure corners for the benefit of hungry property owners and real estate mongers.

L'Enfant's vision of a "Grand Avenue" stretching from the Capitol past the site reserved for the Washington Monument and on to the Potomac was long ignored. He refers to this feature, in the notes that accompany the 1791 plan, as "a Grand avenue, 400 feet in breadth and about a mile in length, bordered with gardens, ending in a slope from the houses on each side. This avenue leads to the monument A and connects the Congress Garden with the President's Park and the well-improved field, being a part of the walk from the President's house, of about 1,800 feet in breadth and three-fourths of a mile in length."

The "Grand Avenue" is at last being realized in the Mall, and the City of Washington is gaining much of the grandeur which L'Enfant visioned for it. This is due largely to the study and recommendations made by the McMillan Commission which was authorized by a bill introduced in the Senate in 1900 by Senator James McMillan of Michigan. This was suggested in connection with the celebration of the first centennial of the Capital City, and provided for the appointment of a committee of experts to study and report on "plans for the development and improvement of the park system of the District of Columbia."

Fortunately for the success of the undertaking, wise choices were made in determining the personnel of this group, which consisted of Daniel H. Burnham and Charles F. McKim, architects; Frederick Law Olmsted, landscape architect; Augustus Saint-Gaudens, sculptor; and Charles Moore, who served as secretary.

This commission of distinguished experts submitted to the Senate, in January, 1902, a series of reports, drawings, and scale models, which formed the basis on which the development of the city plan has been conducted.

One of the most important results achieved was the abandonment by the railroads of their tracks and stations on the Mall, and the concentration of passenger traffic in a great Union Terminal.

Great credit is due those responsible for planning and carrying through this project, but even with the present accomplishment in mind, we must, in justice to all, acknowledge that the City of Washington today owes its dignity and impressiveness primarily to the vision of Pierre Charles L'Enfant.

ANDREW ELLICOTT

The retirement of L'Enfant left the responsibility for developing the city plan in the hands of Andrew Ellicott. He was ordered to prepare a new and corrected plan for publication; and in this he made many changes from the plan submitted by his predecessor in 1791. (Plate 1.) The earlier map had been transmitted by Washington to the House, but was afterward withdrawn. The changes made by Ellicott were in conformity with data gathered by him as acting surveyor, and did not seriously effect L'Enfant's scheme, nor take from him credit for the design.

The new map was engraved at Philadelphia, by Washington's order, in 1792, and was for many years the official map of the city. Even it was not devoid of inaccuracies, and these together with errors in the earlier map were the cause of so many disputes that the commissioners had a map of their own prepared. This was kept and used by them in their own office, but was never published.

Poor L'Enfant received no credit whatsoever on the engraved map of 1792 but Ellicott's name appears, quite casually of course, in very large letters in a statement printed in very small letters. This reads: "In order to execute this plan Mr. ELLICOTT drew a true Meridial line by celestial observation, which passes through the Area intended for the Capitol."

It is said that L'Enfant saw this in the engraver's office at Philadelphia, and noting also that no credit was given him for the original plan that was drawn by his own hand, he walked out in disgust and refused to have anything more to do with the matter.

High-strung temperaments and personal jealousies were the cause from the very start of innumerable squabbles among those associated with the building of the Capitol. L'Enfant's contribution to this phase of the record was referred to by President Washington in a letter, dated February 20, 1792, written by him to the commissioners. He said: "That many alterations have been made from L'Enfant's plan by Major Ellicott, with the approbation of the Executive, is not denied; that some were deemed essential, is avowed; and, had it not been for the materials which he happened to possess, it is probable that no engraving from Mr. L'Enfant's draught ever would have been exhibited to the public; for, after the disagreement took place between him and the Commissioners his obstinacy threw every difficulty in the way of its accomplishment."

Ellicott also, in spite of his ability, proved in some ways to be a thorn in the flesh of the long-suffering commissioners, who lost patience with him in turn, and, on December 23, 1793, reported to the President that, "Major Ellicott after his absence a great part of the summer and all the fall, as we hear on other service, returned to us in the winter, we do not accept his further service. The business we believe was going on just as well without him." The erring major did not, apparently, show sufficient evidence of contrition and reform to soothe their ruffled feelings, for five weeks later, January 28, 1794, the outraged commissioners reported with commendable terseness and finality, "We discharged him at our last meeting."

Andrew Ellicott came of a family noted for its mechanical ability. His father and uncle founded the milling town of Ellicott City, Maryland, and carried on what for that time were extensive industrial enterprises. The town is still a busy manufacturing center, but, unlike most places of the kind, retains its old, picturesque appearance.

Andrew was born, January 24, 1754, in Solebury Township, Bucks County, Pennsylvania. There and in Philadelphia he managed to pick up a rather sketchy bit of schooling, and at fifteen was helping his father build grandfather clocks. However, his natural instinct for mathematics directed his ingenious mind away from clocks, toward the making of surveyors' instruments; and a surveyor he became.

When twenty-one, he married Sarah Brown, and soon afterward joined the militia of Maryland. He attained to the rank of major during the Revolutionary War, and, after the close of that conflict, returned to the family home, Fountainvale, at Ellicott's Upper Mills.

He received an appointment, in 1784, as one of the party to continue the survey of the boundary between Maryland and Pennsylvania, the famous survey that had been begun some years before by the two Englishmen, Mason and Dixon, whose names still are applied to that boundary line.

When through with this work, Ellicott was appointed to the commission delegated to run the western and northern boundaries of Pennsylvania, and to survey the islands of the Ohio and Allegheny Rivers (1785-1786). During this same period he was teaching mathematics in the Academy at Baltimore, and served a term in the legislature.

Ellicott removed again to Philadelphia in 1789 and, with Franklin's assistance, secured a federal appointment to establish the western boundary of New York state. This involved a dispute between Pennsylvania and New York over the site of Presqu' Isle, now the city of Erie, Pennsylvania.

His party encountered stubborn opposition from the British officer in command of Fort Niagara, but in spite of that functionary's strict orders to the contrary, Ellicott contrived to make the first comprehensive study of the Falls. The letter from him to Benjamin Rush, and his report to Washington, give entertaining accounts of his difficulties with the British and his observations of the almost unknown cataract.

The ability and energy displayed by Ellicott on this expedition secured for him the more important appointment, to do the field work in connection with a survey of the ten mile square that had been ceded by Maryland and Virginia for the national seat of government. This work was begun in February, 1791, and led naturally to his association with L'Enfant.

After Ellicott's discharge by the Commissioners of the District, in 1793, he received an appointment from Governor Mifflin of Pennsylvania as one of three commissioners to survey the town of Presqu' Isle, now Erie, in which connection he spent two years working out a road between Reading and Erie, through the almost unbroken wilderness.

His brother Joseph, who had assisted him on earlier surveys, had in the meantime become superintendent of the vast holdings of the Holland Company, and as he founded the city of Buffalo, there must be accorded the clan of Ellicott much of the credit due those responsible for the early development of that rich area that is now included in western Pennsylvania and New York.

In 1796 Andrew Ellicott was once more happily engaged in running state boundaries, this time between Georgia and Spanish Florida. Again in 1811 he ran the line between Georgia and North Carolina, but here he failed to win many laurels for himself, as he placed the line eighteen miles south of where Georgians felt it should be. This thrust at the pride and acreage of Georgia brought down on his head the wrath of its officials and they vented their spleen upon him by refusing to pay more than his actual personal expenses.

Mere trifles like this failed to disturb seriously the poise of a man like Ellicott, and as he had had his fill apparently of lugging transits through the wilderness, he accepted an offer such as L'Enfant had refused, and settled down contentedly in 1814 to teach mathematics at West Point.

During the many years of wandering, the letters that he wrote

PLATE 2. Design for the Capitol; submitted by Samuel Dobie in the competition of 1792. This is one of the best in the group, none of which was accepted. Reproduced by courtesy of The Maryland Historical Society

to his beloved wife, Sally, reflected an ideal devotion, and now for almost the first time they found it possible to enjoy life together. And here at West Point they remained until August 28, 1820, when death came to him and closed the chapter.

Many honors came to Ellicott. He was given the honorary degree of Master of Arts, in 1784, by the College of William and Mary; was made Geographer General of the United States in 1800; and felt obliged to decline the post of Surveyor General which was offered to him in 1801 by President Jefferson. He was vice president of the American Philosophical Society, and papers by him were published by it and other scientific societies at home and abroad. He enjoyed the personal friendship of Washington, Jefferson, Rittenhouse and Franklin. His was a full life.

AN ARCHITECTURAL COMPETITION IS ANNOUNCED

President Washington, in 1792, found himself in possession of a splendid plan, on paper, and a sizable tract of tableland and swamp. This was something, of course, but ahead of him were only eight short years in which to create a complete capital city, in which the nation's government was scheduled to establish itself in running order. The deadline was set for the first Monday in December, 1800.

Fortunate it was that the President and his versatile Secretary of State were personally, and enthusiastically, interested in architecture. These subjects were considered essentials in the education of a Virginia gentleman. Washington had demonstrated his qualifications in the enlargement of his home at Mount Vernon; Jefferson could point to the Virginia Capitol at Richmond, and to his home at Monticello. With Jefferson, architecture had become far more than an incident in his education; it was an absorbing avocation, to which he had devoted continuous study since college days at William and Mary. His residence abroad had afforded opportunity for broadening his grasp of the subject, and it would not be amiss to refer to him, as one of America's ablest native born architects.

L'Enfant had been requested by the commissioners, a few months after his arrival, to submit designs for the public build-

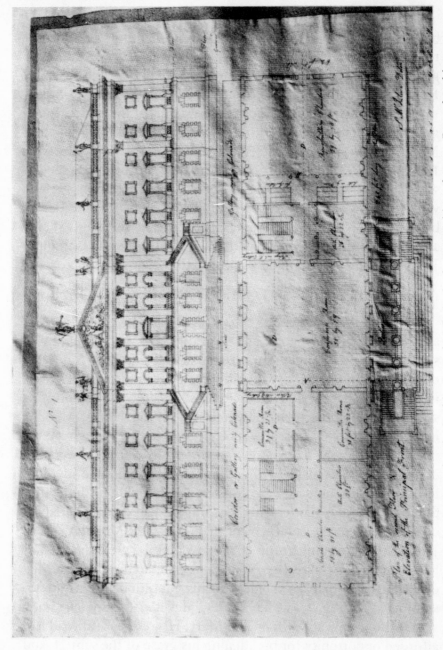

PLATE 3. Design for the Capitol; submitted by Samuel McIntire in the competition of 1792. Reproduced by courtesy of The Maryland Historical Society

ings. This request was mentioned in a letter, dated October 21, from the commissioners to the President. In it they said, "We have requested him to prepare a draft of the public buildings for our inspection, and he has promised to enter on it as soon as he finds himself disengaged. He can have recourse to books in Philadelphia and can not have it here." He made some studies for the buildings, but had accomplished little or nothing at the time he was discharged.

Washington and Jefferson had slight expectation apparently of using his designs, for they had decided definitely on a competition for a Capitol and a President's House. The suggestion had been made by Jefferson who submitted, in the fall of 1791, a form of announcement which he called "a sketch or specimen of advertisement." The original is still preserved in the government archives.

In this preliminary draft are found all the important provisions of the announcement as it was finally printed, excepting the dates, which were left blank, and the city's name, which had not yet been determined but to which he referred as "the chief city of the Federal territory."

Following examination of this paper by the President and commissioners, the name of the city was filled in as, "Washington in the territory of Columbia," and the final date for reception of drawings was set as July 15, 1792.

Jefferson was evidently becoming impatient or worried at the delay, for on March 6, 1792 the forms announcing these two competitions were returned to the commissioners and on the same day he wrote them saying, "It is necessary to advertise at once for plans for the Capitol and President's House." Eight days later the announcements appeared in Philadelphia papers. Clippings were sent to the commissioners by Jefferson, with the recommendation that they insert the notices in other papers, and also secure the services of a superintendent.

The competition program for the Capitol read:

A PREMIUM

of a lot in the city, to be designated by impartial judges, and

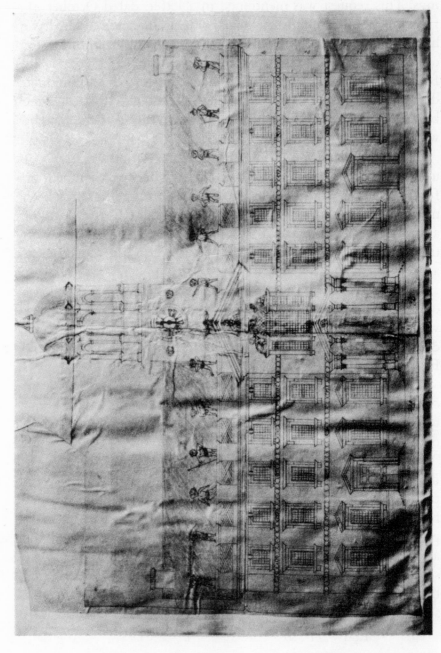

PLATE 4. Design for the Capitol; submitted by Philip Hart in the competition of 1792. Reproduced by courtesy of The Maryland Historical Society

$500, or a medal of that value, at the option of the party, will be given by the Commissioners of Federal Buildings to persons who, before the 15th day of July, 1792, shall produce them the most approved plan, if adopted by them, for a Capitol to be erected in the city, and $250 or a medal for the plan deemed next in merit to the one they shall adopt; the building to be of brick and to contain the following compartments, to wit:

A conference room. ⎫ To contain 300 ⎫
A room for Representatives ⎬ persons each ⎪ These rooms to
A lobby or Antechamber to the latter ⎬ be of full eleva-
A Senate room of 1,200 square feet of area. ⎪ tion.
An antechamber and lobby to the latter. ⎭

Twelve rooms of 600 square feet area each for committee rooms and clerks, to be of half the elevation of the former.

Drawings, will be expected of the ground plats, elevations of each front, and sections through the building in such directions as may be necessary to explain the material, structure, and an estimate of the cubic feet of the brick work composing the whole mass of the wall.

THOS. JOHNSON,
DD. STUART,
DANL. CARROLL,
March 14, 1792.   Commissioners.

The drawings that were received in response to this announcement afford startling evidence, to us today, of the slight extent to which architecture had progressed as a profession on this side of the Atlantic in the late eighteenth century. There were almost no trained architects in the United States.

Domestic architecture was well understood, and house building was usually well done by highly trained master-builders. Such craftsmen were numerous, and the would-be owner of a home had only to make a simple sketch of the plan he desired, determine its dimensions, and give a general idea of the type of design wanted. The builder did the rest. His professional equipment consisted chiefly of a mind well stored with details and formulae learned in apprentice days; a handful of books by Batty

Langley, Abraham Swan, William Pain, or other contemporary publishers of "Builder's Guides"; and a kit of well chosen tools.

Skilful though these builders were in house-building, the requirements of a huge structure adequate to house the legislative and judicial departments of the United States of America were entirely beyond their ken.

Many of the drawings entered in this competition are preserved today by the Maryland Historical Society and, although a few present quite creditable solutions of the problem (Plates 2, 3), most of them are so preposterous in detail that it is difficult to imagine optimism vaulting enough to expect recognition.

Not only were most of the schemes utterly inadequate, but the draftsmanship was pathetic, especially as seen in the weird sculptured figures of men and eagles. If actually executed, these would have crowned balustrades and dome with the effect of a stone circus parade of gigantic size and absurd postures. (Plates 4, 5.)

LABOR TROUBLES

Those in charge of the creation of a capital city for the young nation were not unaware of the many difficulties that stood in their way. As early as November 26, 1791 the commissioners reported to the President that they had engaged a Mr. Cabot to make a tour of New England to "inform himself regarding terms on which men and materials may be had." His report evidently verified certain of their misgivings for, on the sixth of March following, Jefferson wrote from Philadelphia to the commissioners saying, "Do you not think it would be expedient to take measures for importing a number of Germans and Highlanders? . . . If you approve . . . and have a good channel for it, you will use it of course. If you have no channel, I can help you. . . ."

It was quite evident that in spite of the number of good mechanics in the North, few were capable of executing work of the quality required for a building of such importance as the nation's Capitol. The skilled masons were less numerous than the carpenters. At any rate the commissioners followed the matter up carefully, and on June 2nd, wrote quite at length to Jefferson saying, in part: "The introduction of Mechanicks, and Labourers from

Europe being thought by the friends of the City so advisable a measure, we have again taken up that object it may indeed, eventually be useful perhaps almost necessary . . . to hold out additional motives, for Emigration we shall endeavor to concert a plan with some of the Scots Merchants to bring over some stone-cutters and others from that Country. We request you to fall on measures to procure about 100 Germans single men and as many of them Stonecutters, Masons, and Bricklayers, as can be readily had. . . ."

With his customary thoroughness and reliability, Jefferson followed the suggestion in his preceding letter by sending to the commissioners, on June 3rd, a letter of introduction to a firm in Amsterdam, to be used in furthering the arrangements for securing German immigrants.

These plans did not seem to prove workable for, on December 18th, President Washington wrote the commissioners that their failure to "Import workmen from Scotland, equally with that for obtaining them from Holland, fills me with real concern, for I am very apprehensive if your next campaign in the Federal City is not marked with a vigor, it will cast such a cloud over this business, and will so arm the enemies of the measure, as to enable them to give it (if not its death blow) a wound from which it will not easily recover. . . ." He continued with suggestions as to how these workmen might best be procured. After reaffirming the necessity for pushing the work, he concluded by saying ". . . In a word, the next year is the year that will give the tone to the City."

The Secretary of State followed the President's letter, five days later, with one which breathed a spirit of hope for the labor situation. In it he said, "I have the honor to mention to you that in a conversation with Mr. Pierpont Edwards and Colonel Wadsworth of Connecticut, they inform me that any number of house Carpenters may be got in that State, as far perhaps as 500, or 1000, their wages 2/3 of a dollar and to be fed. They have but few Masons, however some may be had, they combine their, the cutting and laying stone, and the laying brick. they mention one Trowbridge as one of the best workmen. however I could not find

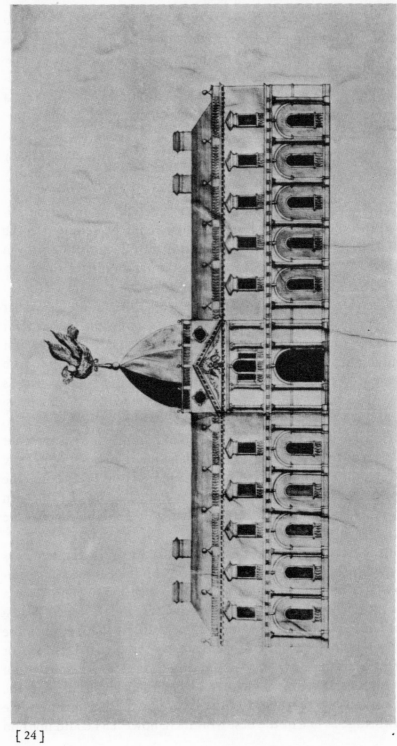

PLATE 5. Design for the Capitol; submitted by James Diamond in the competition of 1792. It is difficult to take seriously a design with a weathercock of such fantastic proportions. Reproduced by courtesy of The Maryland Historical Society

that he had ever done anything higher than stone steps, he never had even cut a column. his wages a dollar a day and fed."

A mechanic who could not cut a column must certainly have rated pretty low in Jefferson's estimation, for to him columns were essential to anything that savored of architecture.

The lack of success in securing workmen from Scotland and Germany turned the attention of the commissioners to France. This suggestion may have come from Stephen Hallet, a French architect, who was keeping a weather eye on the job and might well win friendly regard by assisting in this time of need. A very flowery letter was written to the Municipality of Bordeaux, on January 4th, 1793, the introduction of which should have made the Municipality's collective bosoms swell with satisfaction. Then the commissioners asked meekly if "Mr. Fenwick may have your permission to engage some of your Citizens to come over to us."

In the flourish which led up to this simple request they stated that the job of "raising the public buildings . . . swells our ambition, to express in some degree in the Stile of our Architecture, the sublime sentiments of Liberty which are common to Frenchmen and Americans. We wish to exhibit a grandure of conception, a Republican simplicity, and that true Elegance of proportion which corresponds to, a tempered Freedom excluding Frivolity, the food of little minds."

This appeal to the ego of the Bordeaux Municipality was accompanied by a personal, man to man letter to Mr. Fenwick in which the point blank statement was made that, "Stone cutters are scarce here and must be plenty in France." If this choice bit of diplomatic correspondence came to the eye of Thomas Jefferson, it doubtless gave him a bit of a chuckle, for his sense of humor never failed him, even at the risk of indulging a taste for "Frivolity, the food of little minds."

HOBAN DESIGNS THE PRESIDENT'S HOUSE

All the drawings for the Capitol were rejected, but better fortune favored the President's House. A design submitted by James Hoban was accepted (Plate 6), the contract awarded, and Hoban proceeded with his contract. One of his drawings, that showing

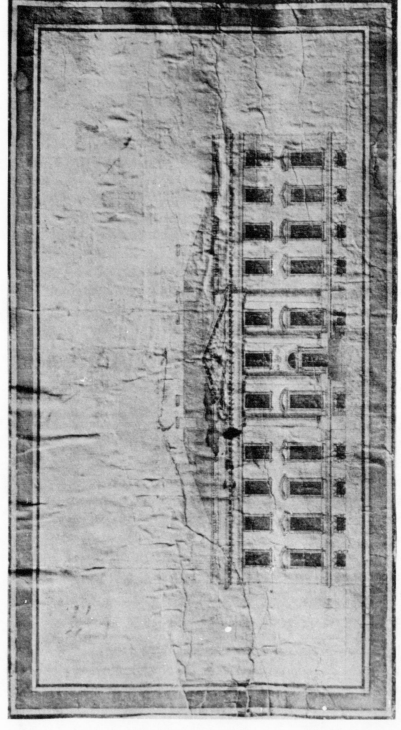

PLATE 6. James Hoban's original drawing for the President's House. This was the accepted design in the competition of 1792. Reproduced by courtesy of The Maryland Historical Society

the north front, is preserved by the Maryland Historical Society, with the rejected drawings for the Capitol. Jefferson himself entered a design for the President's House. This was done anonymously and, as was his custom, he went to Palladio for inspiration and copied the design for the Villa Rotunda which Palladio built near Vicenza.

*   *   *   *

The winner of this competition, James Hoban, was born in 1762 or 1763 at Callan, County Kilkenny, Ireland. In spite of the popular association of Kilkenny with fighting cats, Hoban was one of the few participants in our nation's first great program of building who kept an even keel and steered clear of the petty quarrels in which most of the others were involved.

He had received his early professional training in the school of the Dublin Society of Arts, where he was awarded a medal in 1780 for drawings of "Brackets, Stairs, Roofs etc." He had a part, chiefly as an artisan, in the erection of several important buildings of Dublin and, after the close of the American Revolution, came to this country.

Hoban's presence in Philadelphia was made known by an advertisement which appeared in the papers of that city on May 25, 1785. In this he modestly announced that, "Any gentleman who wishes to build in an elegant style, may hear of a person properly calculated for that purpose, who can execute the Joining and Carpenter's business in the modern taste."

Apparently there were not sufficient "Gentlemen who wished to build in an elegant style," or else they failed to "hear of a person properly calculated for that purpose," for Hoban appeared before long in South Carolina, where he remained until 1792. His ability received recognition there, and he proved himself to be skilled in his profession by designing a number of buildings, including the State Capitol at Columbia. This building was burned at the close of the Civil War.

Hoban returned to Philadelphia in 1792 with a letter from Henry Laurens to President Washington. With the competition in mind he soon turned back south to the Federal City and, having produced the winning design for the President's House or

Palace as it was sometimes called, he settled and remained there for the balance of his life. He was employed almost continuously in superintending governmental work, including that on the Capitol, his activities extending to roadways and bridges as well as to architecture.

His even temper and reliability kept Hoban on friendly terms with all the officials, architects, and superintendents with whom his work brought him in contact, and his ability and integrity may be judged from the fact that he was a member of the Washington City Council from 1820 until his death in 1831.

STEPHEN HALLET COMES INTO THE PICTURE

Most promising of the contestants in the Capitol competition was Stephen Hallet. His designs made such a good impression that the commissioners wrote to him, in care of Secretary of State, Jefferson, at Philadelphia, asking that he come to Washington, and adding, "We ask you to visit us as soon as you can and have a full and free communication of ideas with us. Your design may perhaps be improved into approbation. In all events we will liberally indemnify you for your expenses."

Correspondence indicates that much time and effort were expended during that summer and early fall, trying to find in the various plans submitted, or to develope from these, a design that would meet all requirements. Several more competitors were permitted to enter the lists, under a revised schedule in which the Commissioners stated, "Though limited in means, we want a plan a credit to the age in design and taste."

President Washington not only took an intense interest in the competition, but on him seemed to rest most of the responsibility for decisions, yet he wrote, "I would have it understood, in this instance and always when I am hazarding a sentiment on these buildings, that I profess to have no knowledge of architecture, and think we should, to avoid criticism, be governed by the established rules which are laid down by the professors of the art."

DOCTOR THORNTON WINS COMPETITION

Finally a dark horse appeared in the race, a young physician named William Thornton (Plate 7) who had previously distinguished himself in another architectural competition, in spite of an utter lack of training in this field. Doctor Thornton was born, May 20, 1759, on the little island of Jost van Dyke, in a community of the Society of Friends, which centered at Tortula, in the Virgin Islands.

When five years old the boy was sent to England to be educated, as was the custom with gentlemen's sons. He studied medicine from 1781 to 1784 at the University of Edinburg, finally receiving his degree of M.D. from Aberdeen University.

After spending some time in Paris he returned to Tortula, in 1786, and in the following year migrated to New York, becoming an American citizen, January 7, 1788, in Delaware. The experiments of John Fitch, in propelling steamboats by means of paddles, fascinated him and he was for some time associated with that enterprize.

While so engaged, the versatile genius contrived to find time for the preparation of drawings for a competition originated by the Library Company of Philadelphia. He won the prize and afterward remarked whimsically of this achievement, that when abroad he had, "Never thought of architecture, but I got some books and worked a few days, then gave a plan in the ancient Ionic order, which carried the day." This nonchalance may have irritated the more serious minded and experienced men whom he beat at their own game, and have been somewhat responsible for the turmoil in which he was for many years involved. At any rate the library was regarded at the time as one of the finest buildings in this country, and stood until 1880.

This contest was won in 1789, and in the following year Doctor Thornton married the daughter of Mrs. Ann Brodeau, a successful school teacher of Philadelphia. The bride was of English birth and, in addition to being a person of culture, was possessed of considerable artistic ability, as is to be seen in a miniature, still in existence, which she painted of her husband.

The Thorntons went, shortly after their marriage, to Tortula where he possessed property that had been left to him by his father, and there spent the next two years.

PLATE 7. William Thornton. Original architect of the Capitol. Portrait engraved by Charles Balthazer Julien Fevret du St. Memin. Reproduced by courtesy of The Corcoran Gallery of Art, Washington, D. C. Photograph by Lewis P. Moltz

Learning that another competition was in the offing, Thornton promptly bestirred himself and, with supreme self-confidence, we might say with audacity, he wrote the officials at Philadelphia asking permission to submit drawings according to the first advertisement. This letter was dated October, 1792, three months after the competition had officially closed. In spite of this, the commissioners replied that they would be pleased to consider his design for the Capitol, but it would be unnecessary to make plans for the President's House as that competition had already been awarded to James Hoban.

The consideration shown him may have been due in part to the difficulty experienced in securing a satisfactory design, and also to the fact that the Doctor had been introduced to President Washington by no less a personage than the painter, John Trumbull.

Another letter to Thornton, dated December 4th, stated that Hallet had been retained to prepare a design which was to be ready early in the next month. This was probably done to protect the commissioners in case, as they doubtless expected, the prize should go to Hallet.

This letter was written after Thornton's arrival in Philadelphia some time in November. He soon found, on discussing the contest with those in charge, that the design he had brought with him could not possibly be acceptable and, having been given a glimpse of one of Hallet's designs, he started over again.

Meanwhile Hallet had not progressed as rapidly as he had anticipated and on January 5th he asked for three weeks more of grace in which to get his drawings into presentable shape. Thornton was under an even greater handicap but finally, on January 31, 1793 his still unfinished drawings were submitted to the President. Both Washington and Jefferson were so impressed by the design and commended it so highly that little doubt was felt regarding its acceptance by the commissioners when it was submitted to them at Georgetown. (Plate 8.)

Again the amateur had made good; for records dated February 7, 1793 show that the commissioners and others were generally satisfied with Thornton's plans. On March 3rd he came to George-

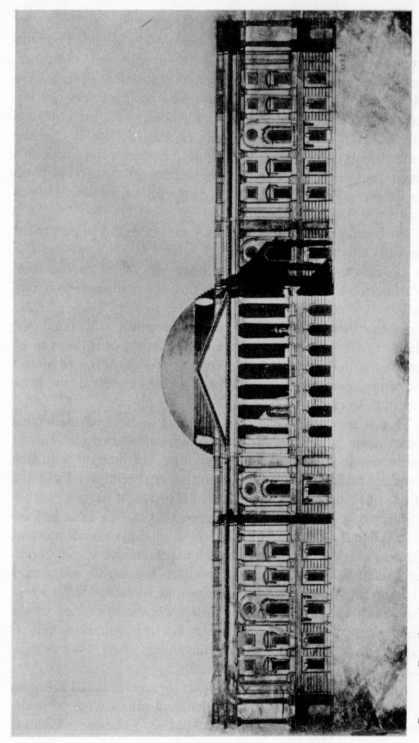

PLATE 8. East elevation of Capitol as redesigned by William Thornton after his appointment as commissioner in 1794. Original drawing is in the Library of Congress

town with a letter from the President in which Washington said, "Grandeur, simplicity, and convenience appear to be so well combined in this plan of Dr. Thornton's," that he felt assured it would meet with the commissioners' approval.

Jefferson expressed himself in about the same words, and on another occasion commented that "Thornton's plan had captivated the eyes and the judgment of all. It is simple, noble, beautiful, excellently arranged, and moderate in size. . . . Among its admirers none are more decided than he whose decision is most important."

HALLET IS CONSOLED — AND STARTS TROUBLE

Following the decision to award the prize to Thornton, a letter was sent to Hallet, which reflects the commissioners' fine feeling of friendship and obligation toward him, and their regret at the disappointment which the decision must cause him. In this letter they said, "The plan you first offered for a Capitol appeared to us to have a great share of merit, none met with our entire approbation. . . . Neither the Doctor or yourself can command the prize under the strict terms of our advertisement, but the public has been benefitted by the emulation excited and the end having been answered we shall give the reward of 500 dollars and a lot to Dr. Thornton. You certainly rank next and because your application has been excited by particular request, we have resolved to place you on the same footing as near as may be, that is to allow compensation for everything to this time, 100 £ being the value of a lot and 500 dollars."

The acceptance of Thornton's plan was announced in the following letter, written to him a few weeks later.

"Georgetown, April 5, 1793.

"Sir: The President has given his formal approbation of your plan. You will therefore be pleased to grant powers or put the business in a way to be closed on the acknowledgments your success entitles you.

"As soon as the nature of the work and your convenience will permit, we wish to be in possession of your explanations with the plan, for we wish to mark out the ground, make preparations, and even lay out the foundations this fall.

"We are, etc.

T. JOHNSON.
DD. STUART.
DANL. CARROLL."

The anxiety of the commissioners to avoid hurting the feelings of Hallet ultimately got them into a peck of trouble. With the best of intentions, they made the fatal mistake of appointing him to study Thornton's plans, and to estimate the cost of the Capitol. He became very busy indeed and, with the whole-hearted co-operation of other disappointed competitors, proceeded to pick Thornton's design to pieces and urge its wholesale modification, if not its actual rejection.

As if this opportunity for sweet revenge were not sufficient, Hallet was soon given the further advantage of an appointment as superintendent of construction. Now he got right down to business, and devoted himself assiduously to the congenial task of searching out defects and proposing alterations.

There was doubtless ample ground for criticism, for Thornton was neither experienced nor trained in architecture or building. Hence a vast amount of bickering and ill feeling might have been avoided if his antagonists had been more charitable in their criticisms, and he had been less cocksure of himself, and less inclined to display a spirit of know-it-all.

The spirit of give and take was quite conspicuous by its absence, and Hallet worked zealously on innumerable schemes in a persistent effort to substitute his ideas for those of Thornton. His drawings are preserved in the Library of Congress, and have caused at least one writer to give Hallet the credit for designing the original Capitol.

Eventually the criticisms of Thornton's plans had their effect and, on June 30, 1793, Washington wrote to Jefferson from Mount Vernon ordering a conference in which the criticisms should be thoroughly aired, and decisions made as to changes that might be found necessary. In this letter he said:

"Dear Sir: You will find by enclosed letter from the commissioners that Mr. Hallet reports unfavorably of Dr. Thornton's plan 'on the great points of practicability, time and expense,' . . . is of opinion that the execution of Thornton's plan (independent of the cost, which would far exceed our means and the time allowed for the accomplishment of the building) is impracticable; and would not in some parts answer the ends proposed. Mr. Hoban seemed to concur in this, and Mr. Blodgett, as far as I could come at his sentiments in the short time I was with him, approved the alterations in it which have been proposed by Mr. Hallet.

"It is unlucky that this investigation of Dr. Thornton's plan and estimate of the cost had not preceded the adoption of it, but knowing the impatience of the Carrollsburg interest and the anxiety of the public to see both buildings progressing, and supposing the plan to be correct, it was adjudged best to avoid delay. It is better, however, to correct the error, though late, than to proceed in a ruinous measure, in the adoption of which I do not hesitate to confess that I was governed by the beauty of the exterior and the distribution of the apartments, declaring then, as I do now, that I had no knowledge in the rules of or principles of architecture, and was equally unable to count the cost. But if there be such material defects as are represented and such immense time and cost to complete the building, it would be folly in the extreme to proceed on the plan which has been adopted.

"It has appeared to me proper, however, before it is laid aside, and justice and respect to Dr. Thornton require, that the objections should be made known to him, and an opportunity afforded to explain and obviate them if he can.

"For this reason, and because Mr. Blodgett is in Philadelphia, and it might not be convenient for Dr. Thornton to leave it, I have requested Mr. Hallet and Mr. Hoban to repair without delay to Philadelphia with all the plans and documents which are necessary to elucidate the subject, and do pray you to get all the parties herein named together and, after hearing the objections and explanations, report your opinion on the case and the plan which ought to have been executed. . . .

"The case is important. A plan must be adopted and, good or bad, it must be entered upon.

"With great regard, I am, dear sir, your affectionate and obedient servant,

"GEORGE WASHINGTON.

"To Secretary of State Thomas Jefferson."

A commission was appointed to examine the plans and make a report. Of the five men chosen, three, including Hallet, had been competitors: Thornton and Hoban were the other two. Hallet industriously drew up a schedule of criticisms and, along with it, presented revised plans which were supposed to correct the errors of Thornton. These plans were accepted by the conferees, with the exception of his suggested treatment for the eastern front of the central unit. Here Hallet had substituted a recessed court for Thornton's rotunda and portico.

Secretary of State Jefferson forwarded this report to the President who, in a letter of transmission to the commissioners referred to this feature with the reservation "that the foundations would be begun upon the plan exhibited by Mr. Hallet, leaving the recess on the East front open for further consideration."

This was in July and, as late as the following January, Hallet was still pegging away with a grim determination to produce a design which would oust that of Thornton. He complained, in a letter to Jefferson, that he had been unable to do himself justice in the designs submitted, "all my time having been employed in working on the ideas of others." He also claimed that the design that was approved at the July conference was his, and in a letter to the commissioners said: "I misunderstood your mind as to the plan so far that I thought to be indebted for the adoption of mine to its total difference with the other as pointed out pretty accurately to the Commissioner's in presence of a number of Gentlemen by Mr. Blodgett and Mr. Hoban. In the alteration I never thought of introducing in it anything belonging to Dr. Thornton's exhibitions. So I claim the original invention of the plan now executing and beg leave to lay hereafter before you and the President the proofs of my right to it." This letter was written on June 28, 1794, nine months after the laying of the corner stone.

It is difficult at this distance to appraise intelligently the merits of the case, especially as Thornton's original competitive drawing has disappeared, and its provisions can be but partially determined by references to it in various documents that have been preserved.

Hallet was an architect of superior training and attainments and had been the recipient of high honors from the schools of France. To him Thornton's design and drawings doubtless appeared very amateurish and unstudied, and it was of course most humiliating to have the competition awarded to this upstart.

Meanwhile, steady going, reliable James Hoban was entrusted with the double responsibility of superintending construction on both the President's House and the Capitol. Hallet was retained as assistant superintendent and draftsman, an arrangement that must have been as gall and wormwood to his soul.

During their joint administration the corner stone of the Capitol was laid, on September 18, 1793, with imposing Masonic ceremonies, "conducted by his Excellency General Washington, President of the United States, a past master of this lodge, which was present and holding the post of honor." The lodge in question was that of Alexandria which still preserves the trowel used on that occasion.

Hallet's services as assistant to Hoban brought him a salary of £400 per year, an arrangement that was made retroactive to June of 1792, but even this liberal (for those days) salary was not without a thorn for Hallet's proud spirit—the superintendent of stonecutters drew pay of the identical amount.

Meanwhile Hallet was getting himself in general ill favor with the commissioners who reprimanded him sharply for failure to complete working drawings, for carelessness, and for making changes in the Thornton plan. He for some reason ignored that little clause in the President's letter to the commissioners which stated definitely that the builders should leave "the recess on the East front open for further consideration." Hallet deliberately went ahead and laid the foundations for a square, open court in this space enclosed by a projecting central mass that dominated the wings. (Plate 9.)

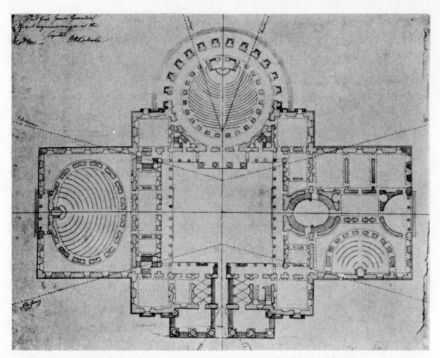

PLATE 9. Plan for the Capitol, as modified by Hallet from Thornton's design. This shows the square central court, the introduction of which was directly responsible for Hallet's discharge. Original drawing is in the Library of Congress

This deviation from official instructions makes it evident that Hoban was devoting his attention pretty thoroughly to the President's House and leaving Hallet largely in control of work on the hill; but even so it seems strange that so radical a change could have been made without a halt being called by someone.

A sharp letter from the commissioners brought matters to a focus. They did not mince words with Hallet but said quite bluntly, "In general nothing has gone from us by which we intended or we believe you could infer that you had the chief direction of executing the work of the Capitol, or that you or anybody else were to introduce into the building any departures from Dr. Thornton's plan, without the President's or the commissioners' approbation.

"Mr. Hoban was employed here before our acquaintance began with you, more especially as chief over the President's House,

of which he was fortunate enough to produce a plan which met
with general, I may say almost universal, favor, and to extend his
superintendence to any other building we might require. We
claimed his service as superior at the Capitol, and this was explained so fully last fall on the spot, with the addition that you
were to communicate with him and be governed by his direction,
that we flattered ourselves that the line of each was perfectly
understood. It is painful to have these things to reiterate, and we
do request that you will signify by letter your understanding of
our agreement to this line, for we can not trust the same piece of
business to the discretion of two heads capable of pursuing different wills. We shall soon separate. Hence a speedy answer will
oblige.
                                        THOS. JOHNSON
                                        DAN'L CARROLL
                                        DD. STUART
                                                Commissioners"

This letter, dated June 26, 1784, demolished the stand taken
by Hallet in a statement that he considered he had been given
power to do as he thought best. Following the receipt of this letter,
he did the obvious thing—sent in his resignation; which was not
accepted.

Another letter written on June 28th to Philip B. Key, Esquire
gives further details of the strained relations that brought about
the rupture. In it the commissioners said that Hallet "has lately
taken up such delicacy that he will not hold intercourse with, or
submit to the Superiority of Mr. Hoban, the Principal. On expla-
nation we have parted, he was on a liberal appointment but re-
fuses to give up the Plans and Essays of Plans as you'll see by the
enclosed."

They asked for a replevin in Prince Georges County Court,
adding that "from Hallet's disposition, as disclosed in this trans-
action we expect he will run out all processes before he'll give up
the papers. . . ."

Finally, on November 15th, 1794, Hallet was formally discharged, and another chapter was closed in the tempestuous
story of the Capitol, in which one actor after another spoiled

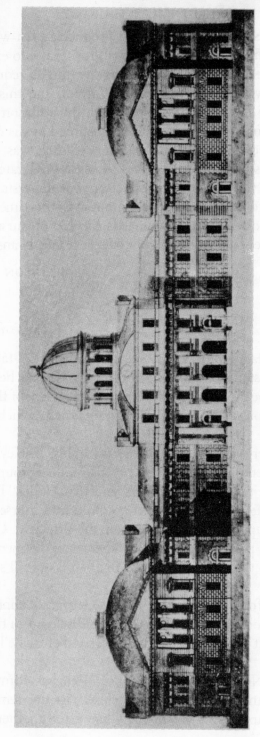

PLATE 10. Design for the Capitol, by Hallet (1793). Original drawing is in the Library of Congress

his record of achievement by temperamental displays of jealousy and vindictiveness.

The self-sufficiency and insubordination of the two talented Frenchmen, L'Enfant and Hallet, justified Jefferson's dry comment on the former, that if a superintendent were brought here from France he would doubtless assume himself to be "the Superintendent of the Directors themselves, and probably of the Government of the State also."

Nevertheless, we have L'Enfant to thank for the ever-admired city plan of Washington; while to Hallet we are indebted for the scheme of a central dome with flanking wings for the two legislative bodies, which has since been adopted from the Capitol and applied to state capitols and courthouses throughout the country. This arrangement was suggested by him on the first design which he submitted before the competition was announced.

To L'Enfant's pique was due probably the loss of the original drawings for the Capitol at Richmond, which he had borrowed from the Virginia authorities. Hallet repeated the unfortunate act by refusing to return the plans for the Capitol at Washington.

ETIENNE SULPICE HALLET

It is evident that the hardy and simple minded Americans found Hallet's name too much for them, so they compromised on its English equivalent, and he is usually referred to as Stephen Hallet. He came to America in 1789, probably to participate in the founding of an Academie des Sciences et Beaux Arts, at Richmond. This plan, which involved branches to be established in other cities, fell through with the outbreak of the French Revolution.

This left Hallet stranded, and we first hear of him as living in reduced circumstances in New York, where the Federal Government was located temporarily. He evidently learned there in advance of the proposed competition for the Capitol and President's House, as he showed Jefferson a design for the Capitol, late in 1791 before the competition had been announced. This design, with its central dome and flanking wings was a type that was common in France, but unknown in this country.

PLATE 11. West elevation of Thornton's revised design (1795-1797). Drawing shows the "Temple" which was to surmount the circular Conference Room. This "Temple" has been misunderstood as an alternative design for the Dome. Original is in the Library of Congress

Following his brief period of work for the Government and his subsequent dismissal, Hallet remained in Washington for at least a year, engaged in developing various inventions, including a crane for lifting stone. The last official record of him was a claim, dated June 19, 1795, for payment due him for services rendered the Government.

He was the first thoroughly trained French architect to come to the United States, and ablest competitor in this, the first of America's architectural competitions. Yet, despite his unquestioned ability, Hallet's professional career ended when his work on the Capitol was finished. Further information regarding him was brought to light in connection with research for this book. An unexpected, and most fortunate meeting with a great-granddaughter afforded the privilege of checking with family records that run back more than two centuries. From these have been gained the following additional facts:

Etienne Sulpicius Hallet, (the son of Claudius Hallet and his wife, Gabriella Rovin) was born in Paris, March 17, 1755. The middle name is spelled in the family records both Sulpice and Sulpicius. It is improbable that any proof, as to which should be considered correct, is available unless it may be in the old records of baptism in Paris, a most unlikely possibility. He married Marie Francoise Gomain, and, in 1789, they fled from the French Revolution, and came to the United States.

The very meager facts regarding his later life are based largely on records of births and deaths. The dates of the births of two children show that the family was at Philadelphia in 1797, while during the ensuing three years they removed to Havana, for it was there in 1800 that the eighth and last child, Stephanie, was born. It is thought that the family remained there several years for it is known that they acquired and used the Spanish language.

Mrs. Hallet died in the city of New York on February 3, 1812, while Hallet himself ended his days at New Rochelle, New York, in February, 1825, at the age of seventy.

HADFIELD COMES AND GOES

As Dame Rumor began to circulate hints that Hallet might not continue long in office, there arose the natural query as to who would take his place. John Trumbull, the painter, who was then at London in the diplomatic service of the United States, wrote a letter to the Commissioners, on September 13, 1794, in which he recommended George Hadfield for the position.

Hadfield was a young English architect of great promise who had formed a habit of carrying off all the available honors in architecture. He was born about 1764 at Leghorn, the son of a hotel keeper. There was evidently an artistic strain in the family, for his sister Maria was a painter of ability, and added to the family distinction by marrying the popular miniature painter, Richard Cosway.

The young architect studied in the schools of the Academy, sent drawings to its exhibitions, was awarded a gold medal in 1781, and, after working for a time as a draftsman in the office of James Wyatt, a leading architect of the time, he won a traveling scholarship from the Academy, which enabled him to spend several years in Rome.

Drawings made by Hadfield, of the temple at Palestrina, received recognition by the Academy, were hung in its galleries, and are still in the possession of the Royal Institute of British Architects.

Upon receipt of Trumbull's letter, the commissioners of the City of Washington, one of whom was Thornton, invited Hadfield to take the position of superintendent of construction on the Capitol. He accepted, and began work October 15, 1795.

He of course inherited some of the difficulties that had grown out of past misunderstandings and conflicting temperaments, but unfortunately he was too inexperienced and lacking in tact to bury them. He began at once to criticize the work already executed and the designs which Thornton had developed. He wished to use a colossal order on the façade, instead of carrying the order on a high base as Thornton's plans specified.

This was not an auspicious beginning. The commissioners vetoed his proposal and Thornton, both as architect and commissioner, did not become increasingly cordial toward his employe-critic. Construction went on, but with growing friction. Thornton's knowledge of classical architecture was just limited enough to make him pedantic in adhering to the rules of the books; while Hadfield was too young and too unfamiliar with the ways of the world to know how to handle or dodge such situations.

Meanwhile, he had designed the Treasury and Executive offices which were burned by the British in 1814, and here again he got himself in ill favor by attempting to exercise supervision over the job, a prerogative for which he had no authority. This, coupled with difficulties at the Capitol, resulted in his dismissal on May 28, 1798.

Hadfield remained in Washington, executing various commissions, both public and private, the most important of which was the City Hall which was completed in 1820. This building has long been used as the courthouse of the District; it was refaced with stone in 1917, and is regarded today as one of the finest examples of classic architecture in the city of Washington.

The Washington County jail was designed by him in 1802, the commission having been given Hadfield on Jefferson's recommendation, and in the following year he planned the Arsenal. The Assembly Room and the Branch Bank of the United States were done in 1822 and 1824 respectively.

Two residences by him were built for Commodore Porter and George Washington Parke Custis, the latter house being the one at Arlington that is best known as the home of General Robert E. Lee. The portico, that is so dominant a feature as seen from across the Potomac, was modeled after that of the Greek Temple at Paestum. Another adaptation is the Van Ness mausoleum in Oak Hill Cemetery, which was inspired by the circular temple of Vesta.

In spite of the success of these commissions, he never overcame his failure in connection with the Capitol and, in the words of Latrobe, "Loiters here, ruined in fortune, temper, and reputation." He remained in Washington until his death on February 5, 1826, a disappointed man and, in the eyes of the world, a failure in spite of his unquestioned ability and the high quality of the buildings which he designed.

Following Hallet's exit from the scene, Dr. Thornton was given the whip hand by President Washington who, on September 12, 1794, had appointed him one of the three commissioners in charge of the District of Columbia.

He showed a refreshing bit of generosity in giving the deposed Hallet credit for having made some valuable suggestions in connection with the design for the Capitol, but at the same time placed on him full blame for diminishing the size of the Senate Chamber, which proved to be too small almost from the beginning.

The unpardonable sin that was fastened on Hallet, like the albatross on the Ancient Mariner, was the change made by him in the foundations for the central unit, where the Rotunda and its surmounting Dome now stand. These Hallet laid in conformity with his own idea of a square court, instead of a rotunda as planned by Thornton. (Plate 9.) This was going altogether too far, and Thornton wrote that "when General Washington saw the extent of the alterations he expressed his disapproval in a style of such warmth as his dignity seldom permitted." And tradition has it that Washington could warm up the English language when necessary.

There was some question as to the advisability of leaving this circular unit an open court or covering it with a dome. The present great Dome is so dominant a feature of the Capitol that, to most of us, it is a surprise to learn that anything else was ever contemplated. However, we find Washington writing to the commissioners, on November 9, 1793, and commenting on a proposal by Hadfield "to add a dome over the open, or circular area or lobby which in my judgment is a most desirable thing, & what I always expected was part of the original design until otherwise informed in my late visits to the City."

Further corroboration is found in a report, dated March 11, 1796, which Alexander White submitted to Congress for the board of commissioners, of which he was a member. In this he stated quite definitely that, "The grand vestibule may or may not

PLATE 12. East front of the old House wing. Designed by Thornton, and
erected by Latrobe. Photograph by the author

be covered with a dome; architects differ in opinion with regard
to covering it. If it should not be covered it will consist only of
an arcade twenty feet high and ten feet wide; and over that a
colonnade sixteen feet high, affording a communication from
the grand staircase to all the other parts of the building."

One might think that the terms "grand vestibule" and "circular
area or lobby" were applied to the circular room originally shown
west of the present Rotunda, the projection of which formed so
effective a feature of the west front in the early designs. Any
uncertainty on this score is dispelled by a statement from the self-
same commissioner, Alexander White. In a memorial to Congress, March 8, 1798, he stated, "That the Capitol in the city of
Washington, if the plan shall be fully executed, will contain a
main body and two wings—the main body is composed of two
parts—a grand circular vestibule to the east, of 112 feet diameter
and a conference room to the west, a circle of 90 feet diameter,
both of full elevation—the first covered with a dome—the second
with a temple—the latter will finish on the outside with a colonnade in the center of the west front." (Plate 11.)

The dimensions given and the use of the term "grand vestibule"
in these two reports by the same man seem to clinch the matter,
and we see also that at some time during the three intervening
years the question of dome or no dome had been settled.

The "temple" referred to in connection with the conference
room is shown on Plate 11, where it may easily be mistaken for
an alternative suggestion for the dome over the rotunda.

The appointment of Thornton on the board of commissioners
was evidently regarded with favor, at least by those conscienti-
ously interested in the situation, for Andrew Ellicott congratu-
lated the appointee and gave the former commissioners a sly dig
by referring to them as being ignorant, and easy prey.

Thornton could go ahead now with the development of his
ideas, unhampered by jealous competitors, and gave out the statement that the President had requested him to restore the Capitol
to conformity with his original plan. This afforded him the congenial task of ordering Hallet's square foundations torn out and
his circular ones restored.

PLATE 13. Detail of old House wing, east front. Compare the detail with that of the Bulfinch gate house and fence post (Plates 57 and 58). William Thornton, architect. Photograph by the author

With a sympathetic and efficient superintendent, in the person of Hoban, Thornton was able to push construction rapidly and satisfactorily. To be sure, Hoban did object to all the extra work that was placed on his shoulders, as a result of having charge of the two big buildings, but the addition of twenty-five guineas per month to his pay envelope smoothed over this difficulty.

The fall of 1795 found the basement story of the north wing about complete. This is the section of the building immediately north of the great Dome, in which is located the room that was occupied by the Supreme Court after the Senate, in 1859, moved into the new north wing. (Plate 18.)

Thornton held the position of Commissioner until May, 1802, when the office was abolished by act of Congress, and during that time had the continued satisfaction of exercising supervisory con- trol over the execution of his designs.

THORNTON THE VERSATILE

Dr. Thornton ceased to direct design and construction of the Capitol when the board of commissioners was abolished. The responsibilities previously vested in them, as well as those of Hoban, were transferred in part to a single executive. This posi- tion was bestowed on Thomas Munroe, who bolstered up his income by serving also as postmaster of the city.

Up to this time Thornton had been the only official architect of the Capitol. Those associated with him, even though possessed of technical training superior to his, were employed merely as superintendents and draftsmen, which may presumably have been a further cause of the criticism and jealousy that produced con- tinuous turmoil.

Termination of this official connection did not result in the loss of Thornton's talents to the Government, for President Jef- ferson immediately appointed him as a clerk, at $1,400 per year, to be responsible for the issuing of patents. This work had been previously in the hands of the Secretaries of State and War, and of the Attorney General. The first patents were issued, so it is said, following special conferences between Jefferson, Knox, and Randolph, who then held these three important offices. The responsibility was placed definitely, in 1793, in the hands of the Secretary of State.

Jefferson's deep interest in mechanics and invention would naturally suggest the establishment of a department devoted to the control of patents, and no better person than Dr. Thornton could be found to undertake the organization of this work. Many of his policies have become established regulations, and he is regarded as the founder of the United States Patent Office. He remained as its head until his death in 1828.

The models, records, and other property of the department were removed by him, in 1810, to one end of Blodgett's Hotel, a building which the Government had recently purchased, and here, with the Post Office Department, they remained until a fire in 1836.

When the British burned the public buildings of Washington in 1814, Dr. Thornton is credited with having saved the Patent Office by an act of heroic bravery. According to the story, he saw a British officer wheel a cannon into position to fire on the building, whereupon he dashed up, threw himself from his horse directly before the mouth of the cannon, and demanded, "Are you Englishmen, or Goths and Vandals? This is the Patent Office, the repository of the inventive genius of America, in which the whole civilized world is concerned. Would you destroy it? If so, fire away and let the charge pass through my body." At this time he removed the records to his farm in the country, so none were lost. During the evacuation of the city he placed a guard at the Navy Yard and the Capitol.

He was noted for his personal bravery, and tradition says that on several occasions he attempted to protect a wife from being beaten by a brutal husband, only to find himself placed on the defensive by a combined attack from the pair.

The sympathies of Dr. Thornton were always with the oppressed, as is evidenced by an expensive and futile attempt on his part to colonize American negroes in Africa. In spite of the failure of this enterprise his interest in negro colonization continued throughout his life.

A contemporary said of him: "He had a well earned reputation

for letters and taste; . . . he was a wit, a painter, and a poet."
Dunlap, early biographer of America's artists, paid him a similar
tribute, writing of him, "He was a scholar and a gentleman, full
of talent and eccentricity, a Quaker, by profession a painter, a
poet, and well acquainted with the mechanics and arts; his company was a complete antidote to dullness."

During the long period of his residence in Washington, from
1793 to 1828, Dr. Thornton developed close friendships and professional relations with most of the important persons of his time.
Washington was a familiar visitor at the Thornton home when in
the Federal City. Jefferson, Madison, Randolph, L'Enfant, Hamilton, Adams, Fulton, and numerous others were numbered among
his close acquaintances. His social circle embraced the Tayloes,
Stuarts, Carrolls, Van Nesses, and many other families of distinction. By them his acquaintance was prized because of his social
graces, his familiarity with the arts and sciences and, perhaps
not least of all, by his love for race horses. This in itself was an
open sesame to the southern heart.

John Tayloe, for whom he designed the Octagon House, was
probably the most noted breeder of race horses in this country at
the time, which was a sufficient reason for the close friendship
between the two men, for Thornton also kept and bred race
horses. He imported blooded stock from Barbary and England,
and his records show that he possessed horses that were valued at
more than $2,000 apiece, a tidy sum of money in those days. The
generosity of Thornton, and his fondness for horses were responsible for the loss of a considerable portion of his fortune.

When President Jefferson appointed Dr. Thornton to develop
a system of handling patents, he was not making a mere political
move; he knew the qualifications of his appointee. He knew of
his interest in mechanics and that, among other things, he had for
many years applied himself to the problems of propelling boats
by steam power. Even before 1790, during his first visit to the
United States, Thornton was engaged to build steamboats for use
on the Mississippi, a scheme that fell through because of lack of
financial backing.

He had been associated with Fitch in his experiments on the

Delaware, long before Fulton attempted to solve the problem on the Hudson, and he defended Fitch's claim of priority in a pamphlet dated June, 1810, that was reprinted, 1850, in the Patent Office Record. He also claimed that Fulton acquired valued suggestions through a study, in 1806, of Thornton's drawings in the Patent Office, and that Fulton's death was due in part to worry caused by Thornton's pamphlet.

A curious commentary on the two men is found in a tradition that Fulton offered to bet Thornton that a steamboat could never go faster than five miles per hour, while the latter optimistically bet on twelve.

Patents issued to the Doctor on the conversion of sawdust into planks, improvements in steamboats, steam boilers and condensers, brought him an offer of £2,000 from Fernando Fairfax for a quarter interest in his patents and manufacturing companies.

His scholarly interests extended to the writing and publication of papers on medicine, philosophy, language, astronomy, government, finance, and art. A book on the elements of written language secured for him the Magellanic gold medal from the American Philosophical Society. This work was published in Philadelphia, 1796, under the title, *Cadmus.*

Painting as well as architecture received due attention from this many-sided genius, and several portraits and miniatures of Washington, Jefferson, the Countess Beauharnais, and others of his friends, are accredited to him.

With all his varied accomplishments, Dr. Thornton is known today almost entirely, it is quite safe to say, because of his design for the Capitol; but by architects, he is as well remembered because of the Octagon House, which he planned for his friend John Tayloe, as a Washington home. This was finished in 1801, and is famous in history as the house occupied by the Madisons after the burning of the White House. It is built of brick, with stone trimmings, and has interior woodwork of unusual richness and beauty of design. The American Institute of Architects now owns the Octagon, which is occupied as the organization's national headquarters.

Tudor Place, in Georgetown, is a more pretentious structure,

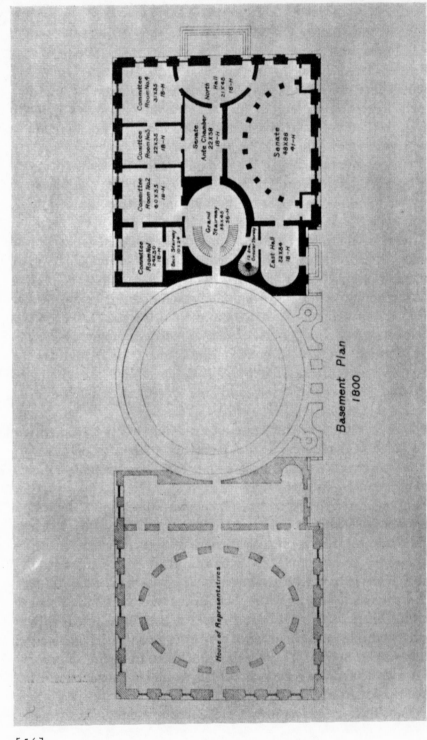

PLATE 14. Plan showing progress of construction of Capitol when first occupied by Congress in 1800. Reproduced from Brown's "History of the United States Capitol"

and has the distinction of being still in the possession of descendants of the original builder. As relatives of the Washingtons
and Custises, successive generations have endowed it with a
wealth of historic objects and family heirlooms, and with associations with the great of our nation's history.

Woodlawn, below Alexandria on the road to Mount Vernon,
and Brentwood in the District, were also built from Thornton's
designs, and there is a possibility that others nearby may be
accredited to him.

Dr. William Thornton made many and diverse contr'butions
to American culture, and was one of those fortunate enough to
receive recognition while still living. His death occurred March
28, 1828, in the city of Washington where he had lived and labored through so many years. He was buried in the Congressional
Cemetery, under a tomb similar to those which cover the graves
of Congressmen, and his body was followed to this resting place,
not only by members of Congress and the Cabinet, but by the
President of the United States.

THE CAPITAL CITY OF 1800

Only an imagination like that of L'Enfant could picture, at the
close of the eighteenth century, the city of Washington as we see
it today. Few visitors to the city of marble buildings, that now
stretches back from the Potomac, can re-create in their minds an
image of the pathetic little excuse for a national capital in which
Congress convened November 17, 1800.

On an isolated hill stood in solitary grandeur one wing of the
projected "Congress House" or Capitol. (Plate 15.) To the south
of it were the site and some foundations of the major portion of
that edifice. A mile or so away to the west stood the imposing
"Palace" of the President. An occasional house or shanty suggested the location of future streets, the direction of which was
indicated partially by ditches, and by stretches of bare ground
from which swirled clouds of dust in summer, and in which
vehicles and animals floundered and partially submerged during
the rainy and muddy seasons.

We can gain our most accurate and vivid impressions of the

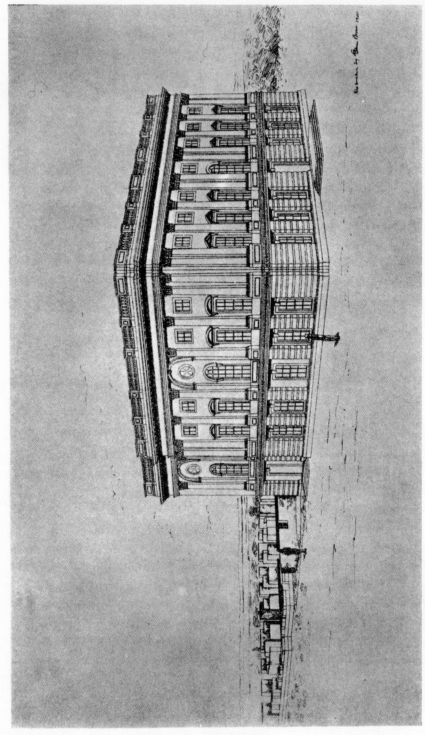

PLATE 15. Drawing by Glenn Brown showing the Capitol when first occupied by Congress in 1800. Reproduced from Brown's "History of the United States Capitol"

[56]

place from the comments of those who lived there and took part in its life. The desolate appearance of the place is reflected without reserve in a letter from Oliver Woolcott, Secretary of the Treasury, who wrote soon after his arrival: "There are few houses in any one place, and most of them small, miserable huts, which present an awful contrast to the public buildings. . . . You may look in almost any direction, over an extent of ground nearly as large as the city of New York, without seeing a fence or any object except brick kilns and temporary huts for laborers."

Mrs. John Adams, fresh from the metropolitan luxuries of Boston, New York, and Philadelphia, expressed scant enthusiasm for the infant capital when writing to her daughter that "Woods are all you see from Baltimore until you reach the City, which is only so in name—here and there a small cot without a window appearing in the Forest, through which you travel miles without seeing a human being."

A letter from Woolcott to his wife was hardly ethusiastic in tone, nor calculated to arouse in her a desire to take up residence in the new city by the Potomac. He told her that there was "one good Tavern about forty rods from the Capitol, and several other houses" under construction, and, he added: "I do not perceive how the members of Congress can possibly secure lodgings unless they will consent to live like Scholars in a college or Monks in a monastery, crowded ten or twenty in one house, and utterly secluded from Society. The only resource for such as wish to live comfortably will be found in Georgetown, three miles distant, over as bad a Road in winter as the clay grounds near Hartford."

Gouverneur Morris wrote facetiously: "We want nothing here but houses, cellers, kitchens, well-informed men, amiable women, and other trifles of this kind to make our city perfect," to which he added, "In short, it is the very best city in the world for a future residence." A certain young lady, in an equally sarcastic vein, spoke of Georgetown as "A town of houses without streets, as Washington is a town of streets without houses."

Yet at that very time Georgetown had a population of about five thousand, and was a busy port with ocean-going ships sailing from its wharves laden with tobacco and wheat for destinations on both sides of the Atlantic. Here General Braddock had landed the troops that marched with him to defeat near Fort Duquesne, and from here had written back to England that he "never attended a more complete banquet, or met better dressed or better mannered people than I met on my arrival in George-town."

John Cotton Smith referred to New Jersey Avenue as "a road, with two buildings on each side of it," and added that "Pennsylvania Avenue was, nearly the whole distance, a deep morass covered with alder bushes, which were cut through the width of the intended avenue," while the city as a whole was overgrown "with scrub oak bushes on the higher grounds, and on the marshy soil either with trees or some sort of shrubbery."

The marshy messiness of the future Pennsylvania Avenue fastened on it a euphonious, if not flattering title, the "Great Serbonian Bog." The wide, lonely spaces between houses prompted Abbe Correa de Serra to describe this pathetic little capital as the "City of Magnificent Distances," a derisive epithet that has stuck, and which time and change have made a term of praise.

In the midst of these unprepossessing surroundings, "the people are poor," according to Woolcott and "live like fishes, by eating each other."

Even the "President's Palace" failed to inspire complete admiration in Abigail Adams, for she found it unfinished and bare, surrounded by rubbish and brickyards. Brickyards in a land of clay where the brick was usually burned at the site on which it was to be used, seemed to be an ever present element of ugliness. Of the Palace Mrs. Adams wrote, "We have not the least fence, yard, or other convenience without, and the great unfinished audience-room I make a drying-room of, to hang the clothes in."

Thomas Jefferson's comment on the Palace, when he moved in on March 4, 1801, was that it was a "great stone house, big enough for two emperors, one pope, and the grand lama into the bargain."

The movement to transfer the seat of government to a city already established gained considerable headway even before British incendiaries fired the public buildings in 1814, and an advocate of this idea, in 1808, called attention to "premature symptoms of decay" all about, and to "so many houses built, not inhabited, but tumbling into decay." The British minister, in the following year, spoke of the city's "wild, desolate air from being so scantily and rudely cultivated." Washington Irving wrote in 1811, during the recess of Congress, "You cannot imagine how forlorn this desert city appears to me, now that the great tide of casual population has rolled away." Yet, in this crude environment Dolly Madison held the gay court that made her and her time famous.   *   *   *   *

The Congress of the United States had led a peripatetic existence. The earliest sessions had been menaced by the threat of British arms, and it has been spoken of as having "met where the enemy was not."

Many a place, where the Continental Congress had held its sessions, nursed a fond hope that to it might come the honor and economic advantage of becoming the seat of government. These hopes were dashed by the Act of July 16, 1790. After the temporary stay of ten years at Philadelphia the little group of officials and clerks, that handled the machinery of government, finally transferred its meager equipment of furniture and records from the Delaware to the Potomac.

When Congress was called to order on November 17, 1800, its wanderings were ended. The government of the United States was established permanently, as President Washington had desired, close to Mount Vernon on the banks of the Potomac. Here Jefferson, Adams, Madison, Hamilton, Monroe, and other great characters of the time guided the early destinies of the young republic.

BENJAMIN HENRY LATROBE

A letter written by President Jefferson in the spring of 1803 placed Benjamin Henry Latrobe (Plate 16) in control of building operations on the Capitol. Following is the text of this letter:

"Washington, D. C., March 6, 1803.

"SIR: Congress has appropriated a sum of $50,000.00 to be applied to the public buildings under my direction. This falls, of

PLATE 16. Benjamin Henry Latrobe. Photograph reproduced by courtesy of
Charles E. Fairman

course, under the immediate business of the superintendent, Mr.
Munroe, whose office is substituted for that of the board of commissioners. The former post of surveyor of the public buildings,
which Mr. Hoban held until the dissolution of the board (at
$1,700 a year) will be revived.

"If you choose to accept it, you will be appointed to it, and
would be expected to come on by the first of April. Indeed, if you
could make a flying trip here to set contractors at work immedi-

ately in raising freestone, it would be extremely important, because it is now late to have to engage laborers, and the quantity of freestone which can be raised, delivered, and cut in the season is the only thing that will limit the extent of our operations this year.

"I set out tomorrow for Monticello, and shall be absent three weeks, but shall be glad to receive there your answer to this.

"Accept my friendly salutations and regards,

"TH. JEFFERSON."

Latrobe immediately accepted the position, which he was eminently qualified to fill. In fact few of the men who have occupied this office have brought to their task training and experience superior to his. He had studied in the schools of England and Germany; worked in the office of a leading London architect; carried on a private practice; held public office. He came to this country as one of the first of a long line of European trained architects. He had not only academic and technical training, but a broad general education acquired in schools, by travel, and through an unquenchable passion for knowledge. Also, nature had endowed him with a retentive memory and rare facility in the use of pencil and brush.

Commissions in both architecture and engineering came to him almost immediately upon arrival in this country, and an early introduction to Thomas Jefferson brought to him eventually this honor of being placed in charge of the country's most important building operation.

*   *   *   *

The name, Latrobe, is of French origin. An immediate ancestor, Henri Boneval de la Trobe, bore the names of two branches of the family, Bonneval and la Trobe. He was a Huguenot who, it is believed, migrated to Holland after the revocation of the Edict of Nantes, and later crossed to England with William III.

His grandson, Benjamin Latrobe, joined the Moravians and became minister at Fulneck, near Leeds. Benjamin married, about 1755 Ann Margaret Antes of Germantown, Pennsylvania, who had been sent abroad for study. Her family too were Moravians, and she was related to David Rittenhouse, distinguished scientist of Philadelphia.

Three sons were born to this couple, one of whom (born May 1, 1764) was Benjamin Henry Latrobe. The boy spent much of his early childhood at school in Yorkshire, and when eleven or twelve years of age he was sent to a Moravian seminary in Saxony, where he remained until prepared to enter the University of Leipsic. His assiduous devotion to study, together with his retentive memory, and diversity of interests, carried him far in scholarship during his three years at the University.

Leaving at the age of eighteen, he spent several months in 1785, traveling through Germany. Then a spirit of dare-deviltry prompted him to enlist in the Prussian Army with some English and Prussian youths, also from the University. This adventure was short-lived, and such military ambitions as he may have nursed were promptly and effectually nipped through participation in a couple of engagements in which his company of hussars was involved. He came out of the fracas severely wounded and, upon recovering, left to others his opportunity to tread the paths of glory, while he chalked up the word "finis" on this foolhardy adventure.

With uniform off and student's togs on, young Latrobe accomplished the "grand tour" of the continent, which was deemed an essential part of every gentleman's education, and returned to England, arriving just prior to the death of his father.

He now spent several years in London studying constantly whatever subjects chanced to strike his fancy. Among other things, he applied himself to the making of two excellent translations from the German.

Architecture proved a fruitful and congenial field of study and he eventually decided upon it as his life work. In preparation for this career he studied engineering with Smeaton, the builder of Eddystone lighthouse, who had retired from active practice and was engaged in preparing for publication works pertaining to his profession.

The scholarly background acquired through his studies of the classics and mathematics, together with his first hand acquaintance with the architecture of the continent, afforded Latrobe a substantial foundation for the specialized studies necessitated in preparation for his chosen field. In 1787 or 1788 he secured a position in the office of Samuel Pepys Cockerell, a leading architect of London and a pioneer in the Greek Revival. This introduction to the new movement, which was receiving impetus from the researches and publications of Stuart and Revett, had an important bearing on Latrobe's future leadership in the Revival that was inaugurated by Thomas Jefferson as a Roman Revival, but which became in time a revival of the Greek.

The facilities of Cockerell's office, together with Latrobe's exceptional ability and studiousness, enabled him to acquire speedily the practical knowledge necessary to qualify as a professional architect and engineer.

He left Cockerell's office after a comparatively brief term and entered private practice. He is known to have built several houses at this time and to have superintended construction of a canal in Surrey, displaying ability which won for him an appointment as Surveyor of Public Offices, in London.

Meanwhile he had married, in 1790, Miss Lydia Sellon, daughter of a distinguished scholar, Dr. Sellon; and sister of John Sellon, an equally distinguished lawyer. She died in 1793, leaving a son and daughter. Her death proved such a heart breaking blow to Latrobe that he determined to leave the surroundings that were so intimately associated with her memory. Declining the office of Surveyor to the Crown, with an annual salary of £1,000, he sold his property, crossed the Atlantic with his two small children and on March 20, 1796, landed at Norfolk, Virginia.

Letters of introduction admitted him to the best society, as may be judged from a letter written some ten days after his arrival. In this he speaks of "doing little odds and ends of services for them—designing a staircase for Mr. A—'s new house, a house and offices for Captain P—, tuning a pianoforte for Mrs. W—, scribbling doggerel for Mrs. A—, tragedy for her mother, and Italian songs for Mrs. T—. The excursion into the Dismal Swamp opened a prospect for professional pursuits of more importance to me. . . . In the meantime the management of the James River

Navigation seems opening for me, and I am going thither to-morrow." Such varied activities crowded into one fortnight, especially after some four months of sea voyage, certainly indicate versatility, to say nothing of boundless energy.

During the following year he designed the penitentiary at Richmond, in which he introduced the almost untried principle of solitary confinement. While engaged on this work he made Richmond his home and undertook various commissions. He completed the exterior of the State Capitol, substituting more severe classical ornament for the Louis XVI detail that was shown on the design prepared by Jefferson and Clerisseau. He also prepared for William Ludwell Lee drawings for the remodel-ing of Green Spring, the residence near Williamsburg that was originally built by the royal Governor, Sir William Berkeley.

On a visit to Philadelphia in March, 1798, Latrobe met the President of the Bank of Pennsylvania, Samuel L. Fox, and dur-ing a casual conversation with him made a hasty sketch suggesting a design for the new bank building which was then under con-sideration. Nine months later he was greatly surprised at re-ceiving word that he had been awarded the contract to design the building, on the strength of his rough, unstudied sketch.

This marked a turning point in his career, and in April, 1799, he moved to Philadelphia to undertake the work.

Erection of the Bank of Pennsylvania was equally important in the life of Latrobe and in the history of American architecture. As the first building of the Greek Revival in this country, it en-abled the architect to give concrete expression to principles and academic knowledge which he had acquired in the office of Cockerell; and to direct the Classic Revival from the Roman types of Palladio, with which it had been clothed by Jefferson, to the Greek forms that were becoming known through the publications of Stuart and Revett, and others.

The building had a portico of six Ionic columns at each end, and a low dome over the middle. The details were adapted from those of the Erectheum at Athens.

We can judge of the beauty of this building from the original drawings, which still exist, and a few engravings in which it is reproduced. Latrobe himself wrote in his journal that "The highest encomium and the most flattering I ever received relative to my architectural efforts, was in regard to the bank of Pennsylvania.

"Walking up Second Street I observed two French officers standing opposite the building and looking at it without saying a word. I stepped into Black's shop and stood close to them. After some time one of them exclaimed several times, 'C'est beau, et si simple!' He said no more and stood for a few minutes longer before he walked away with his companion. I do not recollect distinctly anything that has happened that has given me so much particular satisfaction."

It is a great pity that this building should have been wantonly wrecked as it was shortly after the Civil War to make way for a warehouse. Thus, through the lack of intelligent appreciation, common in that period, American architecture lost one of its important and outstanding monuments.

Another of Latrobe's contributions to Philadelphia was its first water-works system, by means of which a water supply was drawn from the Schuylkill River. In this undertaking he was severely handicapped by the fact that Pierre Charles L'Enfant, the French engineer who planned the City of Washington, had previously designed two buildings for Philadelphia on so grand a scale that neither was ever completed. One was a mansion for the financier, Robert Morris, the other, assembly rooms for the city. These two fiascos, on which large sums of money were squandered, left a bad taste in the Philadelphia mouth, and when another engineer, also with a French name, came along with a weird proposal to run water from the river up to people's doorsteps, it just didn't make sense to the Philadelphia mind.

The customary thing happened, that always happens when someone ahead of his time attempts to do something that his time does not understand. The populace arose in its wrath, and parties unknown began to smash things. When the pipes were laid and the wheels of the machinery almost ready to "go round" public sentiment boiled up to the overflowing point, and "the damned Frenchman" as he was popularly dubbed came in for much villifying, and narrowly escaped physical damage.

However, Latrobe was not to be daunted by a mere trifle like mob violence so, on the day when the pumps were finally ready to be started, he gave orders to have all street hydrants left open. During the night he went with a few trusted friends and one of his workmen to the pumping station, fired up the boiler, and set the pumps in motion.

Next morning when Philadelphia rubbed the sleep from its eyes, it was treated to the amazing sight of Schuylkill water gushing vigorously from hydrants throughout the town.

The "damned Frenchman" now had the satisfaction of hearing jibes turned into praise, and it is to be hoped that he treated himself to a few heartfelt "I told you sos."

This episode of the water-works gives a good slant on the secret of American progress which someone has quite frankly said, is due to the fact that this country possesses men "so dumb that they don't know a thing can't be done, so they go ahead and do it." The attitude of the Philadelphia populace gives a slant on another fact, but one of contrary significance, which is that we have an even greater number of folks who are so dumb that they won't believe a thing can be done until they see it done—and then they have serious doubts as to their eyesight.

LATROBE TAKES ON THE CAPITOL

A survey of a possible canal to connect the waters of Chesapeake and Delaware bays was the next problem tackled by Latrobe but, while engaged on preliminaries, President Jefferson called him to Washington and handed him the appointment as Surveyor of Public Buildings, his chief responsibility to be completion of the Capitol.

He at once (on April 7, 1803) appointed John Lenthal, clerk of works, and delegated to him most of the responsibility for execution of the work, as Latrobe was away much of the time looking after his private practice.

Like his predecessors in office, Latrobe began promptly to suggest modifications in Thornton's design, and as promptly brought down Thornton's wrath on his head. On presenting his suggestions to President Jefferson he was politely referred to Dr. Thornton. The outcome of his conference with the choleric doctor was what might have been expected, in view of the incessant warfare in which Thornton had been engaged with one after another of the men who had been appointed as his associates.

Latrobe wrote rather pathetically to Jefferson, on February 27, 1804, the following letter:

"DEAR SIR: I judged very ill in going to Dr. Thornton. In a few peremptory words he, in fact, told me that no difficulties existed in his plan but such as were made by those who were too ignorant to remove them, and though those were not exactly his words, his expressions, his tones, his manners, and his absolute refusal to discuss the subject spoke his meaning more strongly and offensively than I have expressed."

The President may have suggested this visit with a bit of malicious anticipation of its salutary effect on the new appointee, for he had suffered long and patiently from too much suggestion and not enough execution on this job. At any rate he replied quite noncommittally the next day:

"DEAR SIR: I am very sorry the explanations attempted between Dr. Thornton and yourself on the matter of finishing the House of Representatives have not succeeded."

But Latrobe was not the kind to quit under fire, and continued persistently to push his ideas, eventually gaining his way to a certain extent. Moreover, he proved himself the equal of Dr. Thornton as a tactician, and dodged the steam-roller methods by which the doctor-architect had succeeded in flattening out former opposition.

He was permitted but little leeway on the exterior design of the Capitol, as the north wing was practically completed and it was necessary of course that the two wings should be practically identical in exterior appearance. The south wing was scarcely above the foundations (Plates 14, 15), and within it was a temporary building facetiously called "the oven" in which the House of Representatives held its sessions. The name "oven" referred aptly to both its shape and its internal temperature.

The Library of Congress possesses a letter written to Walter Lenox by Robert Mills, in which he says:

"When I was a student at Washington the room, called the Oven, being of an oval plan, was built upon the original foundations of the south wing of the Capitol for the accommodation of the House of Representatives, in which this body sat for several years, with great satisfaction, being found a most excellent speaking hall."

In view of the persistent embarrassments to which successive architects were subjected by pernicious acoustics in the Hall of Representatives, both before and after the fire of 1814, they might well have learned a lesson or two from this much ridiculed structure.

The space between the two wings, and above which the great dome now rises, was cluttered with foundations. Some of these were scheduled for removal, being the ones built by Hallet, in direct violation of Thornton's plan.

*   *   *   *

Meanwhile the conflict between Thornton and Latrobe gained intensity, involving lengthy statements from both in which charges and counter-charges, explanations and excuses were handed back and forth. Both had keen minds which could word bitter and sarcastic criticisms with either tongue or pen. Each seemed to take unholy delight in harpooning the other, and even after Thornton had ceased, in 1805, to defend officially the integrity of his design, he could not resist an opportunity for derision of Latrobe when some weakness or mistake on his part afforded opportunity.

Strangely enough, Latrobe, with all his ability and training, seemed to lay himself open unnecessarily to such thrusts. He was constantly under fire from various sources because of delays in prosecution of the work, or faulty construction, or of long absences from Washington due to conflicting demands on his time by his private practice.

During these absences, construction on the Capitol was largely in the hands of his clerk of works, John Lenthal, who urged Latrobe, though unavailingly, to spend more time in Washington.

Letters that passed between them have been preserved by

PLATE 17. Old Supreme Court Room. Now used as a law library. Photograph by author

PLATE 18. The old Senate Chamber. Later remodeled for the Supreme Court. Photographed from an old print by L. C. Handy Studios

descendants of Lenthal, and in these may be sensed the manner in which the work was conducted at long range. Latrobe expresses quite freely his annoyance at the tenacity with which President Jefferson sticks to his resolve that the design of the building shall be carried out strictly according to Thornton's original plan, in spite of Latrobe's conviction that his own ways are better. This attitude verifies the statement that he was a man with unbounded confidence in his own ability as an engineer and architect, and intolerant toward anyone who might disagree with his opinions.

Latrobe defended himself convincingly against his critics by attributing delays to the uncertain policies of Congress in making appropriations, and to the difficulties experienced in securing stone. When called to task for not having drawings prepared for certain details of the exterior, he quoted letters previously written to Lenthal in which he asked the latter to work out these drawings from the plates of Sir William Chambers' book. In one of these he wrote, "You have William Chambers book and I have not. I choose rather to refer you to it than involve you in the possibilities of a mistake of mine which might have occurred by rendering the feet and inches of Stuart or Desgodetz into parts of a module; and ten minutes would suffice you who have these things at your finger ends, to have become master of the whole subject."

His reasons for absenting himself for long periods are obvious; he was engaged on construction of the Chesapeake and Delaware Canal, as well as other less important undertakings, and found it desirable to live in Philadelphia, Wilmington, New Castle, or such other towns as were conveniently located near the places where construction was in progress.

Through constant correspondence with Lenthal he felt he was fulfilling his duty to the Government and, at the same time, was earning commissions that were doubtless welcome additions to his income.

His failures in construction are not so easily explained, especially when they have to do with the building of arches. Thornton found wholesome food for his sarcasm in the collapse of vaults in

Richmond, and in the Treasury and Capitol at Washington. Surprising evidence is found in a letter to Lenthal, dated December 31, 1806, in which he says, rather lamely, "I am sorry the arches have fallen, but I have had these accidents before on a larger scale, and must therefore grin and bear it."

It is difficult to understand why an engineer, as well trained and with the experience possessed by Latrobe, should have accepted the collapse of masonry arches as a misfortune to be borne with fortitude, instead of a fault in construction to be studied and corrected. But apparently he did, for, in June of 1808 a large arch in the staircase hall was found to be giving evidence of structural weakness, as may be learned from his letters to Lenthal. In one of these dated July 16, 1808, he wrote:

"I am perfectly horror-struck by the acct. of the motion of the great arch. I fear we are ruined. Has the stairs arch started? Where has the crush gone to? If the sides are sound, how could the panels yield? and as to the piers yielding without cracking I am still more at loss. I can give no advice at this distance, for the failure is beyond my comprehension. Under the circumstances I must try to return as soon as possible. . . . When I have thought a little more about it I will write again, though all I can say must come too late.   "Yours truly,

"B. HENRY LATROBE."

Within two months after this letter was sent, the irony of fate gave tragic emphasis to their fears, and closed the correspondence. Arches under the Senate Chamber collapsed on September 19th, and Lenthal was killed by the falling masonry.

To add to Latrobe's discomfort, acoustics in the new Hall of Representatives were found to be exceedingly poor, affording Thornton the welcome opportunity to give him another dig by saying that if his original plan had been followed, there would have been no such difficulty. As if this were not a sufficiently bitter dose to swallow, it was made still more unpalatable by the caustic comment of no less a person than John Randolph of Roanoke that the hall was "handsome, and fit for anything but the use intended."

Furthermore, on the recommendation of Thornton, Latrobe was ordered by the committee in charge of construction to hang heavy curtains behind the columns which encircled the room, as a means of softening the echoes, and also adding to the decorative effect.

This was in 1808, some five years after he had taken office. Meanwhile he had accomplished much, replacing in the north wing timbers that had rotted away thus endangering the structure; rebuilding certain foundations that had been improperly constructed by an unscrupulous foreman during the absence of a former contractor; and making necessary repairs to the roof, where timbers had decayed as the result of leaky covering.

Various changes had been made in the arrangement of minor rooms designed for committee and other uses, and the plan of the House of Representatives had been changed from an ellipse to a room with two short sides and semicircular ends.

Two alternative designs had been offered by Latrobe for this room, in one of which the great columns, that were to surround it, were of the Doric order, following in detail those of the Theatre of Marcellus at Rome, or the Greek order of the Clepsydra at Athens. This was favored by Latrobe. Mr. Jefferson however chose the more ornate of the designs (Plate 19), in which the Corinthian order was used, and insisted that the capitals be reproduced from the Choragic Monument of Lysicrates at Athens.

He further suggested that the columns be built of burnt brick, with capitals and bases of stone; with the intention probably of covering the brick with a surface of stucco, as was his custom on work in Virginia, notably at his own home, Monticello, and later at the University of Virginia. Ultimately it was decided to cut the columns from freestone.

Use of the Corinthian order was just one more thorn in Latrobe's flesh for, in a letter to the Secretary of the Navy, written in 1811, he complained of Jefferson's mandatory order "that I should introduce Corinthian columns into the House of Representatives, and put one hundred lights of plate glass into the ceiling, contrary to my declared judgment, urgent entreaties, and representations."

PLATE 19. Latrobe's modification of Thornton's design for the Hall of Representatives. Original drawing is in the Library of Congress

He apparently felt a bit apologetic for this evidence of vexation toward Jefferson, who had done so much for him and had been so sincere an admirer and friend, for in the same letter he says: "In other respects, however, the honor which the friendship of this great man has done me obliterates all feeling of dissatisfaction on account of those errors of a vitiated taste and an imperfect attention to the practical effects of his architectural projects." The final phrase rather "vitiates" the implied apology, but reflects the natural feelings of a highly trained professional man toward an amateur who, as in the case of Mr. Jefferson, was entirely self-taught, and without the benefit of school training or professional experience.

Latrobe's tendency to become testy and relieve his mind by "spitting fire" when told how to conduct his own professional affairs had doubtless been aggravated by many such clashes. The following amusing letter, written to Lenthal, evidently served as a safety valve to reduce the temperamental pressure incident to such a collision of ideas:

"Wilmington, Jan. 7, 1805.

". . . You and I are both blockheads. Presidents and Vice Presidents are the only architects and poets, and prophets for aught I know in the United States. Therefore let us fall down and worship them. . . .

"God bless thee. Be moderate with the lime.

"Yours very affecty

"B. H. LATROBE."

In this same letter he hands out some blistering comments on "little Burr and little Hamilton" after which he doubtless felt better toward them all.

A minor dispute occurred regarding the use of glass in the ceiling of the House. The President insisted that "alternate panels in the alternate rows of panels" should be glazed with plate glass. To this plan Latrobe objected strenuously on the score of leakage, condensation, and cross lights.

Convinced that his own judgment in this matter was to be preferred, Latrobe went serenely ahead with the dome, but omitting the glass, until Lenthal was called sharply to task by the following letter:

"Washington, D. C., October 21, 1806.

"DEAR SIR: The skylights in the dome of the House of Representatives' Chamber were a part of the plan as settled and communicated to Mr. Latrobe; that the preparation for them has not been made and the building now to be stopped for them has been wrong; to correct that wrong now they must be immediately prepared, and that the building may be delayed as short a time as possible as many hands as possible should be employed in preparing them.

"Accept my salutations and best wishes,

"Mr. Lenthal."   "TH. JEFFERSON.

The ungrammatical makeup of this letter suggests that the Jeffersonian ire may have been somewhat aroused. He too seemed to spit fire.

The dome when completed was decorated by a painter named George Bridport and, although Latrobe's criticisms of the glazing were to an extent justified and realized, it was otherwise regarded as a successful feature of a much admired room.

In spite of the evident undesirability of the change from the original elliptical plan, and the President's adamant objection to changes from the Thornton scheme, Jefferson wrote to Latrobe, "I declare on many and all occasions, that I consider you the only person in the United States who could have executed the Representative Chamber or who could execute the middle building on any of the plans proposed." At another time he wrote to him, "The Representative Chamber will remain a durable monument to your talents as an architect."

That this was not merely a prejudiced and individual opinion may be inferred from the exclamation of the British officer, responsible for its burning, who said regretfully that it was a "pity to burn anything so beautiful."

The Capitol as originally planned had its more important front to the west, overlooking the city that was to be. Here Thornton had planned a great semicircular colonnade, as the central feature, with an imposing flight of steps following the curve and stretching from the main floor down to the ground level. On the east a portico was planned, with simple arched entrances in the basement wall, (Plates 11, 8) instead of the great sweep of steps that now gives so much distinction to this front.

Latrobe's plans for completing the building, for some reason reversed the importance of the east and west fronts. The semi-circular projection on the west, with its encircling steps, was replaced by a pedimented portico from which steps led down to a small Doric temple, flanked by massive wings of plain masonry, a feature that was quite obviously inspired by the Propylaea at Athens. (Plates 20, 21.) These, happily, were never constructed. On the east front he planned the monumental steps which were constructed later under the direction of Bulfinch.

The difficulties experienced by architect, contractors, and officials having supervisory powers, and by the poor Congressmen who, during the period of construction, had to suffer various forms of physical discomfort and at times actual danger, can scarcely be realized through a casual review of the story.

At one time their patience had become so completely exhausted that the temptation was almost irresistible to throw the whole business overboard; and the House of Representatives actually considered an amendment providing for "finishing the President's House in such a manner as will accommodate both Houses of Congress; and for the purpose of renting, purchasing or building a suitable house for the accommodation of the President." This move was defeated by a vote of 76 to 27.

Meanwhile Latrobe had contrived to find, and continued to find, time to take on outside jobs, designing various buildings, public and private. The output of his facile pencil was amazing. There were houses innumerable; the shops and entrance of the Navy Yard, and St. John's Church at Washington; a number of scattering school and college jobs; a church at Alexandria; a courthouse, a dry dock, and a marine hospital or two; the list is too long to hold one's interest, even if it could be accurately documented. Most important of all his works was of course the

PLATE 20. Latrobe's design for the west front, dome, and entrance of the Capitol. Originial drawing is in the Library of Congress

PLATE 21. South elevation of Capitol as redesigned by Latrobe. Original design is in the Library of Congress

Cathedral at Baltimore, which was not completed until many years after his death.

His fertility of imagination is well illustrated in the capitals and columns which he designed for the ground floor lobby and the small rotunda of the Senate or north wing of the Capitol. In the former he deserted the two thousand year old tradition of loyalty to the acanthus leaf, and bestowed his artistic affections on the lowly cornstalk. His "cornstalk" or "corncob" capitals are among the most unique features of the great Capitol and are the delight of all who are fortunate enough to discover them and appreciate their individuality. (Plates 22, 23.) In them Latrobe made a distinctly original contribution to decorative design and, as might be expected from a man with his ability and discriminating taste, he did it well.

In place of the customary fluted columns, he represented bundles of cornstalks bound at the top with a rope, producing an effect not unlike that of the Egyptian papyrus column. On the capitals were carved ears of Indian corn, with the husks partially separated to show the kernels. Credit for this fanciful design has often been given to Jefferson, but this attribution seems to be disproved by the following letter written to him at Monticello, by Latrobe, on August 28, 1809.

"Dear Sir: I have packed up and sent to Richmond to be forwarded to Monticello a box containing the model of the capital of the columns of the lower vestibule of the Senatorial department of the north wing of the Capitol, which is composed of maize, on a short frustum running about 4 feet from the ground. It may serve for a dial stand, and should you appropriate it for that use I will forward to you a horizontal dial in Pennsylvania marble of the proper size. These capitals during the summer session obtained me more applause from members of Congress than all the works of magnitude or difficulty that surrounded them. They christened them the 'Corn-cob capitals,' whether for the sake of alliteration I can not tell, but certainly not very appropriately."

The capitols in the small rotunda, on the floor above, immortalize the tobacco leaf, source of early Colonial wealth. (Plates

24, 25, 26.) Two rows of conventionalized leaves surround the bell in the customary manner and from between the leaves of the upper row grow stems of natural tobacco leaves and flowers, the whole producing a design so closely approximating the effect of a classic capital that its individuality will be appreciated only on close inspection.

The periods when these two unique features of the Capitol were built are fixed definitely by a letter, dated November 5, 1816, from Latrobe to Thomas Jefferson, who was then living in retirement at Monticello.

"Thomas Jefferson, Esq.
          "Monticello, Virg.

"Dear Sir: Your letter of the 27th. of August received. . . . You have done my capital much honor in making it the support of your dial. The columns and capitals as executed and standing in the north wing of the Capitol on the ground floor were not much injured by the British, so little indeed that I wish some part of the building to remain as they left it. I do not propose to repair them unless the president shall order it to be done.

"By the suggestion of the Senate I devised a very material alteration of their accommodations especially a great enlargement of the Chamber itself.

"The great staircase must give way to the improvements. You probably recollect that, as a curious and difficult combination of admirably executed stone work, it was one of the most remarkable parts of the Capitol, but it was much injured by the Lanthorn, which being of wood, fell burning through the dome, and resting on the stairs, burnt many of the principal stones.

"The staircase has now another situation. It will be less curious but have I think some beauty. The area of the stairs will be occupied by a vestibule, in the center of which a circular colonade will support a dome for the purpose of admitting light. The columns of the rotunda, 16 in number, must be more slender than the Ionic order will admit, and ought not to be of the Corinthian because the chamber itself is of the Ionic order. I have therefore composed a capital of leaves and flowers of the tobacco plant which

PLATE 22. Drawing of "Cornstalk" column and capital. Designed by Latrobe. Reproduced from Brown's "History of the United States Capitol"

PLATE 23. Ground floor vestibule of old Senate wing. The famous "Corn-stalk" columns were designed by Latrobe; they date from before the fire of 1814. Capitals were modeled by Giuseppe Franzoni. Photograph by the author

PLATE 24. Drawing of "Tobacco leaf" capital. Designed by Latrobe. Reproduced from Brown's "History of the United States Capitol"

PLATE 25. Small rotunda in old Senate wing. The columns have the "Tobacco leaf" capitals, designed by Latrobe after the fire of 1814. Capitals were modeled by Iardella. Photograph by the author

has an intermediate effect approaching the Corinthian order and retaining the simplicity of the Clepsydra or Temple of the Winds.

"Iardella a sculptor who has just arrived, has made an admirable model for execution in which he has well preserved the botanical character of the plant, although it has been necessary to enlarge the proportion of the flowers to the leaves, and to arrange them in clusters of three. When we have done with the model I will take the liberty of forwarding it to you. I have neglected so long to answer your very kind letter, that I must entreat you to attribute my silence to anything but a diminution of my respect and attachment. Believe me, that it never can cease.

"Yours very respectfully,   B. HENRY LATROBE."

The capital to which he refers in the first paragraph is the maize or cornstalk design, the model for which he sent to Monticello in 1809, and the sixteen columns of the "circular colonade" are those shown in Plates 24, 25, and 26. The model from which these latter capitals were carved is doubtless the one that is still preserved at Monticello.

Two skilful Italians, Giuseppe Franzoni and Giovanni Andrei, were responsible for much of the sculptured work on the Capitol, having been brought to this country for the purpose on Jefferson's recommendation. To them was entrusted the more difficult work, including figures, and the twenty-four Corinthian capitals of the House of Representatives. Latrobe mentions their arrival in a letter dated March 3, 1806 and says of them that, "Franzoni is a most excellent sculptor, and capable of cutting our figure of Liberty, and Andrei excels more in decoration." They evidently took to their jobs with gusto for, on August 27th of the same year, Latrobe wrote enthusiastically of an eagle that formed a feature of the frieze, "Not in ancient or modern sculpture is there an eagle head which is in dignity, spirit, and drawing superior to Franzoni's."

But even with temperamental sculptors functioning smoothly for the time being, those responsible for building a new capital city, for a new nation, in a backwoods clearing, found other ills to plague them. Latrobe's report, of December 11, 1809, re-

PLATE 26. Latrobe's design for small rotunda in Senate wing. Capitals that
carry dome are ones he designed from the tobacco leaf. Original drawing
is in the Library of Congress

[87]

vealed an irritating complication of easy-going legislators and a happy-go-lucky labor market. "No orders can be given," he wrote, "till the legislative will is known, which has hitherto always been at the latter end of the session."

This complicated matters pretty seriously for Latrobe because, "It is the general practice of all those who hire labor either for agricultural or other purposes to engage their hands on the 1st of January; on that day all the best laborers are disposed of for the season. Those who are afterward hired are few, expensive, and generally inferior hands."

What that meant to the man responsible for the execution of such an immense undertaking as the construction of a nation's Capitol, is perfectly obvious. It was a difficulty that might be encountered anywhere, anytime. But there were further complications; these were definitely local; and with them every devotee of Isaac Walton can sympathize. For he went on to say: "In respect to common laborers, and to almost all the building artisans who have been brought up in this neighborhood, unless they can be engaged and employed during the winter, they can not be depended upon until some time in July. In March the fishing season commences for shad and herrings, and lasts till the middle of May. Every man who has not profitable employment in hand, or who is not under engagement, then resorts to the shores. As soon as the fishing season is over the harvest commences, and until the end of the harvest, no great exertions, which depend upon these numerous classes of our people, can be made."

Certainly a builder's "life was not a 'appy one" and the wonder is that progress on the Capitol was maintained as efficiently as it was.

THE CAPITOL IS BURNED

The utterly senseless burning of Washington's public buildings by British soldiers occurred in 1814. On August 24th the Capitol and the President's House were fired by order of stupid captors of the city. Such vandalism was inexcusable on the part of civilized people, even when engaged in warfare, and not only was the public of the United States stirred up to a fever heat of resentment, but intelligent Englishmen as well regarded this

PLATE 27. Crypt below the Rotunda. Below this is a tomb intended for President Washington. An opening in Rotunda floor formerly afforded a view down into crypt. Photograph by the author.

as an act of barbarism. The *London Statesman* expressed most emphatically the attitude of thinking Englishmen, saying, "Willingly would we throw a veil of oblivion over our transactions at Washington. The Cossacks spared Paris, but we spared not the Capitol of America."

Admiral Cockburn was, apparently, incapable of understanding the futility and undesirability of such an act. He showed a vulgar vindictiveness, both during and after the regrettable episode. Entering the House of Representatives, he strode up on the rostrum and into the Speaker's chair with his muddy boots, and declaimed to the soldiers who followed him, "Shall this harbor of Yankee democracy be burned? All for it will say 'Aye.'" The vote was of course enthusiastically unanimous—soldiers obey their officers—and the building was fired. Afterwards Cockburn's portrait was engraved with a background in which the Capitol was shown in flames.

This portrait, which is reproduced as plate 28, shows the swaggering Admiral warming his coattails before the burning buildings of the Capital City. Beneath the engraving is the following inscription:

Painted by I. J. Hall Esqr. Engraved by C. Turner
To the Earl St. Vincent this Portrait of
Sir George Cockburn, G.C.B.,
Rear Admiral of the Red, & one of His
Majesty's Lords of the Admiralty
Is with permission dedicated by his
Lordship's most obedt humble Servt.
C. Turner
London, Pub. March 1, 1819 by C. Turner
50 Warrent Street, Fitzroy Square

The drawing of the buildings is so accurate that it is evident sketches must have been made by some officer who was on the scene. Even the long corridor connecting the two wings is quite apparent.

Latrobe wrote a vivid description of the building as it appeared after its destruction—

PLATE 28. Portrait of Sir George Cockburn, Rear Admiral of British Fleet, by whose orders Capitol was burned August 24, 1814. Reproduced by courtesy of Library of Congress

"In the Hall of Representatives the devastation has been dreadful. There was no want of materials for the conflagration, for when the number of members of Congress was increased the old platform was left in its place and another raised over it, giving an additional quantity of dry and loose timber. All the stages and seats of the galleries were of timber and yellow pine. The mahogany desks, tables, and chairs were in their places. At first rockets were fired through the roof, but they did not set fire to it. They sent men on it, but it was covered with sheet iron. At last they made a great pile in the center of the room of the furniture and, retiring, set fire to a quantity of rocket stuff in the middle. The whole was soon in a blaze, and so intense was the flame that the glass of the lights was melted, and I have now lumps weighing many pounds run into a mass. The stone is, like most freestone, unable to resist the force of flame, and I believe no known material would have been able to resist so sudden and intense a heat. The exterior of the columns and entablatures scaled off, and not a vestige of sculpture or fluting remained." (Plate 29.)

LATROBE GOES WEST

Meanwhile, the War of 1812 had played havoc with Latrobe's activities. Congress had curtailed appropriations for building operations in order that the money might be used in preparation for war. The south wing of the Capitol had been completed in 1811, and a canal which he was building across the city to the mouth of Tiber Creek was well under way, so he had but little governmental work to require his attention.

He accordingly turned his attention to a project, for supplying the city of New Orleans with a water-works system, which he had been considering since 1809 with Governor Claiborne. His eldest son had already gone to Louisiana to superintend the job, and financial backing had been secured to provide for the construction of such machinery as could best be built in the North.

The war made shipments by sea too serious a risk to be undertaken, so Latrobe decided to move in the fall of 1813, with his family to Pittsburgh, build the pumps there, and ship them to New Orleans by river. Learning that Robert Fulton was consid-

PLATE 29. Appearance of Capitol after fire of 1814. Sketch by miniature painter named Chittenden. Reproduced from Brown's "History of the United States Capitol"

[93]

ering the establishment of engine works at Pittsburgh, he arranged to coöperate with him as agent of the Ohio Steamboat Company.

His interest in this undertaking may be attributed to the fact that the first steamboat to descend the Mississippi had been built in 1812 by his son-in-law, Nicholas T. Roosevelt. Since then two other boats had been built by a son-in-law of Fulton, so the *Buffalo* which Latrobe planned to build as a means of conveyance for his pumping machinery was to be fourth in this line of succession.

This undertaking proved to be a heart-breaking chapter in Latrobe's history. His instructions from Fulton were pathetically inadequate. Neither man seemed to realize the difference in costs of labor and material between those with which Fulton was familiar on the Hudson in pre-war times, and those with which Latrobe was obliged to contend on the Ohio. The obvious result was that appropriations were used up long before the boat was completed; Latrobe drained his own limited resources; Fulton became most critical, unjustly so it seems, making no allowances for errors in judgment, for which both were apparently responsible.

Fulton's censures were a source of deep concern to Latrobe, but it is gratifying to know that Fulton, before his death, acknowledged the injustice of his criticisms.

Completion of the steamboat became impossible. This meant also failure of his plans to build and ship the pumping machinery to New Orleans. Money and hope were gone, and Latrobe broke under the strain in what was apparently a complete nervous collapse.

Fortunately his wife, (for he had married a second time) learned that Congress had passed legislation authorizing restoration of the buildings destroyed by the British. She wrote to Gallatin and others of their friends at the capital, and was rejoiced to learn that her husband was to be asked to resume his old position, and supervise reconstruction of the Capitol.

This stimulating news brought him out of his lethargy and he reported at Washington, where he was given the badly needed appointment. After a return to Pittsburgh for his family he was once more, in the summer of 1815, settled in the capital city and hard at work.

Even during the troublous times at Pittsburgh he had contrived to find time to design a number of residences, including a half dozen at Pittsburgh, one near Lexington, Kentucky, for Henry Clay, and another at Newport for Governor Taylor. Others have been attributed to him but with varying degrees of authority.

The Thirtieth Congress met in 1814 in the building known as Blodgett's Hotel, which has been mentioned in connection with Dr. Thornton's use of it to house the Patent Office. Considerable agitation was directed toward removal of the government to some other city, which would be less accessible to an attacking enemy, and which also would bring into great favor with his constituents the lucky politician who should gather in this delectable plum for his own.

To head off the threat of removal, leading citizens of the city on the Potomac organized the "Capitol Hotel Company" and, on July 4, 1815, began work on a temporary structure for the use of Congress. This was occupied from December, 1815 until 1819 when the Capitol again became habitable, and for many years it was known as the "Old Capitol." During the Civil War it was used as a place of incarceration for southern sympathizers. The site was that now occupied by the Supreme Court Building.

The nervous fear of Washingtonians was allayed when Congress, on February 15, 1815, authorized President Madison to borrow a half million dollars to be expended in restoration of the public buildings. Three commissioners were appointed by the President to superintend the work, John P. Van Ness, T. Ringgold, and Richard Bland Lee, each to draw a salary of $1,600.

Three months later, on May 16, 1815, the commissioners reported to the President: "We have employed Mr. Latrobe as architect or surveyor of the Capitol." They also reported that he estimated the building could be completed before 1816. In this same letter the suggestion was first made that the much discussed and criticized Hall of Representatives be again redesigned.

The optimistic idea that the south wing could be gotten ready for use in 1816 proved to be a fantasy, for it was not completed in its entirety until 1830.

The Hall of Representatives was completely revamped, both Thornton's elliptical plan and Latrobe's pseudo-ellipse being relegated to oblivion in favor of the semi-circular plan with which we are familiar today in Statuary Hall. (Plates 30, 31, 32.) In this room the lower house of Congress met from December, 1819, until the great south wing was completed late in 1857, the first session in the latter being held on December 16, of that year.

In speaking of the north and south wings, it should be remembered that until the middle of the nineteenth century, when the two new wings were added, the term North Wing was applied to that portion of the structure immediately north of the Rotunda, in which is the original Senate Chamber, that was used later by the Supreme Court. The South Wing was the corresponding portion south of the Rotunda, in which was the Hall of Representatives, now Statuary Hall. (Plates 18, 31, 32.)

Andrei was sent to Italy, in August, 1815, to order twenty-four Corinthian capitals for the new columns in the Hall (Plate 33), and six Ionic capitals, four for columns and two for pilasters in the Senate Chamber. The columns for the Hall were quarried in Loudoun County, Virginia, and in Montgomery County, Maryland.

Latrobe's lifelong habit of undertaking a multiplicity of outside jobs, that interfered more or less with the efficient conduct of his official work for the government, again got him into difficulty. The commissioners criticized him severely for giving so little personal attention to the Capitol, and he in turn was resentful toward them for the restraint which they tried, at least, to exert over him.

A source of serious delay in the work was the difficulty in securing the large marble columns and finally, in despair, Latrobe suggested the substitution of sandstone. This suggestion was not however acceptable and the delays were endured rather than make use of an inferior material.

PLATE 30. Latrobe's design for reconstruction of Hall of Representatives after fire of 1814. Franzoni's "Car of History" is shown above doorway (see Plate 35). Original drawing is in the Library of Congress

The destruction of the Capitol by fire had taught in costly terms the folly of using timber in the construction of such a building. Ghastly evidence of this was to be seen in the western portion of the north wing which had been completely gutted by the flames. On the other hand it was found that the portion that had been rebuilt with brick withstood the heat, and much of the masonry was still in good condition.

The shingle roof also had contributed to the destruction and, as there was great need for more space in the Senate Chamber, much tearing out of old construction was necessary, which delayed materially the work of reconstruction.

Especially regrettable was the loss of the Library of Congress which had been housed in the large room that had been used in early days as a meeting place for the House. The nucleus of a new library was supplied by Thomas Jefferson, who sold his splendid library at Monticello to the government for the purpose. He generously offered it at a price to be determined by Congress and it is recorded that his patriotic move was rewarded by payment of considerably less than the actual value of the books. In spite of a later fire, in 1851, a large number of these books still remain in the Library of Congress, treasured among its choicest possessions.

Plans for reconstruction naturally involved provision against such wholesale loss in case of future conflagrations, and Latrobe and Hoban were asked for opinions on the relative values of various roof coverings. Latrobe named his choices, in order of importance, as marble, freestone, zinc, iron, and copper. Hoban on the contrary placed copper first, a choice in which President Madison agreed, and that metal was definitely decided upon.

On April 24, 1816, Congress abolished the commission of three and authorized the appointment of a single commissioner, an office that was conferred upon Samuel Lane of Virginia.

In 1817 a final source of friction arose between Latrobe and other officials. Work was lagging, the roof of the north wing still remained uncovered and in September, with winter approaching, many important details were unfinished. Late in the following month Lane applied the goad by appointing Captain Peter Lenox as Clerk of Works at the Capitol, transferring him from a similar

PLATE 31. Old Hall of Representatives, now Statuary Hall; designed by Latrobe. Above doorway is Carlo Franzoni's "Car of History." Photograph
by the author

PLATE 32. The "Old House of Representatives" from a painting by Samuel F. B. Morse. Between columns are seen draperies that were hung to correct faulty acoustics. At extreme right is Franzoni's "Car of History"; in upper left are Causici's "Statue of Liberty" and Valaperti's eagle. In center of picture a man is lighting the great chandelier which has been lowered from the ceiling. Reproduced by courtesy of The Corcoran Gallery of Art, Washington, D. C., by which the painting is owned. Photograph by Lewis P. Moltz

post at the President's House where he had been responsible for satisfactory progress. The latter office was filled by Shadrack Davis, who was transferred from the Capitol.

This change was as gall and wormwood to Latrobe, for Davis had been his choice; and as far back as 1803, Jefferson had desired to appoint Lenox, but had yielded to Latrobe's request that he be permitted to make his own appointment.

Latrobe and Lane had not hit it off very well from the start, and now they came out in the open with their grievances. Latrobe protested against the transfers. Lane stood his ground; he thought the change necessary in the interest of efficient progress on the building. He also accused Latrobe of frequently recommending incompetent men for positions which they were not fitted to fill. He wished to push work on the Capitol to a conclusion and needed a man in charge who could be depended upon to keep things moving.

He added as a final touch to Latrobe's irritation, "Knowing my duties, I shall scrupulously perform them. All I wish of you is attention to your own." This polite way of telling him to "mind his own business" was the final straw, and Latrobe sent his resignation to the President, who referred it back to the Commissioner.

LATROBE'S CAREER ENDS

The following letters terminated the long and important connection of Benjamin Henry Latrobe with the building of the Capitol.

"Washington, November 20, 1817.
"The President of the United States.

"SIR: My situation as architect of the Capitol has become such as to leave me no choice between resignation and the sacrifice of all self-respect. Permit me then, sir, to resign into your hands an office in which I fear I have been the cause to you of much vexation while my only object has been to accomplish your wishes. You have known me more than twenty years. You have borne testimony to my professional skill—and my integrity has never been questioned. You will, I am confident, do me justice, and in time know that never the delay nor the expense of the public works are chargeable to me.

"I am aware that much inconvenience may arise from my retiring from my office so suddenly. But I pledge myself to furnish drawings and instructions for all the parts of the works that are in hand for a reasonable compensation being made, which my circumstances do not permit me to decline.

"I am, very respectfully, your Obdt. servt.

B. H. LATROBE."

"November 24, 1817.

"B. H. Latrobe.

"SIR: Having seen your letter to the President of the United States, resigning the appointment of Architect of the Capitol, I have to inform you that your resignation is accepted and to request that you will deliver to Captain Lenox all the books, plans, instruments, etc., belonging to the public in your possession.

SAMUEL LANE,
Commissioner of Public Buildings."

Latrobe had carried forward to completion the two wings of the structure, and left drawings for the central portion, now covered by the great dome, which were followed to a large extent by his successors. On his return to Washington, after the War of 1812, he had found the building a ruin (Plate 29), due to the devastation by British vandals, with its stone exterior walls calcined by the flames, and its interior almost completely wrecked. He left it with the interior as largely as possible fireproof, and the exterior restored and painted to cover the discoloration due to fire and smoke.

And by the way, it is probable that the majority of visitors are unaware of the fact that the old, or central portion of the building is not of marble, as are the new wings, but is of sandstone which is painted at regular intervals to preserve the stone and keep its color in harmony with the adjacent marble.

Latrobe left a very definite impress on the design of the building as we know it today, in spite of the fact that Jefferson and others in authority insisted upon adherence to the Thornton plan and to the exterior design of the north wing which had been practically completed under Thornton's supervision.

PLATE 33. Statue of Liberty. Modeled for old Hall of Representatives by Enrico Causici. Eagle on frieze by Giuseppe Valaperti, supposed to have committed suicide because of criticisms of this, his only work in the Capitol. Photograph by the author

The House of Representatives (Plates 18, 30, 31, 32, 33) now Statuary Hall, and the Senate Chamber were his design, and it was at his suggestion that the floor level was raised to that of the main story. He changed the designs for the east portico and the west front of the central section, and added the domed roofs, with their cupolas, that crown both wings. (Plates 53, 54, 55.)

The original "corn stalk" and "tobacco leaf" designs in the north wing were both his. (Plates 22, 23, 24, 25, 26.)

Upon severing his connection with the government, Latrobe moved with his family to Baltimore where he took personal charge of construction on the Cathedral, which had been progressing slowly due to lack of funds, and also began work on the Exchange which he had designed while in Washington. He decided to visit New Orleans for the purpose of completing the water works system. His son had previously undertaken this work, but fell victim to the dreaded yellow fever.

Latrobe resumed operations on the project during a visit to New Orleans in 1819-'20 and began installation of the engines, which had been built in Baltimore. He came back to that city for his family in 1820 and there received flattering testimonials from trustees of the Cathedral and directors of the Exchange.

Returning to New Orleans he devoted himself to completion of the contract with the city, which was to have given him a monopoly on furnishing the water supply for twenty years. Although seven years of this period had elapsed there was every prospect that the contract would enable Latrobe and his family to live in comfort the rest of their lives.

The engines were completed, and but two weeks of work were ahead before they were to be placed in operation. Suddenly, on September 3, 1820, while supervising the laying of pipes, Latrobe, like his son, was stricken with yellow fever, and in a few hours was dead.

The water works system, over which he had labored so long and which had exacted such tragic toll from father and son, passed into other hands. The family left the city in which they had expected to spend their lives and, leaving their sacrifices behind, returned to their former home and friends in the East.

II

THE SCULPTORS

THE SCULPTORS

A SERIOUS PROBLEM for the builders of the Capitol was that of securing sculptors and carvers possessed of ability and training adequate to give proper expression and character to the ornamental details. Both architectural ornament and figure sculpture demanded, for so important a building, the services of artists far more skilful than those who might ordinarily be found in a new country. To be sure there were many wood carvers who had produced excellent work on the trim of the finer houses, and a few of the public buildings, but when the Capitol of the nation was to be built in conformity with classical traditions, it became necessary to interpret style with technique that should not fall too far short of the models by which the designers were inspired.

At the suggestion of President Jefferson, Latrobe wrote on March 6, 1805 to Philip Mazzei, an Italian physician and personal friend of Jefferson, asking his aid in securing competent sculptors. In this letter he wrote:

"The principal sculpture required will be of twenty-four Corinthian capitals, two feet four inches in diameter at their feet, and open enriched entablatures, of 147 feet (both English measure) in length. There are beside five panels (tavole) enriched with foliage and an eagle of colossal size in the frieze, the distance between the tips of the extended wings being twelve feet six inches.

"The material in which this is to be cut is a yellowish sandstone of fine grain, finer than the peperino or gray sandstone used in Rome—the only Italian sandstone of which I have any distinct recollection. This stone yields in any direction to the chisel, not being in the least laminated nor hard enough to fly off (spall) before a sharp tool. It may, therefore, be cut with great precision. The wages given by the day to our best carvers are from $3 to $2.50, or about $750 to $900 per annum. . . .

"There are, however, other qualities which seem so essential as to be at least as necessary as talents. I mean good temper and good morals. Without them an artist would find himself most unpleasantly situated in a country, the language and manners of which are so different from his own, and we should have no dependence on a person discontented with his situation. For though every exertion would be made on my part to make his engagement perfectly agreeable to him, the irritability of good artists is well known and it is often not easily quieted."

He goes on to explain that the expenses of a return voyage will be paid if the artists choose to return. There is also the matter of a seated figure of Liberty, nine feet high, for which he desires a price from Canova, or, in case Canova declines the commission, he wishes to have the name of the next best man, and his price for the work.

FRANZONI AND ANDREI

The correspondence between Latrobe and Mazzei resulted in making contracts with Giuseppe Franzoni and Giovanni Andrei, who appeared in their new field of operations in February, 1806. Franzoni had especially good family connections in Italy, he being a nephew of Cardinal Franzoni and son of the President of the Academy of Fine Arts at Carrara.

Andrei was born in 1770 at Carrara and it is said that he was a brother-in-law of Franzoni and also his instructor. He is reputed to have been the sculptor of the balustrades on the high altar in the Church of Santa Maria Novella, Florence. On hearing of their arrival, Latrobe wrote to Lenthal:

"And so Franzoni and Andrei have arrived. I will trump up all my Italian and write to them tomorrow to keep them in good humor . . Mazzei . . says that Franzoni is a most excellent sculptor and capable of cutting our figure of Liberty and that Andrei excells more in decoration. I wish they would go and seek clay for modelling. Andrews could tell them where to find it and then model one of our capitals."

A little difficulty was experienced in adjusting the minds of the new arrivals to American ideas and ways, and in getting them settled down to work. While wrestling with this dilemma, Latrobe again wrote to Lenthal: "I much fear that our friend Franzoni may be much above the carving of architectural decorations; if so, what can we do with him? In the first place he may model

our eagle . . I would leave to his own management the disposition of this gigantic bird; I shall bring with me the beak of an
eagle which I am promised, or at all events a very good and
measured drawing."

The enormous eagle which Latrobe planned for the frieze in
the Hall of Representatives seemed to be a breeder of trouble,
and even though the architect may have known exactly what he
wanted, difficulty was experienced in getting his ideas across to
the Italian mind. Finally, a month after writing the above letter
to Lenthal, an appeal for help was sent to his friend Charles Wilson Peale. In this he pleads: "MY DEAR SIR: You will say and
I am afraid with truth, that I never write to you but to give you
trouble. At present I have really no other object but to lay myself
under still greater obligations to your kindness than I am already.

"In my design of the Hall of the House of Representatives, an
eagle has become necessary as the principle decoration of the
center of the Hall in the Frieze.

"We have here two most capital Italian sculptors lately arrived. One of them is now modeling an eagle, but it is an Italian,
or a Roman, or a Greek eagle, and I want an American Bald-
eagle. May I therefore beg the favor of you to request one of your
very obliging and skilful sons, to send me a drawing of the
head and claws of the bald-eagle of his general proportions with
the wings extended, and especially of the arrangement of the
feathers below the wing when extended. The eagle will be fourteen feet from tip to tip of the wings, so that any glaring impro-
priety of character will be immediately detected by our Western
members."

This bit of friendly coöperation evidently turned the trick and
saved the Hall of Representatives from harboring ornithological
aberrations. Latrobe certainly heaved sighs of relief, and took occasion in a letter written to Signor Mazzei December 19, 1806, to
express his appreciation for the excellent work that was being
done. He wrote, "Our Italian sculptors continue to give us the ut-
most satisfaction. Franzoni was not very well for a few weeks in
Summer but has been long entirely recovered. . . . Hitherto
Franzoni has been only engaged with eagles. He has finished a

colossal Eagle in the Frieze of the Entablature of the Hall of Representatives 12′ 6″ from wing to wing, and is now engaged on a free eagle, also colossal for the Gate of the Navy Yard. This promises to be the most spirited Eagle I have seen in sculpture either modern or antique."

A commanding feature of this Hall was to be a colossal figure of Liberty, to be placed between two columns, above the Speaker's chair. Latrobe experienced difficulty in securing from Franzoni the type of figure that he had in mind and, on December 31, some two weeks after writing the letter just quoted, he unburdened his mind, while in Philadelphia, in another letter to Lenthal:

". . . By the bye, as I have told you before I do not like his (Franzoni's) model. It may be correct Symbology or emblematology to give Dame Liberty a club or shelalah, but we have no business to exhibit it so publicly. As to the beautiful picture of Peace, which is Canova's, of doves nestling in a helmet; it has no business there at all. I must have one arm close to her side resting in her lap. The other may be raised and rest on a wig or block or capped stick, (which is much more honorable than the wig block, as the cap is more honorable than the wig) for aught I care.

"Your drawing is sufficient to enable me to study the thing, and probably in a day or two I shall give my final orders and reduce her ladyship in height to perhaps 7 feet sitting. . . ."

Meanwhile Andrei had been at work on the capitals for the Hall of Representatives. He possessed great skill, but Latrobe complained, in a letter to Thomas Munroe, that "Andrei although an incomparable artist is the slowest hand I ever saw, especially in modeling, and in fact our clay models of his work have cost us more than the same things in marble."

He continues in this letter to discuss their pay, outside work which they are doing on their own time, and the remote possibility of their completing the work on the Capitol during the coming season, saying, "I am far from believing that they will be spared by the next session. Franzoni has six figures as large as life in hand which will be without arms next session, and Andrei will not have half finished his capitals. They cannot be suffered to remain so."

Both Giuseppe Franzoni and Andrei are known to have worked in Baltimore and, although Latrobe assisted them in arranging this undertaking, it produced results that came back to roost over his doorway. In other words, the ten dollars a day which they received there for doing a rather common class of work, dissatisfied them with their contract with the Government, the outcome being that Latrobe placed them partially on a piece-work basis.

All of this work was of course destroyed when the British burned the Capitol, but the small, preliminary models were saved, and were shipped to Philadelphia by Latrobe on a boat which sailed from Alexandria in December, 1808. They were consigned to the Academy of Arts, as we learn from a letter to Peale. In this Latrobe says, "By Captain Hand. . . . I send to the Academy of Arts four boxes containing the four figures of Agriculture, Art, Science and Commerce which are sculptured in alto relievo over the entrance of the Hall of Representatives here. They occupy 25 feet in length in the original and are rather larger than life filling the frieze of the center map of the colonnade. These are the original small models. I hope they will arrive safe. Commerce has lost a foot I fear. I think I heard it crack in packing but it can be easily replaced with a little White lead. I fear *Lead* will be the only way to put our Commerce *on foot* again. I say let the boxes be brought up by Hand to the Academy for it would be a pity if after having been carried by Hand all the way from hence, they would be ruined by being at last put into a dray.

"They are packed in sawdust. The limbs are relieved, and some entirely free. Great care must therefore be taken in removing it.

"Is Rembrandt really come home?

"Love to all around you.

       "Yours truly,   B. H. LATROBE.

"December 10, 1808."

The vein of humor that runs through Latrobe's letters is a welcome relief from the deadly seriousness of so much official correspondence.

The crisis which preceded the War of 1812, to which Latrobe's little pun referred, together with the diversion of taxes to war preparations, interfered seriously with progress on the Capitol. Plans were made for returning the sculptors and their families to Italy. Fortunately, however, for the quality of later work on that building, an appropriation of $4,000 was made for completion of sculpture in the south wing and, as sea voyages became increasingly unsafe, both men remained in Washington and were available when the work of reconstruction began.

Franzoni died in Washington on April 16, 1815 and, as Latrobe was convinced that such work as carving the Corinthian capitals could be executed much more cheaply in Italy, Andrei was sent to Carrara to contract for capitals to be used in the new Hall of Representatives.

On his return in 1816 he brought with him two more sculptors, Francisco Iardella and Carlo Franzoni (Plate 34), the latter a brother of Giuseppe. A romance soon developed and Iardella married the widow of Giuseppe Franzoni, tradition having it that they had been youthful sweethearts, but had not married because of parental interference in favor of Giuseppe.

CARLO FRANZONI

Like his brother, Carlo was a sculptor of exceptional ability, competent to execute figure work of high quality. His most important contribution to the art of the Capitol is the Car of History clock (Plate 35) which occupies a dominating position above the entrance to Statuary Hall. It consists of a draped female figure, in white marble, standing in a winged chariot that passes over the globe, on which are shown the signs of the Zodiac. The wheel of the chariot forms the dial of the clock, which for many years told time officially for the House of Representatives.

The claim has been made that Giuseppe was responsible for this striking group, and that it was completed by Iardella, but this statement is refuted by an inscription on the statue itself, which reads, "C. Franzoni faciebat 1819." The Franzoni family claim that the model for the figure of History was one of Giuseppe's daughters.

Credit has been given Carlo Franzoni for the bas-relief, "Justice and Fame" on the west wall of the old Supreme Court

PLATE 34. Portrait of Carlo Franzoni; painted in 1818 by Pietro Bonanni. Now in office of the Architect of the Capitol, by whose courtesy it is reproduced

room on the ground floor, but documentary evidence is lacking, and it is difficult to determine with certainty this and many other moot questions because of the destruction by fire of contemporary documents.

Carlo Franzoni was a native of Cararra, where he was born in 1789. He was a man of striking personal appearance, six feet four in height and with handsome features, as is evident from his portrait, by Pietro Bonanni, which hangs in the office of the Architect of the Capitol. His appearance was enhanced by his predilection for rich clothing of the latest style.

He possessed thorough training for his profession, having graduated from a school of anatomy before taking up the study of sculpture. It is said that work by him is to be found in the Vatican at Rome and the Louvre, Paris.

In spite of his fine physique, he became conscious of failing health while in Washington, due probably to overwork, and on the advice of a physician he began to take regular, daily exercise by sawing wood. While working at the sawhorse in his cellar, on May 12th, 1819, he was startled by a sudden and violent ringing of the doorbell, and dropped dead of heart failure.

FRANCISCO IARDELLA

Francisco Iardella, like Andrei and Carlo Franzoni, was a native of Carrara, where he was born in 1793. He was a cousin of the Franzonis and, as has been said, married the widow of Giuseppe. The first work given to him after arrival at Washington was the modeling of the famous tobacco leaf capitals, which distinguish the small rotunda in the north wing. (See page 80, and Plates 24, 25, 26.) He was a carver of architectural ornament and, after Andrei's death, succeeded him in charge of such work on the Capitol.

This position was held by him until 1827, after which time he was recalled when needed until his death on January 23, 1831. He left seven children, a daughter and six sons. His step-daughter, Virginia Franzoni, daughter of Giuseppe, was appointed guardian of the Iardella children, and was also administratrix of the Franzoni estate, which meant that she was responsible for thirteen Franzonis and Iardellas of assorted sizes and sexes. It is to be hoped that Virginia was the model who posed for the figure of History on the clock; she was deserving of a monument.

LUIGI PERSICO

Among the most conspicuous examples of figure sculpture at the Capitol are those found on the east portico of the old building. With one exception these are the work of still another of the

PLATE 35. "Car of History" clock by Carlo Franzoni. It stands above north door of old Hall of Representatives, now Statuary Hall. Photograph by the author

Italian artists who were drawn to this country by visions of golden opportunity. This was Luigi Persico, who was given contracts for the figures on the pediment, the figures of "Peace" and "War" (Plate 36) that occupy niches on either side of the entrance to the rotunda, and the "Discovery" group that stands on the pedestal at the left of the steps. The head of the figure representing Columbus, in the latter group, is supposed to have been copied from an authentic bust of the discoverer in a Spanish art museum. (Plate 37.)

Persico was commissioned to execute both of the groups that flank the steps, but for some reason the "Rescue" group (Plate 43) at the right was awarded eventually to Horatio Greenough.

An interesting sidelight on the sculptured reliefs in the pediment of the portico is found in a letter written from Washington on June 22, 1825 by Bulfinch. In it he says that work on the portico is progressing slowly because of delays in receiving stone:

". . . With respect to the ornament proposed to decorate this, the artists in general feel much disappointed; about 30 persons presented 36 designs, some well and others badly executed, but none answering the President's idea of a suitable decoration for a legislative building. He disclaimed all wish to exhibit triumphal cars and emblems of Victory, and all allusions to heathen mythology, and thought that the duties of the Nation or its Legislators should be expressed in an obvious and intelligent manner. After several attempts, the following has been agreed upon; a figure of America occupies the centre, her right arm resting on the shield, supported by an altar or pedestal bearing the inscription, July 4, 1776, her left hand pointing to the figure of Justice, who with unveiled face, is viewing the scales, and the right hand presenting an open scroll inscribed Constitution, March 4, 1789; on the left of the principal figure is the eagle, and the figure of Hope resting on her anchor, her face and right hand uplifted,—the whole intended to convey that while we cultivate Justice we may hope for success. The figures are bold, of nine feet in height, gracefully drawn by Mr. Persico, an Italian artist. It is intended that an appropriate inscription shall explain the meaning and moral to dull comprehensions." (Plate 38.)

PLATE 36. Figure of War, by Luigi Persico; beside east entrance of Rotunda.
Photograph by the author

PLATE 37. "Discovery" group by Luigi Persico. The head of Columbus is said to have been copied from an original portrait bust in Spain. Photograph by the author

PLATE 38. East pediment over entrance to Rotunda; sculpture by Luigi
Persico. Photograph by the author

The chance that led Persico to these commissions is recalled by
Rembrandt Peale's reminiscences, that have been drawn upon
here before. Peale wrote that, ". . . Persico a few years before
obtained a scanty subsistence in Philadelphia by miniature painting and teaching drawing, till an event occurred which brought
him forth as a sculptor. On the distribution of medals awarded
by the Franklin Institute, there were none for fine arts, but an
honorary committee of three was appointed, of which I was one,
to decide on the merits of two models in plaster—one a portrait
from life, by Wm. Rush, our celebrated ship head carver, the
other a colossal head from memory, by Persico, of Lafayette who
had recently been on a visit to Philadelphia. I was late in joining
the committee, who had kindly agreed in praise of the work of
their fellow citizen; but when I expatiated on the beauty of
Persico's classic creation, as the outburst of a genius that had
been buried in obscurity, and almost in despair, they agreed with
me in voting it the palm of excellence. The language of our
decision aroused the torpid ambition of the young sculptor, who

[119]

PLATE 39. The Rotunda. Causici's "Daniel Boone" panel is above doorway at the left. Photograph by L. C. Handy Studios

proceeded to Washington, to be employed in the costly decorations of the Capitol."

This was not, however, the first time that Persico had been engaged on important work, for while living in Italy he had been employed on the embellishments of various churches and palaces. That he was held in esteem in his native country is evident from the fact that a document in the Museum of San Martino, at Naples, refers to his employment on the Capitol at Washington.

ENRICO CAUSICI

The great statue of Liberty (Plate 33) which stands in a niche, high above the entablature on the south wall of Statuary Hall, is the work of Enrico Causici. This figure is of plaster, means never having been provided for having it cut in marble, if indeed this was intended. Causici was a native of Verona and reputed to have been a pupil of Canova. He made the claim for himself that he had executed the first bronze bust in the United States, a portrait of William Pinkney that he endeavored to sell, in 1823, to the Baltimore Bar. No record of this bust is known to exist.

Causici was awarded a commission to design and execute an ornamental marble clock for the Senate Chamber. This was to have been a fit companion piece to the Franzoni clock in the Hall of Representatives, but unfortunately it was never executed, although a contract, dated March 21, 1823, was drawn up and signed.

The sum of $2,000 was paid to the sculptor for one year of his time, but at the expiration of that period he had completed only the plaster model, and bluntly stated that it would require five years to complete the clock in marble, at a cost of $10,000.

Congress apparently figured that it could keep tab on the time-o'-day for less than $10,000, the project was dropped, and not even a drawing or engraving of the design has been preserved for our edification today.

He fared better with two bas-relief panels for the walls of the rotunda. These are entitled "The Landing of the Pilgrims" (Plate 42) and "Conflict Between Daniel Boone and the In-

PLATE 40. The Rotunda. Photograph by the author

dians" (Plates 39, 42), the former being over the east entrance, the latter over that on the south.

The Daniel Boone panel was the cause of a dramatic scene many years ago. A group of some twenty Winnebago Indians had been induced to make their first visit to a white settlement by coming to Washington. They appeared in full war regalia, with bows and arrows, tomahawks, scalping knives and all. Catching sight of this particular bas-relief, as they approached the door, they stopped short before the representation of Boone in the act of fighting with an Indian brave. The group looked intently at the scene, then with loud cries and war whoops they ran from the building.

The most important work of Causici was not done here at the Capitol, but was the colossal figure of Washington that surmounts the monument designed by Robert Mills for the City of Baltimore.

Little is known of the sculptor's later life, but it is said that he died in Havana, Cuba.

ANTONIO CAPELLANO

Another of the Italians employed on the sculptural work of the Capitol was Antonio Capellano, reputed to be a pupil of Canova. Our first introduction to him is through a letter, dated Washington, August 13, 1816, from Latrobe to William Lee. In this he says:

". . . As to Mr. Capellano, we certainly have urgent and immediate occasion for his talents . . . and nothing would be more serviceable than to obtain the assistance of more able sculptors to restore the figures destroyed by the British."

An entertaining account of the unique introduction of the sculptor to Baltimore's art circles is found in the newsy pages of Rembrandt Peale's reminiscences. This appeared in the January number of *The Crayon,* in 1856.

"The Battle Monument of Baltimore was designed by Maximilian Godefroy. For the execution of the sculptures designed for it, Sig. Capellano, recently arrived in New York, was recommended, who came on to Baltimore; but not finding Mr. Godefroy at home, made his home his domicile, much to the surprise of the black cook who had charge of the house with a limited supply of change. I was informed of the dilemma, and wrote to Mr. Godefroy, but received no answer, as the artist, in a secluded spot was absorbed in making an elaborate drawing of the Natural Bridge in Virginia and forgot everything connected with the Battle Monument. The poor sculptor became impatient and talked of returning to New York. Not to lose the chance of detaining perhaps an excellent artist, an occupation was suggested. Robert Cary Long, the architect of St. Paul's Church, in anticipation of some future occasion of completing his design had caused two large blocks of freestone to be built in the upper front—one for the figure of Christ breaking bread; the other, Moses holding the tables of the law.

"Mr. Capellano was delighted with the idea of getting to work; but it was necessary to decide upon his ability, and I proposed to Mr. Long that I would give forty dollars, if he would contribute an equal amount to pay the sculptor for two small models in clay. They were executed to my satisfaction, and a subscription of a thousand dollars was soon raised for the Church. The sculptor was quickly installed on his elevated platform, and one of the figures was nearly completed before Mr. Godefroy returned to bargain for the proposed sculpture for the Battle Monument. It was not long before he found full employment at the Capitol at Washington, as well as at Baltimore.

"He was a most industrious man and so devoted to his marble that he could not spare an hour to learn either French or English; and his wife who had joined him from New York, told me that she believed that he would turn to stone himself. Fifteen years after this (in 1830) I was surprised one fine afternoon in the Boboli gardens at Florence on being accosted by a well dressed Signor with his gay wife and five fine children. It was Capellano, who acknowledged my timely service to him, and informed me that having made money enough in America, he had bought 'uno picollo pallazzo' to enjoy the remainder of his days in his native city."

Capellano executed the bas-relief of Washington (Plate 41), over the east entrance, between Persico's figures of Peace and

PLATE 41. Bas-relief of Washington, by Antonio Capellano; above east entrance of Rotunda. Photograph by the author

War, and the panel over the west doorway in the rotunda, which shows the Rescue of John Smith by Pocahontas (Plate 42).

He was a competitor for the figure to surmount the Washington Monument in Baltimore, as was Gevelot. However, both were underbid by Causici.

Existing correspondence shows that Capellano had in mind a portrait bust of James Madison, but the price of $800 was too much for the Madison pocketbook, and William Lee was requested by Mr. Madison "to let the matter drop in a manner most delicate towards the artist."

GIUSEPPE VALAPERTI

The eagle (Plate 33) on the frieze of Statuary Hall, below Causici's figure of Liberty, was the work of Giuseppe Valaperti. This was apparently the only work done by Valaperti at the Capitol, although he was recognized as a sculptor of exceptional ability. Latrobe gave him the highest of recommendations when a sculptor was being sought to execute a statue of Washington for the State Capitol of North Carolina, at Raleigh. This letter from Latrobe begins:

"DEAR SIR: I received your letter yesterday afternoon, and give you with pleasure all the information I possess on the subject of the Statue of General Washington proposed to be erected in the State House of N. Carolina.

"The statue may be very admirably made in this country by Mr. Valaperti. He is an Italian artist who after being long employed in Spain, was engaged before the fall of Napoleon in the decoration of his palace at Malmaison. The distracted state of France induced him to seek his fortune in this country, and he has brought

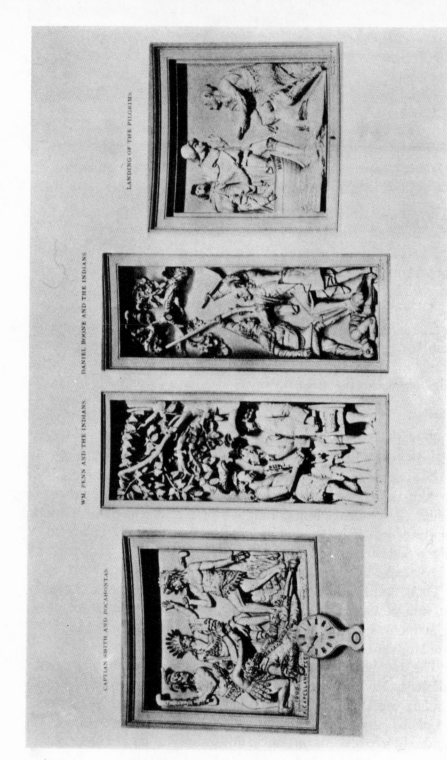

LANDING OF THE PILGRIMS

DANIEL BOONE AND THE INDIANS

WM. PENN AND THE INDIANS

CAPTAIN SMITH AND POCAHONTAS

PLATE 42. Sculptured panels in the Rotunda. Reproduced from Brown's "History of the United States Capitol"

with him the most portable of his works—a few most admirable sculptures in ivory. . . . I wished to have had a bust of General Jackson made for the Corporation of this city, but the project ended in an address. . . ."

The serio-comic ending of his sculptural project "in an address" sounds painfully up to date. He goes on to suggest the possibility of having the statue cut in Italy, under the supervision of Andrei, adding that he "Has a personal knowledge of the temper of our country, and would see that no Italian frippery should degrade the dignity of a figure of Washington."

This letter to Senator Nathaniel Bacon was written on January 9, 1816, and on the preceding day William Thornton had written a letter to the Senator, in much the same vein.

Unfortunately, Valaperti suffered from a complication of poor health and artistic temperament. He became suspicious of any who befriended him, and doubted the sincerity of those who complimented his work.

There was considerable criticism of his eagle in the Hall of Representatives, and it is supposed that he brooded over this; at any rate he disappeared from his lodgings in March, 1817, leaving a will that named his wife and children as beneficiaries or, in case of their deaths, providing that his money was to go to a Catholic church in Washington. He was never located, and it is supposed that he drowned himself in the Potomac. The proceeds of his small estate were sent to his family who lived near Genoa, Italy.

NICHOLAS GEVELOT

Little information is available regarding the French sculptor, Nicholas Gevelot. The most conspicuous record of his work is found in the bas-relief over the north door of the rotunda, on which he carved a representation of "William Penn's Treaty with the Indians" (Plate 42).

Records in the House Journal show that he petitioned Congress for the sum of $1,500 which he claimed as the amount he was to receive for the work. The commissioner had allowed him but $750. Whether or not his claim was allowed is not known.

In 1850 Gevelot proposed to make a medal as a memorial to

the late President, Zachary Taylor. The committee to which the resolution was referred, voted that it be laid on the table. It is evident that his relations with the government were not overly satisfactory.

HORATIO GREENOUGH

The first American to receive a commission for sculptural work on the Capitol was Horatio Greenough. Congress had passed a bill, on July 14, 1832, appropriating the sum of $5,000:

"To enable the President of the United States to contract with a suitable artist to execute in marble a pedestrian statue of George Washington to be placed in the center of the rotunda of the Capitol."

Greenough was the artist chosen, and the statue was modeled in his studio at Florence, Italy. In a letter dated Florence, Dec. 1, 1833, to William Dunlap, he wrote:

"I sigh for a little intercourse with you, gentlemen, at home: I long to be among you; but I am anchored here for the next four years. I will not risk a voyage before my statue is done. . . .

"When I went, the other morning, into the huge room in which I propose to execute my statue, I felt like a spoilt boy, who, after insisting upon riding upon horseback, bawls aloud with fright at finding himself in the saddle, so far from the ground! I hope, however, that this will wear off."

As this figure is not a feature of the Capitol, and is in fact no longer in the building, it will not be considered here, beyond a glimpse at its story. Greenough was a stickler for classical tradition and represented the Father of his Country as clad in a loose drapery that left his body partially naked. This was too much for the ideals of respectability and appropriateness current at the time. A howl of disapproval went up, and it was referred to as "without a shirt," and as suggesting his coming from the bath. After elaborate preparations for its installation in the rotunda, it was subjected to various migrations, eventually being transferred, in 1908, to the Smithsonian Institution.

Greenough's contribution to the enrichment of the Capitol was his so-called "Rescue" Group (Plate 43), which stands on the

PLATE 43. "Rescue" group, by Horatio Greenough; beside east portico. Photograph by the author

north blocking of the east steps. Groups for the two blockings had been ordered originally from Luigi Persico, but eventually this one was transferred to Greenough. It was shipped from Leghorn, Italy, and was set in place some time in 1853. As Greenough died at Somerville, Massachusetts, on December 18, 1852, he never saw his work in position, and the claim is made that the figures in the group are not assembled in relation to each other as was planned by the sculptor.

Horatio Greenough was born September 6, 1805, at Boston, the son of a well-to-do merchant. He attended various schools in and about Boston, and graduated from Harvard University.

As a boy he showed extraordinary skill in carving all sorts of toys and miniature figures. His brother wrote of him:

"His schoolfellows often begged of him to carve them wood cimeters and daggers, as every one he made surpassed the last."

His precocity attracted much attention and, at the age of twelve, Mr. Shaw of the Athenaeum:

"Gave him carte blanche to the 'fine arts' room with its valuable collection of engravings, &c. . . .

"Towards the close of the senior year, a vessel being about to sail for Marseilles, he obtained permission from the government of the college (Harvard) to leave before the usual time, and his diploma was forwarded to him afterwards. He arrived at Marseilles in the first of the autumn, and proceeded directly by land to Rome. This was in 1825."

While in Rome he devoted himself tirelessly to the study of drawing and modeling. A meeting with Thorwaldsen proved inspiring to the young student, but he was compelled to leave Italy within a year by an attack of malaria, brought on in part by overwork. The sea voyage restored his health and, after five or six months at his home, he went to Washington where he modeled busts of John Quincy Adams and Chief Justice Marshall.

Returning to Italy he stayed for a time in Carrara, then settled in Florence. James Fenimore Cooper found him there studying hard, but with few commissions to execute. He gave him a much needed order, brought him before the public, and helped to secure for him the commission for the Washington statue.

III

THEY COMPLETE THE OLD CAPITOL

BULFINCH COMES FROM BOSTON

THE THIRD ARCHITECT to be entrusted with construction of the Capitol was Charles Bulfinch (Plate 44). Like Dr. Thornton, he was without academic training in his chosen profession, but, unlike Dr. Thornton, he had devoted himself seriously to the study of architecture, and had built up a large general practice. He had in fact worked himself up from the status of a cultured dilettante to the position of New England's leading architect.

Charles Bulfinch had been born to wealth, and to position in the aristocracy of Boston. A father and grandfather, both bearing the name of Thomas, had been physicians of prominence in the little colonial city. His great-grandfather, Aldino Bulfinch had come to Boston in 1681 as the pioneer founder of the family. Here he had acquired wealth which helped establish his descendants in positions of economic and social security.

Both Thomas Bulfinches were educated in Europe, the first in London and Paris, the second in London and Edinburg. The latter, before going abroad, had graduated from Harvard in 1749 as valedictorian.

Ten years after returning from Europe he had married Susan Apthorp, whose father was reputed to be the wealthiest man of Boston. Her brother, the Reverend East Apthorp was rector of Christ Church in Cambridge, but left there in 1764 for England where he officiated for a time at the historic London church of St. Mary-le-Bow, in Cheapside, the tower of which is known to every tourist for its "Bow bells" and because it is regarded as one of Sir Christopher Wren's finest works.

Into this family of wealth and culture, Charles Bulfinch was born on August 8, 1763; and in the old house which his grandfather had built in Bowdoin Square he grew up in an atmosphere of security which was his birthright; but surrounded on the outside by the turbulence and political disturbances incident to the breaking away of Massachusetts Colony from the mother country.

He wrote in later years that his earliest recollections were concerned with the exciting incidents that preceded the Revolution—the fight against the Stamp Act, the Boston Tea Party, the Massacre, and finally the battles of Lexington and Bunker Hill. The latter he observed from the roof of the family home.

In spite of turmoil and warfare, the youth attended Latin school and was graduated from Harvard in 1781, the very year that Cornwallis surrendered to Washington at Yorktown.

Following his graduation he deferred to the wishes of his father and, breaking away from the two-generation tradition of medical practice, he entered the office of Joseph Barrell, a prominent merchant of Boston and close friend of the Bulfinch family. This experiment did not prove overly successful however from the business standpoint. Trade was suffering from the stagnation common to post war periods, and the young clerk found more congenial occupation in supervising repairs and restorations on the homes of his employer and other friends than in casting up accounts over the desks of the counting house.

About the time he came of age, a bequest of some $1,000.00 came to the family from the estate of an uncle and this was set apart for his use in financing a European tour. He went first to England and, after visiting friends in various parts of that country, Bulfinch crossed to France where he spent some months in Paris, giving especial attention to the study of its architecture. He was afforded unusual opportunities for research through letters and introductions from Lafayette and Thomas Jefferson, the latter being at that time Minister to France.

A tour of southern France and Italy was then undertaken, following an itinerary suggested by Mr. Jefferson. The year and a half spent in Europe was well invested, and went far in preparing Bulfinch for his later career as an architect.

The professional architect was still almost unknown in the new world, the first to enter this field being Latrobe, Hallet, Hadfield, Harrison and a few others who had secured their training abroad. Mills, Strickland, and others of native birth established themselves a little later on, after study and practical experience in the drafting rooms of the older men.

Bulfinch went abroad as a gentleman with a flair for the arts of building, he returned with a mind stored with knowledge pertaining to architecture, knowledge gained through keen powers

PLATE 44. Charles Bulfinch, Architect of the Capitol (1818-1829). Reproduced from Brown's "History of the United States Capitol."

[135]

of observation, and made useful because of his practical knowledge of building construction. He was admirably fitted to act as advisor to the community and to such of his friends as might be involved in building operations. As such activities had been largely neglected during the period of the war, there was much to engage his attention, and he gave freely of his advice without thought of remuneration. His was the spirit of the true gentleman, who feels that his first duty is to share his ability and possessions with others, for the good of all.

Bulfinch married his cousin, Hannah Apthorp, in 1788 and settled down with the comfortable expectation that their combined estates would insure for them enjoyment of well ordered and useful lives. Eleven children in time shared this life with them. One at least of this numerous brood achieved a successful career as a writer. This was Thomas Bulfinch whose *Age of Chivalry* and *Age of Fable* are still widely known and read.

The first really serious architectural commission undertaken by Charles Bulfinch was a design for the proposed State House to be erected on Beacon Hill. He had returned from Europe in January, 1787, and his drawings were submitted in November of the same year. This was an ambitious initiation for an amateur, but the young man of twenty-five plunged in and produced a design which called for an investment of some $20,000.00. That was no mean sum for those times, and it apparently slowed down the enthusiasm of those in control of affairs. At any rate the matter was shelved temporarily, but was revived by a town action in February, 1795, which authorized a committee to acquire a site for the proposed structure.

Bulfinch was appointed a member of this committee, his design submitted seven and a half years previously was adopted, and its adoption approved by the governor. The corner stone was laid on July 4, 1795, by Governor Samuel Adams, with Masonic ceremonies conducted by the omnipresent Paul Revere, who was Grand Master of the Grand Lodge.

Meanwhile, Bulfinch had been extremely busy. Whether called upon to design a church, a residence, a theatre, or a State House for neighboring Connecticut, he brought to bear upon the problem a mind that was well trained, and endowed by nature with discriminating taste. Unfortunately, records of his connection with individual buildings are sometimes missing, and many of the buildings have long since been destroyed. But those still remaining, together with old engravings and photographs of others that are gone, give ample proof of the uniformly high standards which he maintained in his designs.

An ambitious undertaking, begun in 1793, that proved to be his undoing was known as the "Tontine Crescent." This was a financial venture involving a high grade housing development, as a modern promoter would term it. Bulfinch designed a series of connected dwellings which followed the crescent curve of Franklin Place. Associated with him in financing the scheme were several friends who took care to withdraw when business conditions became uncertain and, in January, 1796, Bulfinch was forced into bankruptcy. His estate and that of his wife were wiped out, their beautiful home and the comfortable life which they had enjoyed were sacrificed, and he was obliged to fall back on the practice of architecture as a means of support.

The devotion and service of Charles Bulfinch to his community, whether in affluence or in financial straits, marked him as an outstanding citizen. For nearly nineteen years he was chairman of the Board of Selectmen in the Town of Boston, his term of office having begun in 1799. Before that time he had served on the board for several years as a junior member.

During those years his contributions to the betterment of his city were so numerous and varied that he was with ample justification called the "Great Selectman."

This long service was rewarded ultimately in a manner that was quite unforeseen, doubtless, by Bulfinch himself. Shortly after the War of 1812, his services were retained as architect of the proposed General Hospital of Boston, and he was commissioned to visit New York, Philadelphia, and Baltimore for the purpose of studying hospital buildings in those cities. He extended the tour to Washington, and while there was introduced to President-elect Monroe, at whose suggestion he was shown over the ruins of the Capitol by Commissioner Lane.

PLATE 45. Plan of Capitol by Latrobe. Reproduced from Brown's "History of the United States Capitol"

Six months later, in July, 1817, the President visited Boston, and Bulfinch as chairman of the selectmen and of the large reception committee, was accorded the honor of reading the official address of welcome. He also found himself shouldering the less dazzling, but much more useful responsibility of arranging details incident to the presidential stay.

While this meant hard work and plenty of it, there was the enviable privilege of close association with President Monroe throughout the week, and this acquaintance was doubtless in considerable measure responsible for the appointment later on of Bulfinch as Architect of the Capitol at Washington.

The outcome may best be told by quoting from Bulfinch's all too brief autobiography, as follows: "About November, 1817, following the visit of the President, I received a letter from William Lee, Esq., one of the auditors at Washington, and in the confidence of the President, stating the probability of the removal of Mr. Latrobe, the Architect of the Capitol, and proposing that I should apply for the place. I declined making any application that might lead to Mr. Latrobe's removal, but before the end of the year disagreements between him and the Commissioner became so serious that he determined to resign, and his resignation was immediately accepted. On receiving information of this in another letter from Mr. Lee I made regular application through J.Q.A., Secretary of State, and by return of post received notice from him of my appointment, with a salary of $2,500 and expenses paid of removal of family and furniture."

The unfortunate ill feeling toward Latrobe had been growing increasingly acute for some time, and early in the fall of 1817 it had become quite evident that a break with him was imminent. Reference to this is made in the letter from Lee to which Bulfinch refers: "I am sorry for Latrobe, who is an amiable man, possesses genius and a large family, but in addition to the President not being satisfied with him, there is an unaccountable and I think unjust prejudice against him by many members of the Government, Senate, and Congress."

A bitter dislike existed between Lane and Latrobe, and it seemed for a time that Lane would be obliged to go. However,

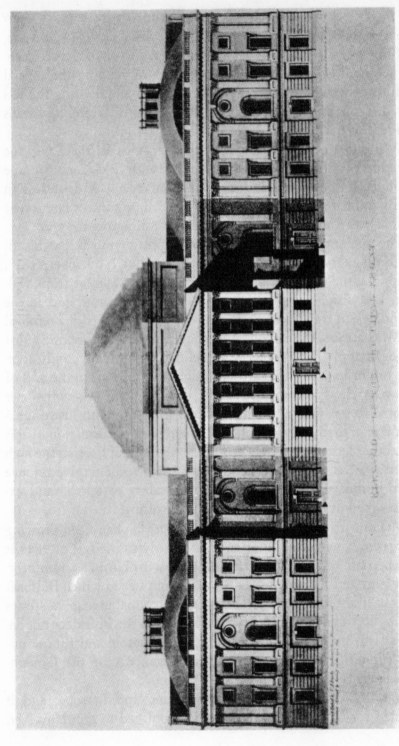

PLATE 46. Elevation drawing of Capitol, by C. A. Busby, an English architect. Measurements taken in 1819; published in 1822

[140]

Latrobe ended the dispute by handing in his resignation on November 20th, and influential friends of Bulfinch at once took steps to secure for him the appointment as successor.

The President in discussing the matter with one of these friends, Harrison Gray Otis, said: "Sir, we are looking to him (meaning Bulfinch), but Mr. Latrobe is a great loss and it will require two persons to supply his place."

The official appointment was signed on January 8, 1818, by Samuel Lane, as Commissioner of Public Buildings. The application for the position had been made through "J.Q.A." as Bulfinch familiarly called John Quincy Adams, and upon receipt of a letter from him confirming the appointment, Bulfinch tendered his resignation to the Board of Selectmen, at a meeting held on December 22, 1817, and two weeks later was in Washington.

A letter to his wife, written a day or two after his arrival, gives details of his first visit to the White House, describing his interview with President Monroe, and his inspection of the Capitol and the various workshops. He goes on to say in a later letter that Colonel Lane has turned over to him many drawings and that, "At the first view of these drawings, my courage almost failed me—they are beautifully executed, and the design is in the boldest style. After long study I feel better satisfied and more confidence in meeting public expectation."

Realizing the difficulties involved in explaining plans and details to the President and members of Congress, Bulfinch employed a young man named Willard, from Boston, to prepare under his immediate direction a wood model of the building. This was about four feet long, and showed various alternative schemes designed by Thornton and Latrobe, together with suggestions for the central rotunda and dome.

This was apparently a wise piece of strategy, for an appropriation was made, with surprising promptness, which enabled him to begin work at once on the central portion of the building.

The dome, as designed by Latrobe (Plates 46, 48), was the subject of considerable criticism on the score of insufficient height. As an aid to settlement of this matter, Bulfinch prepared several drawings showing domes of various heights, including one

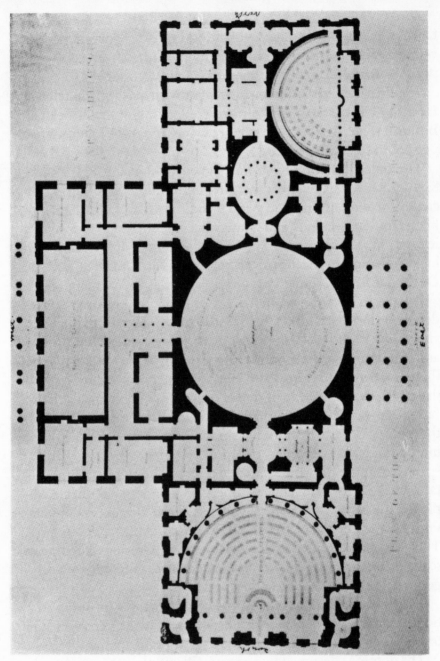

PLATE 47. Plan of the Capitol, by C. A. Busby, showing changes by Bulfinch

drawn much higher than his taste dictated, but shown for the purpose of making comparisons.

Upon submitting these to the Cabinet he was dismayed at having the tallest one selected, while the suggestion was made that a still greater height would be preferred.

Bulfinch was so dissatisfied with the effect when the dome was partially completed that he tried to get permission to reconstruct it in accordance with his lower design. He argued that the saving in copper sheathing would partially offset the additional expense but, finding stubborn resistance to his suggestion, on the part of the commissioner, he dropped the matter rather than become involved in one of the squabbles that had kept the office of the Architect in a turmoil during so much of its history.

(The height of this dome was one hundred and forty-five feet; the present one, designed by Walter, rises two hundred and eighty-five feet above the eastern plaza.) (Plates 48-55, 69, 75, 76, 91, 94-97.)

The first report prepared by Bulfinch tells of the condition in which he found the building, and of the study he had given to plans for carrying the work forward. In this he says, "Great progress has been made toward rebuilding the north and south wings. It will be necessary to complete them according to the designs already adopted and on the foundations already made (Plates 12, 13). I have been engaged in preparing several designs for the central portion, from which the President may choose one."

These words indicate his realization from the outset that it would be his lot to merely carry to completion the ideas of other architects, a circumstance that would be disheartening to any designer with ideas of his own, and that it would be impossible for him to impress his own personality on the great building that was entrusted to his care. All he could hope for was that he could rectify the mistakes and errors of judgment of those who had been his predecessors, and that he could be responsible for good engineering and construction.

The work had progressed too far to admit of important changes in design, and Bulfinch possessed the wisdom and unselfishness

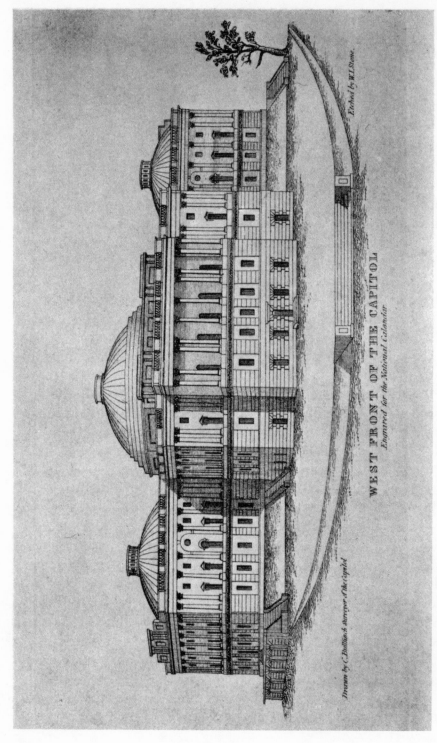

Drawn by C. Bulfinch surveyor of the Capitol.

WEST FRONT OF THE CAPITOL
Engraved for the National Calendar

Etched by W.I. Stone.

PLATE 48. West front of Capitol. Etched by W. I. Stone from drawing by Bulfinch; published (1821), in National Calendar. Reproduced from an original print in the author's collection

PLATE 49. Drawing of Capitol as originally completed. Attributed by Glenn Brown to George Strickland

to avoid the petty attempts of some who had come—and gone—before him, to seek glory by belittling and changing what had already been designed and built. He followed wisely and magnanimously the ideas of Thornton and Latrobe so far as he deemed them practicable, even though not always sympathetic with those ideas.

He not only found drawings completed, with marble and stone in quantities on the ground, but certain details finished and ready for installation. Among these were window frames and sash, marble doorways and parts of doors, and fifty mantels, the latter either designed by Latrobe or selected by him.

Latrobe's design for the east portico was carried out as originally planned, but on the west front various alterations were made. Little attempt was made to change the design, but Bulfinch did improve the plan by diminishing the projection of the central portion to the west, decreasing the size of light wells, and increasing the size of halls (Plates 47, 48).

The restored Hall of Representatives (Plates 31, 32) was found

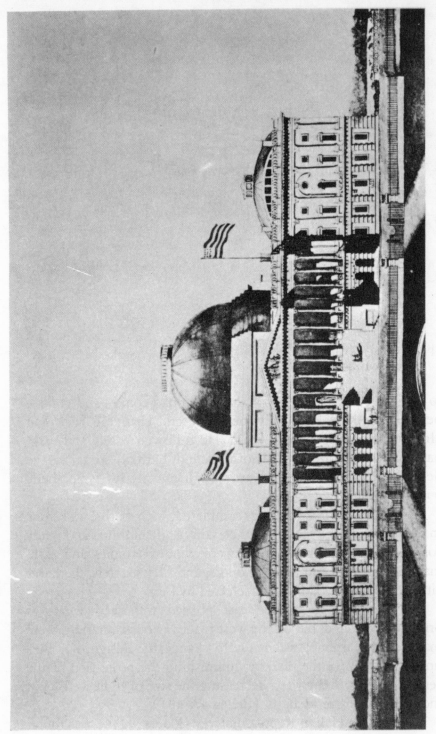

PLATE 50. Water color showing east front of Capitol, with steps, portico, and fence, as built by Bulfinch. Date probably 1832-1834. Artist unknown; it may belong with plans signed Alex. J. Davis. Original drawing in the Library of Congress

to have perpetuated in it the echoes that had caused so much difficulty and criticism in the past. Committees were appointed to investigate the difficulty. Bulfinch was called upon for his opinion, as were William Strickland and Robert Mills, both of whom had formerly been assistants and associates of Latrobe.

A variety of theories and suggestions were propounded and expounded, no two of which were in agreement, and none of which seemed to have much effect in remedying the poor acoustics. A canvas ceiling was stretched above the columns. This stopped the echoes, but also stopped the voice of the speaker, a consummation that would certainly not prove appealing to a legislative body all primed with pent up oratory. A wooden partition was built between the columns, but this came down ignominiously after a week's trial.

Sunken panels were prescribed in place of the flat, painted ceiling. One expert wanted the floor raised; another contended that the ceiling should be lowered; a third proposed a rearrangement of the furnishings; and after all suggestions had been discussed or tried out, over a period of fifteen years or more, they apparently gave it up as a bad job. Today the room is used as a repository for statues of the great and near great, and the guides entertain visitors by demonstrating the freak echoes which enable them to hear whispers from certain remote positions on the floor.

Bulfinch, like the others who had worn the not too enviable crown in this little architectural kingdom, ran afoul of his share of political disturbance. A new appointee to the office of Commissioner of Public Buildings, replacing Thomas Lane, rediscovered the age old formula for making good with those in authority. He inaugurated a policy of financial retrenchment and started in by aiming at his most shining target, the highly (?) paid Architect of the Capitol. The idea seemed to be a good one and the first shot took the form of the following letter to Bulfinch:

"Washington, D. C., September 30, 1822.

"SIR: I have a painful duty to perform. It is that of announcing a general reduction of salaries, to take place at the end of the present year.

PLATE 51. East front of Capitol. From an old engraving in the author's collection

"Subsequently to that period yours will be $2,000 per annum.
"Very respectfully, your most obedient servant,
"J. ELGAR,
"Commissioner of Public Buildings.
"To Charles Bulfinch."

Painful though this duty may have been to Commissioner Elgar, the idea in general seemed to have been even less happy in the estimation of Architect Bulfinch; in fact he seemed to reciprocate very little of Elgar's enthusiasm. He quietly brought the matter to the attention of his friend, John Quincy Adams, claiming that his salary was fixed by contract, hence was no affair of the commissioner.

There seemed to be a peculiar absence of governmental red tape in those days, that we find difficulty in understanding in our own more enlightened age. When the matter was brought to the attention of President Monroe, he wrote a hurry-up letter to Attorney General Wirt, on January 31, 1823, and on the self-same day Wirt sent a formal reply to the President in which Bulfinch was sustained and the opinion rendered that his contract with the Government was "Unalterable by the mere will of either party." Thus ended another reform movement, and the subject of salary cuts seems to have been dropped abruptly and permanently so far as Mr. Bulfinch was concerned.

The architect's report of progress made during the year 1822 is well worth reading because of the picture its few words present of the manner in which the great dome was carried up.

"Washington, D. C., December 9, 1822.
"JOSEPH ELGAR, ESQ.,
"Commissioner of Public Buildings.
"SIR: . . . The principal labor of the season has been devoted to raising the dome of the center. For this purpose, the interior walls of the Rotunda were continued: As soon as the appropriations were made in the spring, they were raised to the full height, and covered with the entablature and blocking course. The exterior walls were carried up with stone, formed into large pannels, and crowned with a cornice and four receding gradins; about two

PLATE 52. The Capitol, seen from White House (1840). From an engraving published by N. P. Willis, after a painting by Bartlett

thirds of the interior dome is built of stone and brick, and the summit of wood. The whole is covered with a wooden dome of more lofty elevation, serving as a roof; it is hoped that a few days of favorable weather will enable the workmen to sheathe it securely, when it will be in readiness for the copper covering. It will be finally crowned with a balustrade, to surround a skylight of twenty-four feet diameter, intended to admit light into the great Rotunda. . . . I cannot omit this occasion to mention the ingenuity and persevering diligence of the superintendents of each branch of the work, and cheerful and unremitted exertions of the workmen, in their endeavors to execute their orders, and to bring this part of their labors to a close. . . .

"Respectfully submitted,
"CHARLES BULFINCH,
"Architect of the Capitol of the United States."

(This dome should not be confused with the present one that was built by Walter forty years later.)

Heating a building as large as the Capitol with open wood fires must have been a real job. The mere problem of storing fuel was a serious one, and one that evidently worried the architect. In a letter written to the chairman of the Committee on Public Buildings, in March of 1826, Bulfinch "considered it proper to provide suitable places of deposit for the large quantities of fuel annually consumed, amounting to about 400 cords." As this was "stowed in the vaults forming the cellars of the North and South wings" he recognized the seriousness of the fire hazard, which was increased by the fact that "every attendant on the fires . . . must use lights of some kind, either lamps or lanthorns, for getting the daily supply of fuel."

In enumerating the items necessary "to complete the Capitol and its appendages" he includes "Iron gates, with stone piers, on four sides of the square, to the garden, with two porter's lodges." The estimate for these lodges was as follows: "4 lodges at North and South entrances, containing Engine-house, Guard-house, and Porter's houses, with piers to Carriage-way, at 7,000 dollars each —$28,000.00."

PLATE 53. The Capitol from Pennsylvania Avenue (1840). From an engraving published by N. P. Willis, after a painting by Bartlett

Congress was evidently keeping a close watch on expenditures for, in a report dated February 7, 1827, the committee pared away what was deemed not absolutely essential, and the four lodges were placed in that category. Piers and gates were recommended, presumably with vagrant live stock in mind.

The same thing happened a year later, but by that time two lodges were specified for the west, with the guard-houses still at the north and south. The cost of the latter had shrunk to $1,450 each.

The Capitol was reported as practically completed at the close of 1824, at least so far as the interior was concerned. Various features of the exterior, however, still remained unfinished, among them being the colonnade of the east portico, and the approaches from the west, together with the necessary grading, planting, and other improvements required on the surrounding grounds.

Bulfinch devoted himself very largely to this work during the years 1826 and 1827, designing the enclosing fence with gate lodges and posts of stone. The details of these were kept in close conformity with the details of Thornton's early work, as may be seen by comparing them with the central windows of his east front (Plates 13, 56, 57, 58).

It is to be regretted that these features were removed in 1873 when extension of the Capitol grounds was necessitated by the addition of the great north and south wings. Fortunately two gate lodges and three posts have been preserved for us by their reërection on Constitution Avenue at 15th and 17th Streets, near the Washington Monument.

The long service of Bulfinch was terminated by a bill passed in Congress, May 2, 1828, abolishing the office of Architect of the Capitol. However, he remained until June 25, 1829, when the following official letter was written to him:

"Washington, D. C., June 25, 1829.

"SIR: I am directed by the President to inform you that the office of Architect of the Capitol will terminate with the present month.

"Respectfully, I remain your faithful and obedient servant,

"J. ELGAR."

PLATE 54. "Principal Front of the Capitol Washington." Engraved from a painting by Bartlett. From an old engraving in the author's collection

[154]

As no mention of pain on the part of the writer was made in this letter, as had been done in the previous one when introducing the subject of pay cuts, it is quite possible that Elgar may not have been deeply regretful of this action.

Although no longer in office, Bulfinch prolonged his stay in Washington still another year, the date of his final departure being made known to us in a letter written by him on June 3, 1830, in which he said, "I date from this place for the last time. We have taken places on the stage and leave for Baltimore at 2 o'clock."

During his residence in Washington Bulfinch had designed the Unitarian Church, which was demolished in 1900, and the penitentiary, that was destroyed to make way for the Army War College. He also designed, in 1828, the State House that was erected in Augusta, Maine. His works were so numerous that they cannot be enumerated here.

After returning to Boston Mr. and Mrs. Bulfinch lived quietly among their friends, and in the fall of 1838 visited Washington where they spent the winter. The following year they accepted an invitation from his nieces to make their home in his old birthplace in Bowdoin Square. Here, at the age of seventy-four Mrs. Bulfinch passed away, and three years later, on April 15, 1844, he followed.

Funeral services for him were held in King's Chapel, the building of which was made possible largely through the generosity of his grandfather, and of which he had long been a loyal supporter.

As an architect no one, probably had, up to that time, exerted so powerful an influence in New England; and as a citizen he was looked up to as a leader in all that made for the betterment of his native city.

SALARIES

The salaries paid at this time seem pathetically low, when compared with those of today, but this is of course a matter that is determined by general economic standards. A fair idea of the current salary scale may be had from Elgar's report for the year 1827. From this are taken the following figures:

[156]

PLATE 55. East front of the Capitol. Drawn by H. Brown, and engraved by J. Andrews for Hinton's "History of the United States." From an old engraving in the author's collection

Charles Bulfinch, architect, salary for one year $2,500
Antonio Capellano, sculptor, salary for one year 1,500
Luigi Persico, sculptor, salary for one year 1,500
Francisco Iardella, carver, salary for one year 1,250
George Blagden, superintendent, salary for one year 1,500

MEN WHO SUPERINTENDED THE JOB

JOHN LENTHAL

The story of Latrobe and his distinguished services as Architect of the Capitol would be incomplete without mention of John Lenthal, who worked with him for five years in direct superintendance of the work of construction and of the men engaged on the job.

Lenthal was born in England in 1762. His great-great-grandfather was Sir John Lenthal, fourth to bear the name, and a member of Parliament. He in turn was the son of William Lenthal, who had been a Speaker of the House of Commons.

Latrobe appointed Lenthal, Clerk of Works on the Capitol, immediately after receiving his own commission as Architect. The complete confidence that was placed in him is evident from the letter written him, on April 7, 1803, announcing the appointment. This letter reads in part:

"I have taken upon myself the fullest responsibility for your conduct, and . . . have to inform you that it is clearly understood by the President of the United States and the superintendent of the city that you are to be the sole judge of the merits of the workmen and are authorized to discharge any man without appeal. . . . You are also the sole judge in my absence of the fidelity with which contracts are fulfilled . . . no money will be paid without your certificate."

Latrobe's long absences, while engaged on his own private undertakings, worried Lenthal who was well aware of the adverse criticism which was aroused by his apparent neglect of work on the Capitol. He tried to induce Latrobe to spend more time in the Federal City and devote himself more closely to the progress of construction, but without avail. He was content, when absent, to keep in touch with the work by correspondence with Lenthal.

PLATE 56. The Capitol from the west, showing fence designed by Bulfinch. Photographed from an old print by the L. C. Handy Studios

Many of his letters are preserved in a book which belongs to a great-great-grandson of Lenthal, Hamilton Abert. These letters are decidedly entertaining as well as revealing but, with the exception of a few quotations here and in Brown's *History of the Capitol,* little of their contents has been made public.

SHADRACH DAVIS AND PETER LENOX

The office of Clerk of Works, left vacant by the death of Lenthal, was not filled officially until 1815 when Shadrach Davis received the appointment. Little is known about him, but he seems to have been held in good favor by Latrobe and in ill favor by Commissioner Lane. As has been stated previously, the latter transferred Davis, in 1817, to a position at the President's House, replacing him at the Capitol by Peter Lenox, an action that precipitated the resignation of Latrobe. Lenox had made an excellent record for himself at the President's House in pushing work to completion, while work at the Capitol under Davis had lagged.

Peter Lenox was a man of superior ability and good family connections. He was born in March, 1771, at Williamsburg, Virginia, where the Lenox family had lived since 1700 when their pioneer ancestor came to this country from Scotland. His mother was a Miss Carter, also of Williamsburg.

Walter Lenox, the father of John, had been well to do before the Revolutionary War, but had lost his property during that conflict, and the son came to Washington in 1792 with the hope of mending his fortunes. He secured a position as foreman on the President's House, and later was made Clerk of Works.

This position was held by him during the period of construction, prior to the War of 1812, and during the reconstruction made necessary by the vandalism of British soldiers.

The services of Lenox at the Capitol were evidently as efficient as before, for he retained the position until the building was considered completed, in 1829.

Like others holding public office at the time, Lenox conducted outside business of his own, and succeeded in amassing a comfortable fortune by dealing in lumber. He built for himself a large, four story, brick house on Maryland Avenue, near the river.

PLATE 57. Gate Post; designed by Charles Bulfinch. Removed in 1873 to Constitution Avenue, corner of Fourteenth Street. Photograph by the author

PLATE 58. Old Gate House; formerly at west entrance of Capitol grounds, now at Constitution Avenue and Fourteenth Street. Compare detail by Bulfinch with that by Thornton on east front of old Capitol (Plate 13). Photograph by the author

Peter Lenox was a prominent citizen of the Capital City in its early days and, judging from his portrait, was distinguished in his personal appearance. He served at various times on the city council, was a successful investor in real estate, and received a commission as captain during the War of 1812. His death occurred in 1832.

GEORGE BLAGDEN

One of the few men who saw long service on the Capitol, and kept out of politics and the jealousies that involved so many, was George Blagden. Like Hoban, he worked on friendly terms with all the warring factions of architects and commissioners from 1794, shortly after his arrival in this country, until 1826. On June 3rd of that year he, as did Lenthal, met his death by accident when a bank of earth at the south angle of the Capitol caved in upon him.

Blagden held the position of superintendent of stonework and quarrying. He was a skilled mechanic, with an old world training, and possessed the confidence of all the officials with whom he was associated, his advice being sought on many occasions. During his long stay in Washington he managed to accumulate a comfortable fortune.

WATER FOR CAPITOL HILL

A vivid realization of the primitive conditions that existed in the city of Washington, a third of a century after its founding, may be obtained by reading reports on the struggle to obtain an adequate water supply, and otherwise make Capitol Hill presentable and habitable.

Commissioner Elgar reported, in 1826, that "The ground around the Capitol has been so encumbered with materials and shops, as to prevent any systematic attempt to regulate it; and no plan for that purpose has, as yet, been arranged."

Three years later, Bulfinch urged "The expediency of having two lines of iron scroll railing from the western lodges to the first flight of steps, for the purpose of securing the grounds from the intrusion of cattle." As late as 1874 it was found necessary, as a prelude to improving the grounds "to move the frame stables, sheds, workshops, etc., from the spaces belonging to the United States at B streets north and south, and First street at the foot of the grounds."

Old shacks could be destroyed very easily, but a water supply was something different. The two wells that had once formed oases in the barren space between the two wings, had long since disappeared when the Rotunda was built over their site. Tiber Creek ran not far away, and the canal came well up toward the west entrance (Plate 65), but purer sources were sought for the drinking supply.

A report in 1829 stated that "there is not a well on the hill but may be pumped dry in fifteen minutes; . . . the canal and the Tiber Creek are the only places from which a supply of water could be obtained; and the distance is too great, the population too thin, and the fire engines too few in number, and too inefficient to justify any hope of success in a contest with that most terrible of destroying elements, fire."

Levels were run to the upper reaches of Tiber Creek which was followed up to its head, in a swamp about three miles distant, and as it was fed entirely by springs there seemed to be no great difficulties in the way of collecting the water "by means of covered drains, into a reservoir at a clump of cedar bushes near a small brick house on the west side of the swamp."

This source would "discharge 124 cubic feet in two minutes and four seconds, or 13,935 cubic feet, equal to 104,241 wine gallons, in 24 hours." Apparently wine gallons left less to the official imagination than would the same statistics in the less familiar terms of water gallons.

Furthermore, this very liberal flow of water could be conveyed by gravity to "a large reservoir, say at the highest point of the Capitol square . . . and from that point it could be taken to every part of the Capitol and public grounds, . . . not only for security against fire, but for other purposes, among which may be enumerated objects of cleanliness, watering the grass, shrubbery, trees, &c. &c."

Other "useful and necessary purposes" were enumerated for the use of water but, curiously enough, nothing was said about drinking it.

This report came to the Commissioner of Public Buildings in January, 1829; a year later, on February 2, 1830, an investigator with an inventive turn of mind submitted specifications and drawings of a device, the model of which would, he assured Congress, "be at your service, if called for." He was prepared, "if requested, to furnish calculations which exhibit the superiority of the plan for supplying pure water from springs in the neighborhood of the Capitol, over any plan which proposes to bring water through pipes a great distance by means of its own gravity."

And then he dangles before the dry, and presumably thirsty Congress, the challenge that "A fountain of pure spring water, affording four hogsheads per minute, can be obtained within five or six hundred yards from the Capitol, which may be raised by steam or other power, into a reservoir on the hill, in the vicinity of the Capitol. That portion of the water which may not be wanted about the Capitol, can be carried off to other parts of the city."

Another scheme of dazzling proportions involved the construction of a "grand common basin, 200 feet in width, and about 400 perches in length, extending from near the foot of the botanic garden, through the center of the mall, to the Potomac river; containing a sheet of water of about thirty acres." This was to be fed by a "contemplated canal from Georgetown," and the water was to be pumped to tanks that should afford needed fire protection to all public buildings. These specifications were worked out carefully in every detail, including an estimate of costs, and as its sponsor, I. L. Skinner, proposed elaborate landscaping, and the development of hydraulic power, there was much to recommend it.

Robert Mills also submitted a very carefully studied plan, on March 30th, 1830, a month later than the preceding one, in which he reported on the possibilities of both Tiber and Rock Creeks. He quite naturally referred to what had been accomplished at Philadelphia and Baltimore, he having been associated with both undertakings, especially with the latter, of which he was engineer and president. He stated that the supply of each was furnished "by a pump engine, worked by a water power, derived from the source that irrigates the city. There was more economy, simplicity, and certainty, in this mode of operation, than by steam."

He dwelt on the respective merits of water from springs and streams, and anticipated the seriousness of denuding a country of its forests. In this connection he said, "Again, to depend on one or two springs for a *public* supply is very precarious—springs frequently sink, or dry up; they never increase, but on the contrary, decrease in quantity; there is a natural cause for this in cultivated country; first, the cutting off the trees, (the natural conductors of moisture) and the consequent exposure of the surface of the ground to the sun's rays; second, the draining of marshy grounds etc."

Meanwhile, Mr. Skinner's letter outlining his scheme for a "Grand Central Basin" had been referred to the Committee for the District of Columbia. This committee was enthusiastically favorable to the whole idea, but—"believing that the object falls more properly within the functions of another committee, asks to be discharged from its further consideration." On its recommendation the matter was shunted over to the Committee on Internal Improvements.

Here the matter was deemed to be of "such importance to the public, as well as to the city of Washington, as to merit a survey and examination. And that the President of the United States be, and he is hereby, requested to procure the same to be made, by the Board of Engineers, under the direction of the Secretary of War, and to cause a report thereof, together with an estimate of the cost, to be laid before congress, as early as may be at their next session." This resolution was dated May 22, 1830, and apparently provided a safe place of sepulture for the whole business.

However, the matter refused to stay buried and we find, tucked away among the items of business approved on May 25, 1832, provision "For bringing in pipes to the Capitol, and the construction of reservoirs and hydrants, and the rights of individuals to the water, forty thousand dollars."

There was, apparently, a slip somewhere in someone's calculations, for Mr. Noland included in his annual report of 1836, the following memorandum:

"Mr. John A. Smith's spring, with one acre of land, has been purchased for the sum appropriated by Congress for that purpose, and a deed, certified to be good by the district attorney, has been executed for the same, and recorded in the proper office. It may be proper here to state, that, by a contract heretofore entered into between Mr. John A. Smith (the former proprietor of the spring which supplies with water the reservoirs of the Capitol,) and my predecessor in office, Mr. Smith conveyed to the United States, for a valuable consideration, all the water within an enclosed wall of eight feet square. It was ascertained by several measurements, that the spring within the enclosure yielded only sixteen gallons of water per minute—a quantity barely sufficient to supply one of the reservoirs with pure water. By the late purchase a supply of sixty-six gallons per minute has been added to the head fountain, as will appear by the accompanying report of Mr. Mills, the architect, marked A."

Included in this report, among other statistical items, is the following:

"For the purchase of Smith's spring, including one acre of land, and for enclosing the same; for building culverts, and keeping the water-pipes in order—$5,115.72½."

Whether the half cent was expended for land, fencing, culverts, or maintenance of water-pipes is, unfortunately, not stated, but aside from that one item the expenditure for an assured water supply seems fair enough.

Numerous reports and estimates were received by Congress during the period that the matter was being agitated, a second one coming on January 13, 1832, from the ever nimble pen of Robert Mills. It is evident that every water hole and stream within pumping or flowing distance, including the Potomac, was surveyed by hopeful and appraising eyes.

Tiber Creek has been mentioned frequently in connection with the study of water supply for the Capitol region. It was a stream that flowed formerly around the base of the bluff known as Jenkins Hill, now the site of the Capitol, from which it turned to the west through a stretch of swampy woodland that is now the Mall.

This stream was known originally as Goose Creek but was later christened Tiber by a man named Pope, who lived on an adjoining estate called Rome. He contended that if a Pope lived in Rome, the nearby river must be the Tiber, and so the Tiber it became.

The unruly little stream had such a habit of overflowing the swamps on both sides that it was enclosed ultimately between stone walls, after which it became Tiber Canal. (Plate 65.) It extended the length of the Mall, following the line of what is now Constitution Avenue, from the foot of Jenkins (Capitol) Hill to the approximate site of the Lincoln Memorial where it emptied into the marshy borders of the Potomac.

Tiber Creek has long been filled in, but even today its waters are a source of concern to the engineers responsible for foundations adequate to carry the monumental buildings that line the Mall.

ROBERT MILLS, PROTÉGÉ OF JEFFERSON

By a curious irony of fate, the next architect to be placed in control of the Capitol had practically no influence on its design,

PLATE 59. Robert Mills; Architect of the Public Buildings (1836-1851).
Reproduced from Brown's "History of the United States Capitol"

and did not possess the official title of Architect of the Capitol.
Yet he was closely associated with the building, off and on, for
nearly fifty years, and was in charge of construction and repairs
for fifteen years.

His early career was directed by no less a person than Thomas
Jefferson; he became one of the first native born architects of this
country, and one of the most able. He was probably second to
none in the number of buildings which he designed and erected;
and his work may be found today scattered through the eastern
states from Massachusetts to Louisiana.

This man was Robert Mills (Plate 59), a native of Charleston, South Carolina. He was born August 12, 1781, his father
being William Mills, a Scotchman who came to this country in
1772 from Dundee. His mother was Anne Taylor, whose grandfather, Thomas Smith was Governor of South Carolina from
1690 to 1694, and was one of five Carolinians to hold the title of
Landgrave, bestowed by the British Crown.

Thanks to the wisdom of his father, Robert was enabled to obtain an academic education at Charleston College, where he remained until twenty years of age. His taste for architecture was
due, perhaps, to the facts that an uncle in Scotland was an architect, and that he had early associations with James Hoban, the
Irish architect who, as we have seen, lived in Charleston for a
time before going to the Federal City.

Mills followed Hoban north in 1800, and almost immediately
secured a position with him as draftsman, working on the President's House. Here he attracted the attention of Thomas Jefferson,
and the acquaintance ripened into a lifelong friendship, the last
evidence of which was a letter written to Mills only two months
before Jefferson's death in 1826.

Both men were omniverous readers and seekers after knowledge; both were intensely interested in architecture; and to both
no field of research seemed uninviting. Both had inventive minds
and were responsible for inventions of practical value.

Both wrote prolifically, and Mills like Jefferson had to his
credit a goodly number of books. Among these were guides to the
Capitol and the National Executive Offices at Washington; a re-

markably accurate atlas of South Carolina with twenty large cop-
perplate maps drawn to a scale of two miles to the inch; and
treatises on lighthouses and inland waterways. His *Statistics of
South Carolina* contains seven hundred pages of data that make
the work comparable to but much larger than Jefferson's famous
Notes on Virginia. Both books are regarded today as valuable for
their source material.

Mills' qualities of mind, that later became so highly developed,
were doubtless evident to Jefferson in the young man, and drew
them together in spite of the disparity in ages. It is generally believed, though not definitely proven, that the young protégé was
taken to Monticello for a prolonged stay, of perhaps two years,
and that while there he gave instruction in draftsmanship to Jefferson's granddaughter, Cornelia Randolph. At any rate we know
that the young man made a careful drawing of Monticello, in
which he introduced minor changes in design; that he was given
the freedom of Jefferson's library; and that Cornelia had a knowledge of drawing that was of great assistance to her grandfather
in later years.

The drawing of Monticello has been responsible for the errone-
ous idea that Mills was architect of the house. This fantastic no-
tion has no basis except pure fiction, for the original Monticello
was begun in 1770, eleven years before Mills was born, and the
remodelling was undertaken in 1796 when he was fifteen years
old and living in Charleston. Mills may have been a genius, but
we really can not expect him to go around the country designing
mansions at that tender age.

At Jefferson's suggestion he made a tour of the eastern states
giving especial attention to the architecture, and visiting many
architects, to whom he had letters from Jefferson and Hoban.
Among the men whom he met in this way was Charles Bulfinch of
Boston.

MILLS SECURES A POSITION WITH LATROBE

On returning to Washington the young student secured a position with Latrobe, under whom he studied both engineering and
architecture. He had as fellow draftsmen, Peter Lenox and Wil-

liam Strickland, with whom he surveyed the city of New Castle, Delaware. He also worked for a considerable time on Latrobe's pet project, the Chesapeake and Delaware Canal.

While in Washington he lived for a time with the family of Colonel Joseph Nourse, first Register of the Treasury, paying for his board $2.50 per week. The Nourse home is now known as Dumbarton House and is owned by the National Society of the Colonial Dames of America, by whom it is maintained as headquarters and as a museum of Colonial family life.

Serious as young Robert Mills seemed to be and doubtless was, he found time for a bit of romance, and Mrs. Gallagher quotes in her biography a sly little note that obviously breathes coquetry or ardent emotion.

Note.

Robert Mills, Esq. Debtor to Catherine   Wilmington, Del.

May   1805.

For the pleasure of mending 2 waistcoats . . an evening walk, when time, weather, & inclination permit.

(Signed) A.M.A.

The position with Latrobe was most helpful to the young architect from a professional standpoint, but financially it left much to be desired. In fact his condition might be described as critical when he became engaged, or hoped to achieve that happy relation, to Eliza Barnwell Smith, daughter of General John Smith of Hackwood Park, Frederick County, Virginia.

For an impecunious young draftsman to seek the hand of a girl accustomed to the comfortable life of a Virginia plantation required courage that bordered on heroism. In addition to his pathetically small income, there were long separations due to his detention in Philadelphia on Latrobe's work. Most serious of all was the prospect of meeting the young lady's military father, for no young man of those days could claim, or even seek, fair lady's love without first securing the parent's sanction.

However, the spirited girl hatched up a scheme, which included what is known today as a "pull." A little maneuvering resulted in letters of recommendation being sent to the awe-inspiring father from no less personages than Thomas Jefferson, President of the United States, and Paul Hamilton, Governor of South Carolina. Such a distinguished bombardment proved effective as an introduction to even the inner circles of the F.F.V., and in due time Eliza Smith became Mrs. Robert Mills.

But this did not come about in a day, for, like many another young couple, they found that "getting engaged" did not bring them at once to wedded life, even though that engagement were achieved through the connivance of a President of the United States and the governor of a sovereign state. Robert was under the necessity of earning a living, first for himself, and ultimately for a wife. His job was in Philadelphia, his fiance was in Virginia, and as the journey from one to the other was then a matter of days, instead of hours as at present, the periods of separation were long and seemingly unbearable.

She probably made the customary remarks about his loving his profession more than he did her; but her devotion was sincere, as was proven later through long years of financial stress and privation.

MILLS ESTABLISHES A HOME AND AN OFFICE

Finally the separation ended. They were married and settled down to housekeeping in Philadelphia, with one of the old family servants from the Frederick County plantation.

It is to be regretted that the story can not picture them as enjoying all the comforts of life ever after. Unfortunately, Robert Mills, with all his ability, scholarship, and versatility, was not gifted with business acumen, and life with him was an almost constant struggle against poverty.

Six years were spent in Philadelphia endeavoring to establish himself in practice as an architect, for he had left Latrobe's office in hopes that he might improve his financial condition. But, there was little demand for the services of a professional architect, so in 1814 they moved with their three small children to Baltimore that he might supervise construction on the Washington Monument which was being built from a design that had won for him a five hundred dollar prize.

This was the first important monument erected in memory of the first President, and to this honor Mills added the distinction of designing two other monuments to Washington, the one in the Capitol Grounds at Richmond, Virginia, and most famous of all the great obelisk that dominates the City of Washington. Also, he claimed that the Bunker Hill Monument was built after a design submitted by him, although another received credit for being the architect. To this list of memorials may be added Washington Hall, which he designed for the Pennsylvania Benevolent Society of Philadelphia.

While in Baltimore, Mills planned various engineering enterprises including canals, a drainage system and, perhaps most important of all, a water-works system. He was particularly well qualified in this last field as he had been associated with Latrobe on his Philadelphia project. He was made president as well as chief engineer of the Baltimore Company. He also interested the authorities of Baltimore in the subject of railroads, with the result that three such roads were built in that locality.

Six years in Baltimore brought no great pecuniary reward, so another progress southward was made, this time to his old home, Charleston. During these years of struggle their plight was often pathetic, and at times only the ability of Mrs. Mills to teach drawing, music, and other subjects saved them from actual want. At one time they were reduced to such straights that they had to return the rented piano on which she was giving music lessons.

An appointment as "Civil and Military Engineer of the State" went far toward making life smooth for them in South Carolina, and also gave him wide opportunity for the exercise of his varied talents. The state is rich today in the creations of his versatile mind. At Charleston, Columbia, Camden, and other places are to be found churches, courthouses, residences, and an occasional library, monument or college building. It is sometimes difficult to determine which are his works and which the works of others, but the authenticated examples are sufficient to maintain his reputation.

His engineering works embraced roads, canals, and drainage; he aroused interest in railroad building and helped promote the road which, in 1831, first carried passengers, in actual service, out of Charleston, and led the country in transportation by steam power.

Richmond is another city that owes much to the ability of Mills as an architect. He was winner of the competition for the Monumental Church on Broad Street, and designed a number of the finest residences in the city. The church was erected on the site of a theatre that was burned in 1811, entailing the loss of about sixty-five lives, among the victims being some of Richmond's most prominent citizens. It was decided to replace the burned theatre by a permanent memorial, and a prize of five hundred dollars was offered for the most satisfactory design. Mills entered several designs in the competition, and from one of these the church was erected.

His multiplicity of interests paralleled those of Jefferson, and it is not surprising to find that when Mills organized "The Society of Artists" in Philadelphia for the purpose of promoting interest in art and architecture and of holding exhibitions, the name of Thomas Jefferson appears as its first President while Robert Mills served as Secretary. No adequate appraisal of Mills' interests and activities can be made without expanding a chapter to the proportions of a biography.

The final move of Mills and his family, made in 1830, was from Charleston to the City of Washington. There he was given an appointment as principal draughtsman to the Land Office, and later was transferred to a similar position in the Patent Office.

In 1836 President Andrew Jackson made him Architect and Engineer for the Government, and during this period he designed a large number of buildings, principally customs houses, and marine hospitals, that were erected in various parts of the country. Most important of his works for the government were the E Street front of the Post Office, the F Street front of the Patent Office, and the long colonnade of the Treasury Building on 14th Street. These still stand, though they have been added to and more or less remodeled.

It was after holding this position for fifteen years that the greatest opportunity of his lifetime slipped away from Mills. This was the project for enlarging the Capitol. The necessity for providing more commodious working quarters for Congress had become evident within twenty years after the building had been completed, thus verifying the contention of Thornton that the reduction in size of his design was a serious mistake. He was in fact about the only one of the group concerned with the original construction who seemed to sense the vast growth that lay ahead of the young country, and the demands which this growth would make upon the building that was to house its lawmakers.

To meet this need, it was decided in 1850 that extensions of the Capitol must be made at once, and Mills accordingly submitted a report, accompanied by drawings. This report was received by the Senate Committee on Public Buildings but the Senate refused to accept it, insisting that a competition be held as a means of securing a suitable design, thus following the precedent set in 1792.

An official announcement was drawn up according to the wishes of the Senate, and was published daily through the month of October, 1850. The munificent sum of $500.00 was offered for the design that should be accepted, the further provision being made that in case more than one design should meet with official approval, the prize money should be divided equally among the lucky contestants. All the premiated designs were to become the property of the government, which might take from each such features as should be deemed adaptable to the finished design.

The competition closed December 1st, four designs were selected, and the money divided between the four winning contestants, a rather slim reward for all the work involved.

The Senate Committee on Public Buildings, which had this contest in charge, consisted of R. M. T. Hunter, Jefferson Davis, and John H. Clarke. Mr. Davis was made chairman of the committee. A decade later he became President of the Southern Confederacy.

Upon receiving the committee's report, the Senate instructed

Mills to work out a plan in which should be embodied the best features of the winning plans.

However, there seemed to be the customary absence of felicitous coöperation between the President and Congress, for Millard Fillmore, who then held down the presidential chair, proceeded to sidetrack the entire train of action. He ignored Mills completely and appointed as architect of the extension of the Capitol, Thomas U. Walter, a competitor who had entered two sets of drawings in the Senate's competition. Walter went to work at once preparing a final plan and on June 11, 1851, took the oath of office.

This erased Robert Mills completely from the picture, so far as the Capitol was concerned, for not only had he no further connection with the preparation of designs, but supervision of the work was placed in control of the Department of the Interior.

Mills was of course an old man at this time, and it is not surprising that the President should have deemed it advisable to replace a man of seventy with one having a longer future to anticipate. If this were the motive in making the change, it seems to have been justified, for Robert Mills died March 3, 1855. He was buried in the old Congressional Cemetery, and although no commissions were appointed to raise a monument over his grave, the monuments which he had raised over the graves, or in memory of others, and the many, many buildings which he had constructed throughout the length and breadth of the country were in themselves sufficient memorial.

IV

THE EXTENSION OF THE CAPITOL

WALTER GOES AHEAD WITH THE CAPITOL

ANY SUGGESTIONS were made for solving the problem of a suitable extension of the Capitol. One of Mills' plans involved a high masonry dome, smaller but in some respects similar to the one finally erected. He placed new wings to the north and south of the old building, with the two halls of Congress on its longitudinal axis, and designated the old chambers of the Senate and House for use by the Supreme Court and for the display of art. All of these ideas were ultimately embodied in the final plans. (Plates 60, 61.)

One of the competitive plans by Walter provided for the erection of a building east of the old one, and almost equal to it in size. The two were to be connected by corridors, thus practically obliterating the old east front, the remaining portions of which would face inner courts. Otherwise the old building would remain intact. Perspective views prepared by him, show a huge rectangular building with Latrobe's entrance removed to and dominating the east front and with the low dome practically lost to sight.

Work was begun at once, and on July 4, 1851, the corner stone was laid with elaborate ceremonies, both civic and Masonic. These were participated in by President Fillmore, Walter Lenox, Mayor of Washington (a son of Peter Lenox, for thirteen years Clerk of Works on the old building), and a throng of notables.

The oration of the day was delivered by Daniel Webster, then Secretary of State, and a copy of his words was deposited with other documents in the stone.

The entire undertaking must have been handled in a somewhat dictatorial fashion for, during the winter, the Senate began to manifest a certain curiosity as to the sort of quarters the architect was inclined to vouchsafe them. It asked pertinent, or impertinent, questions about the lighting, ventilating, and even the acoustics. Perhaps some of the members had heard of the torrid discomforts of the old oval "oven" of early days; and all had doubtless suffered from the difficulty in hearing or being heard in the Hall of Representatives. Certainly nothing could be more painful than the

PLATE 60. Design by Walter for extension of the Capitol. Approved, 1851, by President Millard Fillmore. The present lofty dome authorized in 1855. Reproduced from Brown's "History of the United States Capitol"

knowledge, on the part of an orator, that his flights of speech were being lost somewhere up around the skylight.

Taking it altogether, the Senate apparently entertained the quaint idea that it possessed a right to know what was being done for it with the people's money that was being so generously voted into the hands of the builders. The desired information was politely handed to it in various reports and messages.

Then the House began to show a similar curiosity, and wanted to know something about the stone that the builders were using. This body of lawmakers was informed that the stone came from the Potomac River above Washington, and its qualities were carefully determined for their benefit and enlightenment.

Most elaborate tests were made, crushing tests, absorption tests, and freezing tests, of various samples of marble submitted for use on the exterior. This work of research was conducted by a commission of leading scientists, and as a result it was decided to face the walls with the product of quarries at Lee, Massachusetts.

Meanwhile political rumblings were heard. The Capitol was under the jurisdiction of the Commissioner of Public Buildings and Grounds, but the new work was placed in charge of the architect, who in turn was under the Secretary of the Interior. This wounded the feelings of the current commissioner, William Easby, who felt apparently that he was being deprived of something that he ought to have. Realizing that an investigation is the easiest and most direct way of getting a political rival into trouble, Easby instituted charges of fraud and misconduct in nearly everything he could think of in connection with the job.

After seven months of investigation a House committee reported a few criticisms of minor importance regarding methods of computing values of stone. Methods of letting contracts were discussed; the foundations were reported as excellent; a brick contractor was found guilty of turning over his contract to the superintendent; the luckless superintendent was fired; and the work went on.

This disturbance was stirred up, as is often the case, by a disgruntled official; the witnesses were mostly men who had been unsuccessful bidders for contracts, or workmen who had been dis-

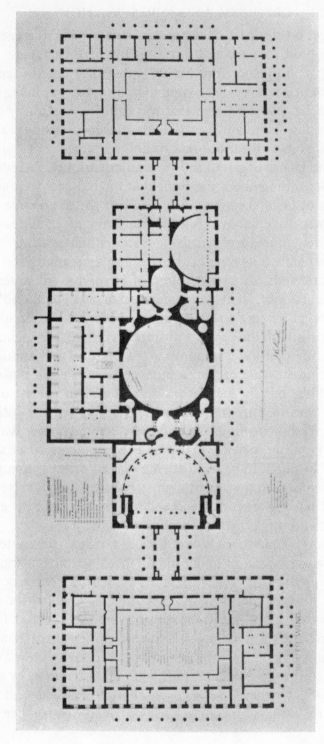

PLATE 61. Plan of the Capitol as completed by Walter. Reproduced from Brown's "History of the United States Capitol"

charged. But despite the bias of prosecution, and the favorable character of the report, the affair had its effect, and the newly elected President, Franklin Pierce, issued an order that superintendence of building operations on the Capitol should be made a responsibility of the War Department.

As Jefferson Davis was at that time Secretary of War, the undertaking which he had sponsored in the beginning, while chairman of the Senate Committee on Public Buildings, was now returned to him for further guidance.

With the order for transfer came a request from the President that a competent officer be detailed to take charge of the work. This responsibility was conferred on Montgomery C. Meigs, captain of engineers. He at once called in experts to study the plans for ventilation and acoustics, while he himself suggested various changes in the arrangement of rooms in the two wings. Most important of these was the relocation of the two halls of Congress which were placed in the center of their respective wings, on the main axis of the old building. Previous plans had shown them at an end of each wing, while extensions of the main corridors followed the axes.

The architect, Mr. Walter, and the new superintendent worked together amicably on these changes, each apparently having a wholesome regard for the other's ability.

The changes proposed by Meigs were improvements in many respects on the original plans, and were approved by the President. Wide corridors were carried entirely around the two chambers, and monumental stairways afforded convenient communication between the main and gallery floors. (Plate 61.) These features were quite in contrast with the narrow hallways and out of the way staircases of the old building.

Ceilings over the two chambers were of iron, hung from iron trusses, and were divided by heavy beams into panels which were filled with ornamental glass, affording well diffused light. (Plates 63, 64.)

The Hall of Representatives was equipped with three hundred desks, which were arranged in semicircles on a floor 137 feet long by 92 feet wide. The gallery on three sides was planned to accommodate 1,200 visitors.

By placing the large chambers in the center of the wings it was possible to surround them with a large number of small rooms to meet various needs. The smaller size of the Senate Chamber allowed even more space in the north wing for committee rooms and lobbies, many of which were given elaborate architectural treatment.

Considerable discussion was stirred up regarding the manner of letting contracts. The architect, Mr. Walter, advised general contracts, including both materials and labor, but his suggestions were overruled by the President and Congress. As a consequence, much of the work was done by day labor.

Along with work on the two wings, the architect was also engaged in reconstructing the interior of the extension west of the rotunda, in which the Library of Congress had long been housed. A destructive fire, on December 24, 1851, had caused a tragic loss of books and manuscripts, emphasizing the necessity for using fireproof materials when providing storage for such valuable and inflammable material.

Walter met this requirement by the use of cast iron for all the structural and ornamental features of the interior, including the shelves. His plans included refitting the quarters already occupied by the library, together with suggestions for future expansion. The sum of $72,000 was appropriated on March 19, 1852, for the restoration of the original space, and in 1865-1867 the entire west extension, above the basement floor, was given over to the library.

This included three large rooms occupying the entire west, north and south sides of the extension. The first of these was built up above the floor with two galleries of book stacks surrounding a long, narrow central court; the other two had three gallery levels. The detail throughout was very elaborate in design, quite in contrast with the stark simplicity of a modern library book stack. (Plate 62.)

These quarters were used until 1897 when the new Library of

PLATE 62. The Library of Congress as rebuilt by Walter after fire of 1851.
Photograph by the L. C. Handy Studios

Congress was completed. Since then the space has been cut up into small rooms for various uses.

The new Hall of Representatives (Plate 63) was reported as ready for occupancy in Captain Meigs' report of November, 1857, and on December 16th the House of Representatives held its first session in the new quarters. Completion of the Senate wing was delayed by difficulty in securing ironwork, and it was not until January 4, 1859 that the new Chamber (Plate 64) was occupied by the Senate.

Among other "modern improvements" provided for the Capitol was gas lighting, and to provide for this a ten inch main was run into the building. It was found however that the demand for gas thus created was greater than the company's plant could supply, without building a new gasometer, and Captain Meigs advised that the government manufacture its own gas.

[185]

PLATE 63. Hall of the House of Representatives; Thomas U. Walter, architect. Photograph by the L. C. Handy Studios

Meanwhile, trouble for the architect was once more brewing. Walter and Meigs, who at first had worked together in peace and amity, began to wrangle over those age-old sources of dispute and warfare—priority and authority. Jefferson Davis consistently upheld Meigs in these dissensions, but when James Buchanan became President, in 1857, the feud broke out with renewed energy.

Meigs demanded possession of all drawings pertaining to the Capitol, and obtained an order to that effect from the Secretary of War. The architect replied that he believed the order called for only such drawings as were necessary for use in carrying on the work, and wrote a letter of self defense to the Secretary, explaining in detail that the captain demanded all existing drawings that had ever been made for the Capitol. He on the other hand contended that the proper place of deposit for them was in the office of the architect. He concluded by saying, "If it is your wish that Captain Meigs shall control the architecture of the public works, of which I am Architect, and you will so inform me, I will retire from them without a moment's delay." He gave a parting shot by adding the malicious taunt, "If Captain Meigs is to have control of the architecture I shall take pleasure in retiring."

The war of words went on. Meigs intimated in another letter that Walter had stolen the drawings, because he refused to transfer them to a house on A Street where Meigs had moved his office. He also referred to the architect as "my subordinate." He finally became so obstreperous and unbearable in his attitude toward Walter, and even toward the Assistant Secretary of War, who had the temerity to uphold Walter in a letter written during the absence of the Secretary, John B. Floyd, that the latter found it necessary to squelch the bumptious captain.

The assistant's letter, to which Meigs had taken exception, was returned by the Secretary with the following official endorsement: "The paper to which this is appended contains the opinions and views of the Secretary of War, which were then and are now deemed to be proper and correct. The conduct of Captain Meigs in thus interpolating the records in his possession with a paper manifesting such flagrant insubordination and containing lan-

PLATE 64. The Senate Chamber; Thomas U. Walter, architect. Photograph by the L. C. Handy Studios

guage both disrespectful and insulting to his superior is reprehensible in the highest degree."

Hearing that an order for his discharge had been written, Meigs made a last grandstand play to save himeslf, by going over the heads of all his superiors with a letter to President Buchanan, in which he asked that his "Last letters to the War Department be read before you decide the case." This letter was written November 1, 1859, and on that same date Captain Montgomery C. Meigs ceased to function as Superintendent of Construction of the Capitol.

His place was at once filled by Captain W. B. Franklin, of the topographical engineers, who possessed tact as well as efficiency, and carried on the work of superintendence without friction.

The policy of placing a military engineer in authority over the Architect of the Capitol became the subject of vitriolic debate in Congress. On December 29, 1854, Mr. Stanton of Kentucky made a scathing indictment before the House of this procedure, asserting that it was "A great mistake to suppose, because these gentlemen acquire a theoretic knowledge of architecture at West Point, . . . that therefore they are qualified for the construction of any edifice, no matter how elaborate or complicated its architectural details. . . . Men who may erect a log hut are not, necessarily, qualified to build a palace; nor does it follow, because a military engineer may plan a fort, or lay out a road, he is, therefore, qualified to construct a stately portico, or erect a splendid dome. The building you propose to erect must have a civil architect. . . . You can not get along without such an officer. Were you to place a dozen military engineers in charge of the work you could not dispense with his services. . . . The presence of a military engineer is but an incumbrance, and serves only to embarrass the architect. . . . I do not know of any civil work in progress, which is placed under the control of a military engineer, that some half-paid civil architect is not employed to do the work for which the credit is given to the Army officer."

These caustic criticisms naturally stirred up hot discussions, but the military supervision continued until the Civil War drew the engineers from constructive into destructive activities.

PLATE 65. Capitol from the west; showing unfinished dome and extension. Tiber canal in foreground. Photograph by the L. C. Handy Studios

WAR BETWEEN THE STATES

Captain Franklin had been in his new office scarcely a month when work was discontinued, due to lack of appropriations. It was not resumed until July 1, 1860. A month later a contract was made for thirty-four monolithic columns, to be quarried in Baltimore County, Maryland. These columns, for the porticoes, were to be 25 feet 2⅛ inches high, 3 feet in diameter at the base, and 2 feet 6⅛ inches at the neck.

By the end of that year the platforms of all the porticoes were ready to receive the columns; the foundations for all steps were laid; and interior work was completed, except for the decorations.

Opening of the Civil War in 1861 interfered seriously with progress on the Capitol, little work being accomplished during that year. In February Captain Meigs was detailed to his old post again, but soon afterward was ordered to the Southwest, and was replaced by J. N. Macomb of topographical engineers.

By midsummer a portion of the old building had been transformed by the military into a bakery, while the crypt became a place of storage for flour; and it was not long before the entire building was taken over for hospital purposes with 1,500 beds installed.

A protest against this high handed act was registered by the Commissioner of Public Buildings, and on October 15th President Lincoln ordered the building vacated by the army, just in time to permit of its being cleaned and damages repaired before the fall session of Congress.

On April 16, 1862, Congress passed a bill transferring supervision of the Capitol Extension and erection of the new Dome to the Department of the Interior. This order must have brought joy to the soul of Thomas U. Walter, for by it he was given supreme authority as both architect and superintendent, thus removing an irritating thorn from his flesh.

THE DOME

In the meantime, while work on the new wings had been progressing according to Walter's original plans, an important modification was being made on the old building. The plan as originally decided on involved no changes of importance on the build-

PLATE 66. The old Capitol as seen today. The colonnade of present dome replaces original flat dome. Photograph by the author

ing as it was left by Bulfinch but, just before adjournment on March 3, 1855, Congress authorized replacement of the old, low dome, which was built of wood sheathed with copper, by a cast iron dome of much greater size.

The drawings which Walter made in compliance with this order are quite extraordinary examples of draftsmanship, and show engineering ability of a high order. Much of the credit for them should go, doubtless, to August Schoenborn who was Walter's chief architectural draftsman. Schoenborn held a position in the office of the Architect of the Capitol from 1850 to 1902, a term of service that places him in a class with Hoban and Mills. He was born October 20, 1827, and died January 24, 1902.

The dome as shown, and as constructed, is 228 feet in height, with a lantern above it 52 feet high by 17 feet in diameter, while surmounting all is the famous figure of Freedom, that was executed by Thomas Crawford at three times life size, or to be exact, 16 feet 6 inches tall.

An elaborate system of trusses ties together the outer and inner domes, and on Plate 68 is a carefully worked out detail of the scaffolding by means of which men and material were raised to the points where work was being carried on.

This drawing solves the baffling problem that has worried many an uninitiated visitor, the problem of how that big, bronze goddess ever achieved her position on top of that lofty lantern.

It is quite simple, if one knows how. Walter merely built scaf-

PLATE 67. Section of Dome; designed by Thomas U. Walter. Original
drawing is in the Library of Congress

folding straight up in the middle of the rotunda, through the eye
of the dome, and from there swung out a derrick by means of
which the ironwork could be hoisted up on the outside, from the
roof of the old building. Another derrick on that roof started the
material on its upward journey. Donkey engines, one on the
roof, furnished the motive power. (Plate 68.)

Above the dome the scaffolding was carried on up, both inside
and out of the lantern. At last, when all was completed, the five
sections of the bronze statue were hoisted up and bolted in position.

The interior of the rotunda (Plates 39, 40) remained un-
changed up to the top of the cornice, which was 44 feet above the
floor. On this was built a wall nine feet high, supporting a colonnade from which the inner dome was carried on up to a crown,
surrounding an opening 65 feet in diameter.

A curious feature of the outer dome is the manner in which the
great peristyle is supported. This is the colonnade that encircles
the drum, on which the dome rests, just above the octagonal base.

The inner dome is supported on the old walls of the rotunda,
so any construction outside of it must have some outside means
of support. This condition presented a serious problem in connection with the peristyle which was thrust far out beyond the
wall. The difficulty was overcome by carrying the columns on
brackets attached to the outside of the rotunda wall, and surrounding them by a curtain wall which gives the effect of a supporting base (Plate 67).

In spite of all the demands which war made on man power and
finances, President Lincoln insisted that work on the Capitol be
carried on as a symbol of the permanency of the Union.

Architect Walter, in his report on the progress of work during
the season of 1863, mentioned the difficulty experienced in securing marble, because of war conditions. Nevertheless, work had
progressed so satisfactorily on the porticoes and dome that, on
December 2nd, the great bronze statue of Freedom was placed
in position as the crowning feature of the Capitol. At exactly
12:00 o'clock noon, the head of the statue was hoisted from the
ground, and in twenty minutes it was in position, a flag was un-

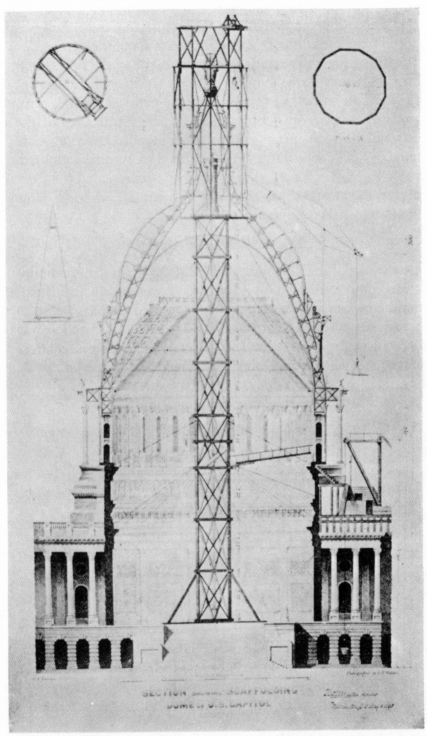

PLATE 68. Section of Dome, showing construction of scaffolding and temporary roof; designed by Thomas U. Walter. Original is in the Library of Congress

furled and a salute of thirty-five guns fired from Capitol Hill was echoed by similar salutes from a dozen forts about the city.

In spite of the bitter struggle that was dividing the states, both North and South were bound by a strong sentimental attachment for the building that had been so long the nation's Capitol. This was evident when, on February 3, 1865, representatives of the North and the South met on a ship in Hampton Roads to negotiate a termination of hostilities. As soon as opportunity permitted, Senator R. M. T. Hunter of Virginia, who represented the Confederacy, asked eagerly of Secretary William H. Seward, "How is the Capitol? Is it finished?"

WALTER STEPS OUT

Dedication of the crowning statue did not mean that the building was completed; on the contrary, there were many details still unfinished when Thomas U. Walter submitted his resignation to the Secretary of the Interior on May 26, 1865. This action was prompted by an order from the Secretary cancelling a contract with the man who was building the enlargement of the Library of Congress in the western extension of the Capitol.

A few words from the letter of resignation will explain Walter's position.

"Hon. James Harlan,
"Secretary of the Interior.

"Sir: I have the honor to acknowledge the receipt of your letter of yesterday inclosing a copy of a communication addressed by you to the contractor for the enlargement of the Library of Congress, in which you state that the contract entered into between myself, on the part of the Government, and Mr. Charles Fowler, the aforesaid contractor, 'is void,' and that 'no accounts or claims for service performed or materials furnished under it will be allowed.' You also state that 'the Commissioner of Public buildings will be instructed to take the necessary action to prevent the further progress of said work under said supposed contract, and also to preserve the public buildings until the work can be legally resumed, after advertisement for bids.' This of course removes

PLATE 69. The great Dome against the night sky. Photograph by the author

all jurisdiction of the work from me, which, it is proper for me to say, I do not at all regret.

"I may, however, be permitted to remark that I consider the stoppage of the work at this time as particularly unfortunate. . . . I regret that so important a movement as the abrogation of a contract, in which I stand as the representative of the Government . . . should have been effected without any consultation whatever with me. . . . I have likewise received a letter from the Commissioner of Public Buildings and Grounds, inclosing a copy of a communication received by him from the Department of the Interior, . . . in which you direct him to take immediate 'charge of all work on public buildings in the District of Columbia in course of construction, extension, or repair, now in progress, that are legally subject to the control of the Secretary of the Interior.' This, of course, places me in a position subordinate to the aforesaid Commissioner of Public Buildings and Grounds.

"These changes . . . suggest the present as the proper time for me to retire altogether from the charge of the public works."

It was a long letter in which he gave a dignified statement of his connection with the public buildings and of his accomplishments during the fourteen years of his stay in Washington. It was not unmixed with pathos. As we read between the lines, there seems to be more than a suggestion of just another of those miserable quarrels that strewed the pathway along which we follow the history of our Capitol building; quarrels which seem an inevitable result of mixing politics with artistic temperament. So many of these have already been uncovered by this recital that it may be as well to leave this one buried.

Thomas U. Walter was too much of a man to allow the vexation of such an episode to crush him, as it had some of his predecessors, and it had little effect apparently on his professional reputation. Returning to his native city, Philadelphia, he accepted a position as assistant to John McArthur, architect of the new city hall, devoting his attention largely to the great tower, and to the decorative work on the building. He held this position until his death on October 30, 1887.

PLATE 70. Ground floor corridor, new south wing; designed by Thomas U. Walter. Photograph by the author

PLATE 71. Thomas Ustick Walter, Architect of the Capitol (1851-1865). From an old print

LIFE OF WALTER

Thomas Ustick Walter (Plate 71), son of Joseph S. and Deborah Walter, was born September 4, 1804, and was named after Thomas Ustick, a prominent minister of the time. He was apprenticed, while still a young boy, to his father who was a bricklayer and mason, as was also his grandfather who came to Philadelphia from Germany. In 1825 he became a master bricklayer. Meanwhile, he found time to acquire a good education, with mathematics as his especial interest, and also studied mechanical drawing in the office of William Strickland. Leaving this office after a short time, he spent several years studying mathematics, physics, construction, drawing, and painting. In 1828 he again entered Strickland's office, this time devoting himself to architecture and engineering.

He struck out for himself as a practicing architect in 1830, and on October 14, 1831, was awarded a commission to design the Philadelphia County Prison, usually called Moyanmensing, which was built in the so-called "castellated manner." In 1833 his drawings were selected in a competition for the Girard College for Orphans, which he completed in 1847. His premiated design was not used, a classic temple form being substituted, at the suggestion of Nicholas Biddle.

While engaged on the Girard building, he was sent abroad to study European institutions of learning and, on completion of the contract, was elected a director of the college, serving on this board for three years.

The unhappy arrangement of the interior, with its four great rooms, fifty feet square, whose groined ceilings rise to the attic, can not be attributed to him; it was forced upon him by terms of the Girard will.

This stately but impracticable building marked the high spot in the Greek Revival, and also the beginning of its decline.

Walter had developed an extensive practice in Philadelphia and neighboring towns, and when he removed to Washington left as a record of his professional ability a large number of buildings, including residences, hospitals, churches, prisons, and banks.

He visited Venezuela, in 1843, at the invitation of its govern-

PLATE 72. The Capitol with city and Potomac River in background. The Washington Monument is shown with square base, designed by Robert Mills, but never built. Tiber canal occupies present location of Constitution Avenue from which it turns to the south. From an old engraving in the author's collection

ment, to report on the desirability of building a breakwater, for the protection of shipping, at the port of La Guaira. The work was carried out according to his drawings and specifications, being completed in 1845.

Early in his career he saw the desirability of bringing members of the architectural profession together and, in 1837, was active in promoting "The American Institution of Architecture," of which he was elected secretary. This organization lasted only a short time, but it is evident that Walter maintained his belief in the idea for, in 1857, he was one of the founders of "The American Institute of Architects." He became the second president of the Institute, succeeding Richard Upjohn, and held that office from 1877 to 1887.

While in Washington, serving as Architect of the Capitol Extension, he executed many other governmental works for which, he stated, no increase of salary was awarded him. The east and west wings of the old Post Office were designed by him, as were the north, south, and west wings of the Treasury Building, the extension of the old Patent Office, the Hospital for the Insane, and the State, War, and Navy Building. Only the interior of the latter can be attributed to him, the efflorescence of colonettes on the exterior being a later growth. He also designed the Marine Barracks at Brooklyn and Pensacola.

His scholarly attainments brought him many honors. He received the honorary degree of Master of Arts from Madison University, New York, in 1849; that of Doctor of Philosophy from the University of Lewisburg, Pennsylvania, in 1853; and Doctor of Laws from Harvard University in 1857.

The professorship of architecture in Franklin Institute, was held by him from 1829 until his death. He delivered many lectures on architecture in Washington and Philadelphia. He was a member for thirty years of the American Philosophical Society, and was a contributor to the *Journal of the Franklin Institute* of articles on various subjects, among them being "Formation of an Artificial Spectrum," "Orders of Architecture," and descriptions of certain buildings which he had built.

He was a tireless student, and zealous worker for whatever

PLATE 73. Corner of Bulfinch's west extension; Thornton's House wing; connecting corridor and new House wing by Walter. Photograph by the author

PLATE 74. West front of new House wing; designed by Thomas U. Walter.
Photograph by the author

promoted his chosen profession of architecture. His strong mind was endowed with a powerful physique, and his impressive face was crowned with a mane of white hair in his later life that added to his distinguished appearance.

THE ROTUNDA FRIEZE

The nine foot frieze that rises above the Rotunda cornice was the subject of much planning and discussion. The wall that forms this frieze was built according to Walter's plan above the old cornice of the original Rotunda, and against it was to have been placed a series of high relief sculptures, forming a continuous frieze three hundred feet in length. These sculptures were to tell the story of America's growth.

The scheme was discussed fully by Meigs and Crawford, their correspondence showing that Crawford advised the use of plaster instead of marble, as a means of saving in both expense and weight. He felt that the great height at which these figures were to be seen would make the cheaper material as satisfactory as the marble, from a decorative standpoint.

The death of Crawford, the outbreak of the Civil War, and the transfer of Meigs to military duty put an end to these plans, and it was not until October, 1877, that we hear of them again. Then the architect stated in a report that "the belt of the rotunda intended to be enriched with basso relievos is being embellished in real fresco representing in light and shadow events in our history, arranged in chronological order, beginning with the landing of Columbus and ending with a period of our revolutionary history."

This work was undertaken by Constantino Brumidi, but his death, on February 19, 1880, left the work but partly finished. It was continued, however, by Filippo Costaggini who carried out Brumidi's scheme, drawing the full size cartoons from the small sketches that had been prepared by Brumidi. Costaggini executed about two-thirds of the frieze, but he in turn died before it was completed, and the frieze remains unfinished today, just as it was left by him. (Plate 78.)

PLATE 75. Walter's Dome, rising above the east portico that was designed by
Latrobe and built by Bulfinch. Photograph by the author

PLATE 76. Capitol from the southwest, showing House wing and Dome by Walter, and west extension of old Capitol as completed by Bulfinch. Photograph by the author

PLATE 77. Constantino Brumidi, Decorator of the Capitol (1854-1880).
Photograph by M. B. Brady

BRUMIDI AND COSTAGGINI

The dramatic career of Constantino Brumidi (Plate 77) closed with a record of more than twenty-five years devoted to the decorative paintings on the walls of the Capitol. He was born July 26, 1805, at Rome. His art education was secured at the Academy of Fine Arts and the Accademia di San Luca, in Rome, where he studied modeling under Thorwaldsen and Canova, and painting with Baron Camuccini. He was commissioned by Pope Pius IX to restore the frescoes of Raphael's Loggia in the Vatican, and found time also to serve as a captain of the national guard.

His career in Rome came to an abrupt end when he refused to order his command to fire on the people. For this he was confined in prison for fourteen months without charges being preferred against him. Luckily he was on friendly terms with Pope Pius X, who secured his release without trial and, on the advice of the Pope and other friends, he left Italy to avoid the enmity of Cardinal Antonelli, then Minister of State.

In a statement, made by Brumidi for the Architect of the Capitol, he wrote that "The French occupation of Rome in the year 1849 for the suppression of republican institutions determined" him to come to America. He arrived at New York in 1852, and two years later secured his naturalization papers in Washington.

He was interested, most naturally, in progress on the Capitol and suggested to Meigs that a structure of such importance deserved decorations of permanence such as those found in the monumental works of the Italian builders. He recommended the use of real fresco, a suggestion that appealed strongly to Meigs, who promptly put Brumidi to work.

His initial undertaking was, according to this own statement, "The committee room on Agriculture in the south wing of the Capitol (which) was painted in 1855 as the first specimen of real fresco introduced in America."

Brumidi's long service of twenty-five years or more gives him a legitimate place among the builders of the Capitol, especially as his work, like that of the sculptors, is an integral part of the structure.

Filippo Costaggini, like Brumidi, was born at Rome, though

PLATE 78. Upper portion of Rotunda, showing fresco frieze by Brumidi and Costaggini. Photograph by the author

much later, his birth date being August 13, 1837. He too studied at the Accademia di San Luca, but the two were unknown to each other while students at the school. He was versatile and painted many portraits, as well as religious and historical subjects for cathedrals and churches. His death occurred April 13, 1907.

V

SCULPTORS OF THE EXTENSION

THOMAS CRAWFORD

THE STORY OF THE SCULPTORS and sculptures, that give the final touch of character to the Capitol Extension, lacks much of the dramatic element that added zest to the earlier one. The nation had made rapid progress culturally during the intervening years; it had produced artists who were taking their places on an equality with those of the old world; and it was no longer necessary to place all dependence for sculptural work on the artists of Italy.

Captain Meigs, in spite of his unfortunate differences with Mr. Walter, was intensely conscientious in the administration of affairs pertaining to the Capitol. Before recommending to the President anyone to execute sculptural work, he made most careful investigations into their records and ability, writing numerous letters to men who were regarded as authorities on the subject.

His greatest fault seemed to be his supreme self assurance, and his disregard of the opinions of all who were not vested with superior authority. He regarded himself as subject to the will of the President only, for he was well aware of the fact that the Capitol had always been a definite responsibility of the President. Washington, Jefferson, and Madison, especially, had regarded the building as almost a personal possession, and that early tradition has continued. Even today "the position of Architect of the Capitol is filled by Presidential appointment and without the advice and consent of the Senate." (The quotation is from a statement prepared in 1933 in the Architect's office.)

As a result of his painstaking investigations, Meigs satisfied himself that the figure work called for by Walter's drawings could be entrusted safely to at least two of America's sculptors, Hiram Powers and Thomas Crawford. This opinion was strengthened by a letter from Edward Everett, who wrote from Boston:

". . . I have no hesitation in expressing the opinion that Mr. Hiram Powers, of Ohio, now at Florence, and Mr. Crawford, of New York, I believe now at Rome, are at the head of the artists of this country; and perfectly competent to design and execute the proposed works in a manner to do honor to the country. I consider Mr. Powers in some respects the first living artist; he is the author, as you are aware, of several first rate works. . . . Mr. Crawford, now engaged in a great monumental work for Richmond, is also a first-rate artist and quite competent to design and execute a work like that proposed."

Meigs realized the danger that commissions involving so much money might, if not discreetly handled, become involved in politics, for we find him writing to Crawford a letter marked "Private" in which he says:

"I have no hesitation in asking first the assistance of yourself and Mr. Powers, as I am well aware that you are at the head of your profession, but if it gets abroad too soon we may have jarring interests and claims urged by personal influence to make members of Congress interfere. The whole construction of the building is expressly committed to the President by law, by him placed in the hands of the Secretary of War, under whose order I am in charge."

That he was a little fearful of the ultra-classical tendencies of the day is made evident in a gentle hint written to Crawford:

". . . Permit me to say that the sculpture sent here by our artists is not altogether adapted to the taste of our people. We are not able to appreciate too refined and intricate allegorical representations, and while the naked Washington of Greenough is the theme of admiration to the few scholars, it is unsparingly denounced by the less refined multitude. . . . In our history of the struggle between civilized man and the savage, between the cultivated and the wild nature are certainly to be found themes worthy of the artist and capable of appealing to the feeling of all classes."

The readiness with which the sculptor accepted this point of view may have had something to do with the volume of commissions which Meigs poured out for him. It was certainly good diplomacy for Crawford to reply from Rome:

". . . I fully agree with you regarding the necessity of producing a work intelligible to our entire population. The darkness of allegory must give way to common sense. I have faith enough to believe that poetry and grandeur are inseparably connected with the history of our country's past and future and that the dignity of sculpture may well be devoted to the perpetuation of what the

PLATE 79. Bronze doors by Thomas Crawford; east entrance of Senate wing.
Photograph by the L. C. Handy Studios

people love and understand. . . . The Washington monument I am now engaged upon for the state of Virginia will serve as a practical exponent of my desire to illustrate American history without having recourse to sculpture as practiced in the age of Pericles."

The invitations to submit designs for the pediments were responded to quite differently by the two Americans, resident in Italy. Powers tersely but politely declined to enter the lists, saying in his reply:

". . . I fully coincide with your views which seem both natural and just and I thank you much for the frank and kind spirit in which you have written to me. But I have not the time to prepare designs for the decoration of our Capitol Buildings even if it were a desirable object with me to *propose* for a commission from the government of my country. . . ."

Crawford accepted the invitation, and transmitted his design and estimate to Meigs, who recommended its acceptance in a letter, dated November 29, 1853, to Jefferson Davis, Secretary of War. In this letter he quotes Crawford's proposal to prepare and cast the full size models for the east pediment of the south wing for $20,000, which work he estimated could be completed within thirty months. He stated in the letter:

". . . There are fourteen figures and numerous accessories and I think that the price is reasonable and respectfully request authority to give him the order for the execution of the models should the design meet the approval of yourself and the President."

On the next day after this was written, a formal acceptance was sent to the sculptor in Rome, authorizing him to undertake the work.

The refusal of Hiram Powers to consider the commission for the Senate pediment caused a change in plans, and this more important position was awarded to Crawford, the House pediment being reserved for another.

The sculptor recommended that the figures be cut in marble at Carrara, Italy; but Meigs, with his customary attention to details, checked up on the weather resisting qualities of various marbles and decided to use marble from the quarries at Lee, Massachusetts. This was a most fortunate decision, for sculptured figures of Carrara marble have suffered seriously from atmospheric conditions at the Capital City.

Italian workmen were employed to do the cutting at Washington, working in shops built near the Capitol. As the individual pieces were completed, they were set up in the grounds for public inspection.

The subject of this pediment is the progress of the white race and the decadence of the Indian; hardly a happy subject. The group was completed and set in place during 1858. (Plate 80.)

This work by Crawford proved so satisfactory to those in official positions that he was given other important commissions. He modeled the figures of Justice and History, above the east doorway of the Senate, and had them cut in Italy, these being the only ones to be executed there.

He also designed the bronze doors for the east entrances of both wings, but died in London, England, on September 10, 1857, before their completion. Work on these models was carried on for a time under the supervision of his wife, but during the following year the models were turned over to W. H. Rinehart for completion.

A letter, dated June 22, 1863, from Walter to the Secretary of the Interior, states that models for the doors, now in the Senate wing, were completed and ready for casting but, according to his information, "nothing has been done to the other, except the original sketches remain as Mr. Crawford left them. Should this be the case," he continued, "I am of the opinion that it would be proper to withdraw the order, and have the second door modeled in this country." (Plate 79.)

He further recommended that the completed models be shipped at once to this country for casting, and that a tentative contract, with a Bavarian firm for making the castings, be canceled. This was done evidently, for the doors were cast in 1868 at Chicopee, Massachusetts. The models for those of the House wing, which Rinehart completed, were stored in the Capitol for many years, and it was not until 1905 that these too were cast in the foundry at Chicopee and the doors installed.

Most widely known of Crawford's works is the gigantic figure of Freedom that surmounts the Dome. For making the model of this he was awarded $5,000. His plaster model passed through a series of adventures that sound like fiction and make us wonder that it ever survived to reach its lofty position above Capitol Hill.

The sculptor's death occurred while the model was still in Italy, and it was not until April 19, 1858, that it was shipped from Leghorn. The bark on which it was being transported sprung a leak, and, a month after departing from the port of Leghorn, it put in at Gilbraltar for repairs. All the cargo except the heavy model was unloaded, and the vessel was calked. This meant delay of another month, but finally a second start was made for New York.

The voyage had scarcely begun when heavy gales were encountered, the bark again developed serious leaks, and much of her cargo of citron and baled rags was thrown overboard. The end of this month found the ill fated little craft at Bermuda, where it was found to be in such bad condition that it was sold and the cargo sent on to its destination in another ship.

Only a portion of the model was included in this cargo, which arrived in New York on December 27, 1858, and it was not until the following March that the last sections of the model were shipped by schooner from New York to Washington. Nearly a year had elapsed from the time the big crates left Leghorn until they were finally unloaded at the United States Capitol.

Arrangements had been made to have the figure cast at a foundry near Bladensburg, and work was under way, when the outbreak of the Civil War brought an abrupt stop to operations. Work was soon resumed, however, and on December 2, 1863, the statue was placed in position as the crowning feature of the Capitol. (See page 194.)

LIFE OF CRAWFORD

Thomas Crawford was born in 1813 or 1814, probably at New York. As a child he showed a decided bent toward art and at the age of fourteen went to work for a wood carver. When nineteen

PLATE 80. East pediment of Senate wing. Sculpture by Thomas Crawford. Photograph by the author

he apprenticed himself to Frazee and Launitz, makers of monuments, and studied in the evening classes at the National Academy of Design.

He tried his hand at marble busts, and carved such unusually delicate detail on the regular marble work of the shop that his employers advised him to pursue his studies in Italy. Accordingly, he sailed in May, 1835, for Leghorn, and was received most cordially in Rome by Thorwaldsen, to whom he had a letter from Launitz, who assisted him and gave him the run of his studio.

The young man worked far beyond his strength while in Rome, at one time modeling seventeen busts in ten weeks. His health broke and for a time his outlook was dark, but with recovery commissions began to pour in upon him. Charles Sumner gave him a commission and spread his fame in this country. This necessitated a return from Europe and while here, in 1844, he married a sister of Julia Ward Howe.

After a stay in the United States, Crawford returned to Rome, working there from 1850 to 1856. He contracted a serious disease

[221]

in one of his eyes and went for treatment to London, where he died on September 10, 1857.

His most important commission in this country, aside from those on the Capitol, was that for figures on the Washington Monument at Richmond, which was designed by Robert Mills. For this, Crawford modeled the equestrian figure of Washington, and the two figures of Thomas Jefferson and Patrick Henry. Following his death the other figures were completed by Randolph Rogers.

WILLIAM H. RINEHART

William H. Rinehart, who completed the models for the bronze doors that were left unfinished at Crawford's death, was born in 1825 in Carroll County, Maryland. He left his father's farm in 1846, secured employment as a stonecutter, and devoted his evenings to study at the American Institute. He went to Rome in 1855, but after a short stay there returned to this country and opened a studio in Baltimore.

In 1858 Rinehart received from the widow of Crawford a commission to complete the models for the bronze doors, work on which had been continued under her supervision until her remarriage. There is some uncertainty as to just how much credit is due Rinehart for these doors. The claim has been made that he designed one of the doors for the House wing, but a photograph of the original clay model shows Crawford's signature.

Other bronzes in the Capitol that came from Rinehart's hand are the figures of an Indian and a Pioneer that support the clock in the House of Representatives, and a fountain with the figure of a reclining Indian. This fountain was originally in front of the Post Office Building, but was removed in the course of building operations to the office of the Architect of the Capitol.

Rinehart's death occurred on October 28, 1874, in Rome.

RANDOLPH ROGERS

Most important of the Capitol doors are those of the east entrance to the Rotunda. These were the work of Randolph Rogers (Plate 81) and, because of the subjects from the life of

PLATE 81. Randolph Rogers. Photograph made in Munich (1860). Reproduced through courtesy of Charles E. Fairman

Christopher Columbus that appear in the panels, are generally known as the "Columbus Doors." (Plate 82.)

Again the sculptor was chosen by Meigs, and the rather sketchy information regarding the manner of his employment tends to raise one's opinion of the headstrong captain. Reverence for red tape did not seem to be one of his virtues, but he did get things done.

He wrote a letter to Rogers, on February 16, 1855, in which he refers quite casually to photographs of work by the latter, which had been submitted to him, with the evident purpose of paving the way to a possible commission. Within a month another letter, in which the casual spirit is definitely absent, conveys information regarding a suggestion for doors to be installed in an entrance to Statuary Hall, and throws out hints regarding a colossal figure to crown the new dome. Two months later a communication to Thomas Walter states that:

". . . Young Mr. Randolph Rogers is . . . making a sketch for a bronze door for an interior. He has taken the life of Columbus as his subject. If the sketch shows ability he will probably receive a commission for executing it. I wish it were not so incumbent upon our sculptors to live abroad. . . ."

Two weeks later, on May 24th, an estimate was submitted by Rogers. On the same day, Meigs forwarded the estimate to the Secretary of War, and on the following day his letter which accompanied it received the following endorsement:

"Approved, Jefferson Davis, Secretary of War, War Department, May 25, 1855."

In this letter Meigs indicated the careful manner in which he sized up his man, by the following comment:

"Mr. Rogers is young, full of ambition, self-reliant, not younger than Ghiberti when his designs secured him the preference over all competitors for the gates of Florence Baptistry. If he can succeed as well with these as with his Ruth, of which you have seen a photograph, it will be enough. . . ."

The models were prepared in Rome, where the sculptor worked on them until 1859, and then were shipped to a firm of bronze founders in Munich who did the casting.

PLATE 82. "Columbus Doors" by Randolph Rogers; east entrance of Rotunda.
Photograph by the L. C. Handy Studios

The commission for these doors was given with the under-standing that they were to be installed in the south entrance of Statuary Hall, from which leads the corridor to the House wing. They proved to be so beautiful that this location was deemed un-worthy of them and in 1870 they were removed to their present location in the most important entrance to the Capitol.

*   *   *   *

Randolph Rogers spent his boyhood at Ann Arbor, Michigan, where he received a scanty education in the public schools, and gained some business experience in a general store. He was born July 6, 1825, at Waterloo, New York, but his father, who was a carpenter, had the western urge and, after several migrations in that direction, settled in Grand Rapids.

Here the boy's natural taste for art expressed itself in various ways, and in 1840 he received ten dollars from an Ann Arbor newspaper for a woodcut of a log cabin and some flags, which became the party emblem used in the Harrison presidential cam-paign.

This success evidently fired the boy's ambition for, at the age of eighteen, Rogers established himself in New York and for five years worked as a clerk in the wholesale drygoods store of John Stewart. Here he apparently found opportunity to follow his bent for art with an emphasis on sculpture, for it is recorded that he quite diplomatically modeled portraits of the children of Ly-curgus Edgerton, one of his employers. This work, together with a bust of Lord Byron made such an impression that members of his firm advanced funds which enabled him to go abroad for a period of study.

Rogers worked from 1848 to 1851 in the Academy of St. Mark, at Florence, under Lorenzo Bartolini, and through the sale of two pieces of sculpture repaid the loan and established himself for two years more in a studio at Rome.

Returning to the United States, in 1853, he secured the contract for the Capitol doors, and two years later was again in Rome. He remained there most of the time until his death, returning to this country only on occasional business trips. While here in 1857 he married Rosa Gibson, of Richmond, and raised a family of nine children.

He completed the sculptural work on the Washington monument, at Richmond, which had been left uncompleted at the death of Crawford in 1857. This monument was designed by Robert Mills, but Crawford's equestrian figure of Washington is so dominant that credit for the design is more apt to be accorded the sculptor than the architect.

Roger's tremendous energy and vitality were backed by a powerful physique which carried him through a life of unremitting industry, and enabled him to achieve an amazing output of sculpture. This included soldier's and sailor's monuments in Cincinnati, Detroit, Providence, and Worcester, Massachusetts, as well as innumerable smaller works.

He died at Rome, January 15, 1892, a leader in the American colony, the possessor of many honors and a wide circle of friends that included the most distinguished residents and visitors of Rome.

During his later years Rogers sent the original casts of most of his works to the University of Michigan, including duplicate casts of the Columbus doors, where they are preserved in Ann Arbor, the town in which a newspaper woodcut gave first public recognition to his artistic talent.

About the time that Rogers was being awarded his commission for the doors, the expected happened. Those large orders that Captain Meigs was handing out began to attract attention. The transfer of authority over the Capitol from the Secretary of the Interior to the Secretary of War had stirred up a few hornets' nests; and the Meigs method of putting things across stirred up a lot more. A sample of the criticism to which the military management of the work was subjected is found in the House proceedings of June 14, 1854, as reported in the *Congressional Globe*. A Congressman pounced on the offending Captain Meigs in these words:

"He makes contracts with whom he pleases; he purchases materials when and where he chooses; he employs mechanics and laborers, and pays for all them by his own check or order. I can not see the authority for all this. I look in vain for the law of Congress which authorizes it; and if I say that Captain Meigs occupied his position against the expressed enactment of this body I give utterance only to what any candid man will believe who examines the subject."

With such feeling as this added to the animosity engendered by his attitude toward Walter, it is not surprising that Captain Meigs was made to walk the official plank. The wonder is that he remained on board as long as he did.

A contributing cause of his downfall is found in the appointment in 1859 of a committee to look into the matter of giving out commissions. Captain Meigs, as usual, drove straight at the heart of the matter when he wrote in a letter to Randolph Rogers—

". . . The artists have as you know, looked with some jealousy upon what has been done for the Capitol Extension in art, and they succeeded in getting such provisions attached to the appropriation bills during the past two years as to prevent my giving orders for more sculpture or painting.

"Messrs. H. K. Brown, J. R. Lambdin and J. F. Kensett, have under the law been appointed a 'Commission of three distinguished American Artists' to whom all designs for sculpture or painting must be submitted before being executed. The designs after passing this ordeal must be approved also by the Library Committee of Congress. . . . There is no provision for paying for designs. These gentlemen seem to hold only a veto power. . . ."

"The Commission of three distinguished American Artists" presented a voluminous report on the art of the Capitol; Congress voted to:

". . . confine the expenditure of the $300,000. for the Capitol extension simply to complete the building, and excluding the expenditure of any money for painting or sculpture. As, therefore, there will be no employment for the art commission next year, it is suspended or abolished."

"Thus passed," comments Mr. Fairman, "the first and only Art Commission which has been permitted to interfere in the art matters pertaining to the Capitol."

The *Congressional Record,* or rather the *Congressional Globe* as it was then called, bristled with discussions of the military control of governmental building operations. During the Senate session of March 5, 1862, a discussion of a proposed "transfer of the superintendency of the Capitol extension from the War to the Interior Department," was concluded by Mr. Hale with the following pithy remarks, "When this Capitol was commenced, it was commenced under civil superintendency, and a decent, Christian plan of building a house was devised and begun. The foundations were laid for a respectable building; one that would have given us the benefit of a little light and air from heaven, instead of having our air pumped up from the cellar and our light come down as it does. The foundations of the building were all laid for it in that way. Then Mr. Pierce came in, with Mr. Davis as Secretary of War, and he thought the arrangement of the Almighty for supplying light and air was not quite so good as he could devise, and he moved it (the Senate Chamber) into the center of the building, like a mouse trap in a pot, so that no air could come to it and went to work, at an immense cost, pumping up air from the cellar. And that is the way we get our air here, by a steam engine that is constantly at work. This is one of the worst ventilated rooms I ever was in in my life, not excepting stables; . . . Why, Mr. President, it has got so now that this Government cannot do anything under heaven, but the Army has to come in to do it. It seems to me . . . that the Army has got quite enough to do, without holding on to anything and everything there is to do, and the Secretary of the Interior has not quite enough."

CONGRESSIONAL ART CRITICS

The embellishments of the Capitol came in for pitiless panning on the part of Congressmen. They enjoyed themselves hugely as they fired their barbed arrows of oratory at the art, and at the artists whose decorations failed to fit in with the aesthetic ideas and ideals, if any, of the lawmakers. These gentlemen were outraged by the many-colored effects, to be found on walls and ceilings, which they compared with great self-satisfaction to Joseph's well known "coat of many colors."

One speaker took a double barreled shot at army and artists, in a single paragraph, saying:

"Now, sir, these military men are to be found everywhere. The superintendent for constructing this Capitol must be a military man; and if you ask for their monuments . . . look at the meretricious and garish gilding of these walls. . . . And then go down into the Agricultural Committee-room—at one end is a representation of Old Put leaving his plow; and at the other end is Cincinnatus, also leaving the plow. . . .

"The picture of Putnam would have been very well in the committee-room of Revolutionary Claims, but has no significance where it is. . . . In the place of this should have been the picture of a western plow, with its polished steel mold-board, with the hardy yeoman, with one hand resting on the plow-handle, and with the other holding a span of bays, with arched neck and neatly trimmed harness. Pictures are symbols of ideas, and this would have told to the future the present mode of culture of free labor. At the opposite end, in the place of Cincinnatus and his plow, (the plow of two thousand years ago,) there should have been a negro slave, with untidy clothing, with a slouching gait, shuffling along by the side of a mule team, with ragged harness and rope traces, drawing a barrel of water on the forks of a tree. This would represent the idea of slave labor. Thus we should have a symbol of the two systems of labor now struggling for the ascendency."

This picturesque bit of oratory by Mr. Lovejoy was followed by a long debate over the bill under consideration, which was to provide means for the completion of the Capitol without permitting any of it to be diverted to embellishments.

Some ten days later, on May 28, 1858, to be exact, another tilt took place. This time it was the sculpture that served as a shining mark for disgruntled Senators. Senator Sam Houston of Texas entertained himself and his colleagues at length, beginning with the innocent query:

"Who are the sculptors that are employed in the shanties out here, in preparing the different statues . . . the goddess of Liberty, I believe is one . . . I object to its attitude. It appears to me

PLATE 83. Paul W. Bartlett; from a sketch by E. Laurent. Photograph by the
L. C. Handy Studios

to be in anguish . . . had it been physical, I should have imagined that it really had a boil under the arm."

"Then there is an Indian woman, or squaw, to be more technical, seated on a slab of marble. That may be very well executed; but she has a little papoose in her arms, and its little head is sticking out like a terrapin's. . . . its little neck, without the least curve or grace, is very stiff, like an apple on a stick."

"And then there is a poor Indian boy, who looks as if of Oriental stock. He has a large shell on his shoulders; and, in this agonizing attitude, water is to spout continually on him. . . . I am a man of sympathy; I feel for human suffering; and I could not contemplate one of these three figures without the extremest agony. They are in torment. . . ."

To this touching stream of ridicule, the Secretary of War, Jefferson Davis, replied in kind: "The Senator's sympathetic heart is greatly moved at this mother of stone's rude treatment of her child; and his sympathy getting possession of his judgment, and his industry not having induced him to acquire any information on the subject, he supposes these statues are to go in the Capitol. One is a faun, a piece merely intended to be put under a fountain. He mixes up the group made for the pediment with the idea of statues for the niches in the Capitol: and after all that his eyes had drunk in had been exhausted, he turned his imagination loose. . . . If the Senator will inform himself a little more, his criticisms hereafter may be spared the corrections which they now provoke."

And after this happy interchange of compliments, the two probably went out and had a drink together.

PAUL W. BARTLETT

The final episode in the embellishment of the Capitol was concerned with the sculpture for the pediment on the House wing. The refusal of Hiram Powers to submit a design for the Senate pediment, and the subsequent transfer of this work to Crawford, had left the House pediment unprovided for.

Various artists had made application for the commission, and it seemed for a time that it would be awarded to Erastus Dow Palmer, but the necessary appropriation was not forthcoming.

Finally, following a recommendation by the National Sculptors'

PLATE 84. East pediment of House wing; sculpture by Paul W. Bartlett. Photograph by the author

Society, Paul W. Bartlett (Plate 83) submitted a sketch model that was approved in 1909 and on which work was at once commenced. Delays were experienced due to the World War and the fact that his studio was in Paris. The difficulties involved in trans-Atlantic shipments were so great that he found it necessary to execute most of his large figures in a studio which he maintained in Washington. When all had been placed in position formal dedication exercises were held on August 2, 1916. (Plate 84.)

The sculptor, Paul Wayland Bartlett was born on January 24, 1865, at New Haven, Connecticut. He showed precocity as a child and was taken abroad at an early age in order that he might enjoy the educational advantages of Paris. There, at the age of fourteen, he exhibited in the Salon a bust of his grandmother.

He won honors on both sides of the Atlantic, and his work is to be found in many collections, both public and private, and as embellishments of important buildings. Several figures by him, aside from those on the pediment, are to be seen in and about the Capitol. His death occurred on September 20, 1925, in Paris.

[233]

VI

THEY COMPLETE THE CAPITOL

THEY COMPLETE THE CAPITOL

ALTHOUGH THE CAPITOL seemed to be practically complete when Walter retired, there were still many details to be looked after, and there continued to be never-ending changes as the personnel of Congress changed and grew, and as new inventions outmoded existing equipment. To meet these demands and the necessity for having someone in charge to maintain competent supervision of the building and grounds, Edward Clark was appointed successor to Walter, a position which he held from August 30, 1865, to January 6, 1902.

Under Clark's direction work was continued on uncompleted details, the last porticoes being completed in 1867. The balustrades and other exterior marble work were put up during the following year, and in 1870 the last of the exterior stonework was cleaned and pointed.

EDWARD CLARK

The services of Edward Clark (Plate 85), in connection with the Capitol, continued over a period of fifty-one years. He was in the employ of Walter when the drawings were first prepared for the Capitol extension, and was Architect of the Capitol at the time of his death.

Clark was born, August 15, 1822, in Philadelphia, the son of James Clark who was also an architect. He attended public schools and academies of the city and was given special instruction by his uncle, Thomas Clark, who was an army engineer. He also received lessons in free-hand and mechanical drawing from his father.

While still quite young he secured a position in the office of Thomas U. Walter, and was made superintendent of construction on the Patent Office and General Post Office, in 1857, when Walter was placed in charge of the extension of those buildings.

Clark devoted himself closely to his government work, thus avoiding the difficulties that had complicated matters for others who had carried on private practice at the same time. He did, however, give freely of his services to charitable institutions.

He was closely associated with the Corcoran Gallery of Art,

having served as chairman of the committee on works of art, as well as the building committee, and at the time of his death was the oldest member of its board of trustees.

Many scientific, literary, and musical societies numbered him in their membership, among them being the American Institute of Architects, of which he was a Fellow. He was a lover of books and music, and at his death on February 6, 1902, left what was probably the largest collection of music in Washington.

"MODERN IMPROVEMENTS"

The first elevator was installed, 1874, in the Senate wing. In 1878 an investigation was made of the possibility of lighting with electricity instead of gas, and in 1880 an expert reported that he felt this form of light was too unsteady to be satisfactory. However, in 1884 the United States Lighting Company was given the privilege of installing, at its own expense, arc lights at the tops of three of the approaches.

A similar concession was made to the Brush-Swann Company, which installed, on the Dome, batteries of lamps which were planned to illuminate a wide area around the Capitol. A further experiment was conducted by the Edison Company, which placed incandescent lamps inside the building—in lobbies, stairways, and cloak rooms. These were pronounced much superior to the gas lights, but the arc lamps on the exterior were definitely unpopular because of the passionate emotions which their brilliant rays aroused in flying insects.

The Capitol was pretty thoroughly electrified by 1897, one of the last installations having been in the space over the glass ceilings of the two legislative chambers. This change was found to be especially desirable above the Senate Chamber as the heat generated there by the gas lights had been sufficient in cold weather to crack the skylights.

Electric bells came in 1891, but it was not until 1895 that push buttons at all of the desks did away with the old and very primitive custom of summoning pages by clapping hands.

Crude types of plumbing and drainage had long existed in the building, but in 1893 this was replaced by a modern, efficient

PLATE 85. Edward Clark; Architect of the Capitol (1865-1902). Photograph by M. B. Brady

system. The original fireplaces gave way ultimately to hot air furnaces, and in 1863 the suggestion was made that steam be substituted.

With completion of the two great wings, and the occupation of their new quarters by the two branches of Congress, the former Senate Chamber was given over to the Supreme Court. Necessary remodeling for this purpose was done in 1860, and the former court room was adapted for use as a law library.

The most important change since that time has been the removal of the Library of Congress in 1897 to its new building a few rods east.

As these changes and repairs were made, fireproof materials were substituted for the earlier construction which had constituted so serious a hazard. The wisdom of this procedure was evident when, on November 6, 1898, a severe explosion that was followed by fire threatened to destroy the building completely, and might have done so had it not been so carefully reconstructed of fire-resisting materials.

LANDSCAPING

The extensions of the Capitol to the north and south necessitated the acquisition of additional land to give the great structure an adequate setting. Walter had made a study for the landscaping, which he submitted with his report of 1864. A bill authorizing the purchase of land necessary to the development of the landscaping scheme was passed in 1866, but little if anything was done in the way of grading until 1873. In that year Clark recommended that a landscape architect be employed to lay out the grounds, and an act of June 23, 1874, placed this responsibility in the hands of Frederick Law Olmsted.

The broad plaza on the east was planned by Olmsted, together with the marble terraces and grand stairway on the west, as we know them today. The work on the grounds, including grading, boundary walls, and other features of the scheme was done between 1875 and 1881, at which time Olmsted urged an appropriation for the marble stairway and terraces on the west, which had not been included in the former bill. Work on the terraces was begun two years later, the foundations being laid in the form of 194 wells sunk to an average depth of twenty feet and filled with concrete.

As this work was purely architectural in nature, Olmsted voluntarily retired from the undertaking which was placed in charge of the Architect of the Capitol.

The marble and granite work of the terraces was reported as finished in July of 1890, but the stairway and balustrade and the

PLATE 86. The east front at night. Photograph by the author

connection with the building proper were not complete until two years later.

The addition of the terraces was made to serve a practical purpose as well as one of beautification, for beneath them were built ninety-three rooms, a large proportion of which could be used for committee rooms.

The care with which Olmsted thought out the plans for these architectural terraces, and the practical sense he showed in utilizing the extensive space underneath, are convincingly indicated in a report which he published, with illustrations, and submitted to the Hon. E. H. Rollins, chairman of the Joint Committee of Congress on Public Buildings and Grounds. The following excerpts are self explanatory:

"SIR: "Illustrations are here presented for the more convenient consideration by your Committee of the plan of an architectural terrace, designed to supercede the present earth-work covering the unfinished base of the Capitol."

"The perspective (Plate 88) . . . is taken from the point which would be occupied by a man coming up the hill in a carriage, where the first unobstructed view of the building would be had." He explains that the height of the terrace and its effect in concealing the granite base had been indicated and made clear by temporary "poles with cross-bars at top (which) have been set in the ground south of the building showing the height and position of the parapet of the terrace. . . . The granite base-course of the present marble walls of the Capitol will be found in looking from the road within the grounds to appear a little *above* the cross-bars. What remains to be seen of this granite above the line, will in the end be obscured by the foliage to be introduced upon the terrace, and the effect of the arrangement will be to re-establish a granite base on the natural surface of the ground, all the visible structure above being of marble."

One plan (Plate 89) shows the manner in which space under the terrace is to be utilized.

"The additional space is 1,400 feet long by 60 feet wide, divided into rooms opening from a central corridor. Ten of these correspond in form and dimensions with the best of the present

PLATE 87. Frederick Law Olmsted, Landscape Architect. In charge of planning and developing grounds of the Capitol (1874-1885). Reproduced by courtesy of Olmsted Brothers

Plate 88. Drawing of Capito

upper committee rooms, each having two or three windows looking upon the existing courts. . . . These courts are to be made attractive winter gardens. (The rooms in question are marked A on the plan.) A small perspective" on the other plan "shows the character of the rooms. . . . The other rooms are expected to be used (1) for the storage of coal and other materials now within the walls of the Capitol; (2) for the keeping . . . of the archives and documents, now stored in bulk . . . (3) for the temporary deposit of current documents of Congress, sorting, folding, packing and other working purposes; (4) for extraordinary committee and clerk's rooms when needed. These rooms will be fire-proof, dry, and may be gas-lighted and steam-heated at pleasure."

"The (second) plan (Plate 90) shows the esplanade or deck of the terrace . . . to be in two parts . . . the inner one to be level with the foot of the several short flights of steps opening from the porticos, the outer one four feet lower . . . following the di-

ids, by Frederick Law Olmsted

vision between the two levels there is to be a channel eight feet wide and four feet deep, the bottom of it on the lower level, the top a little higher than the upper. . . . This is to be filled with soil and planted and decorated in the Italian manner of gardening. . . . By thus setting the outer part of the terrace at a lower level than the inner parts, its parapet will not harmfully obstruct views from or toward the building."

The committee is asked to consider:

"That it is twenty years since the problem of suitable treatment of the northern, western and eastern bases of the Capitol was first forced upon Congress; that the present plan has been prepared under special orders of Congress as a solution of it; that it is five years since it was presented and adopted by Congress as a satisfactory solution; that while other plans have from time to time been devised for occupying the ground, none of them have met with favor, none have contemplated as small an outlay; none would involve as little destruction of work already done, and

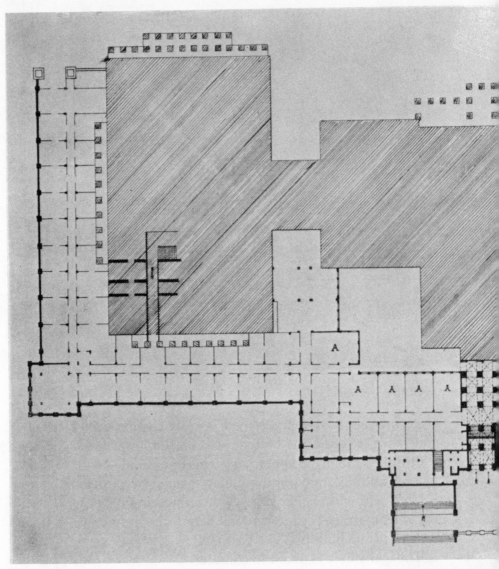

PLATE 89. Plan of Capitol

none have been designed with a single eye to support, sustain and augment the primary architectural motive of the Capitol; finally, that the merit neither of what has been obtained in the Capitol, nor upon its grounds, can be realized until the gap between the two is harmoniously closed, as it is designed to be by the proposed construction."

"And in view of these considerations the question whether it

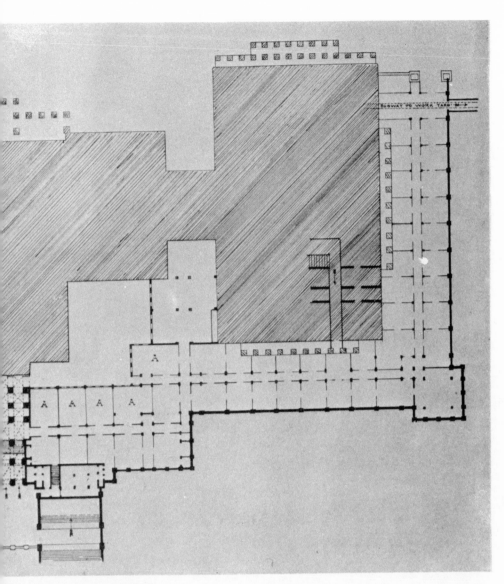

s, by Frederick Law Olmsted

can be sound economy to further delay entering upon the work is respectfully submitted."

"FREDERICK LAW OLMSTED, *Landscape Architect.*"

This forcefully worded statement, clarified by evidence provided by the dummy stakes with cross-arms, which he had set up to indicate the location and height of his proposed terrace walls,

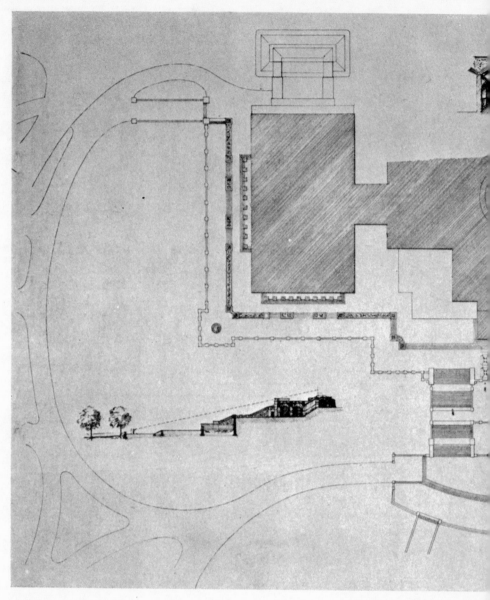

evidently turned the trick, as had the wooden model which Bulfinch had prepared when he took office. At any rate, the desired
approval was forthcoming from Congress and, when Olmsted
decided that his work had been accomplished, he left further
execution to other hands. The architectural features were de-

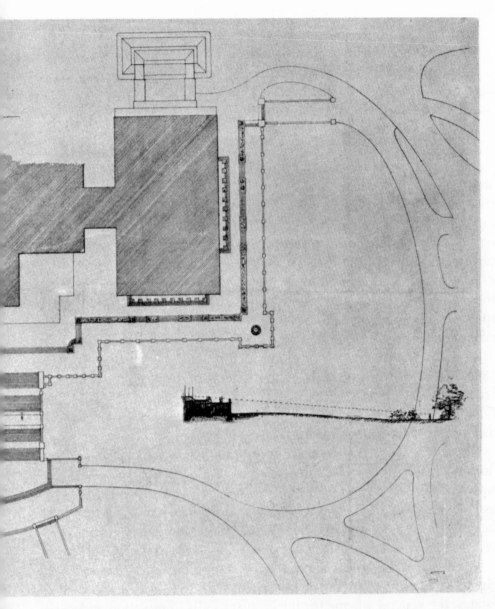

nds, by Frederick Law Olmsted

signed by Thomas Wisedell who worked under Olmsted's direction. He added one of the few really jarring notes in the entire composition, for his fountains, lamp pedestals, and gate posts are of the unhappy type fashionable in that period, and have little in common with the classic style of the building.

The dignified gate lodges and fence posts, designed by Bulfinch in harmony with Thornton's details, were ignominiously "cast into outer darkness," but someone had the wisdom and good taste to set up several of them beside Constitution Avenue, exiles that are unfortunately almost forgotten. (Plates 56, 57, 58.)

FREDERICK LAW OLMSTED

The career of Frederick Law Olmsted (Plate 87) as a landscape architect was preceded by a long period of preparation in scientific channels. Two years were devoted to gaining a practical, working knowledge of agriculture, after which seven years were spent on his own estate putting into practice his knowledge of agriculture and horticulture.

His love of nature prompted him to take many journeys on foot and on horseback, and four trips were made to Europe. There special study was devoted to parks, forests, zoölogical and botanical gardens, and city plans.

A study of economic conditions in the South was made in 1853 and 1854, when he traveled more than four thousand miles on horseback. In 1857 he was selected to design and lay out Central Park, New York, his design having been selected from thirty-three competing schemes.

He served on the National Sanitary Commission for two years during the Civil War, and then removed to California where he was appointed Chairman of the California State Commission, and assumed custody of Yosemite and Mariposa Reservations. Returning to the East in 1865, he entered on a long and brilliant career as a landscape architect in New York and Boston.

The list of achievements by his firm is staggering, and includes eighty recreation grounds; many towns, suburbs, and private estates; the general scheme for the Niagara Falls Reservation and the Columbian Exposition grounds; innumerable parks, college campuses, and the grounds of public and semi-public buildings.

He was the author of several books, one of which *A Journey in Texas* was reprinted in Leipsic and Paris. His death occurred on August 28, 1903, at Waverley, Massachusetts; his birth on April 26, 1822, in Hartford, Connecticut.

PLATE 91. West front at night. Photograph by the author

ELLIOTT WOODS

The office of Architect of the Capitol passed, on February 6, 1902, to Elliott Woods (Plate 92) who had served for seventeen years as chief clerk and assistant architect. This wise policy of promoting men who are thoroughly conversant with the department which they are to head might well be followed in other departments that are all too frequently placed at the mercy of political appointees. Woods in turn held this office until May 22, 1923, when he was removed by death.

DAVID LYNN

The next architect to take over the responsibilities of this office was David Lynn, who, by heritage and training, was well fitted for the task. He came from an old family, of Frederick and Allegany Counties, Maryland, which for many generations has been distinguished in the judicial, military, business, and social life of the state. (Plate 93.)

His great, great-grandfather, Judge David Lynn, came from Dublin, Ireland, in 1717; served for several terms in the General Assembly of Maryland; was one of three commissioners appointed in 1751 to lay out the town of Georgetown; was justice of the Frederick County Court from 1756 to 1775, and in 1758 was made a member of the quorum of that court.

Judge Lynn's son, Captain David Lynn, served with honor throughout the Revolutionary War, after which he settled in Cumberland, Maryland, on the large estate known as Rose Hill. He represented Allegany County in the General Assembly, and was a Commissioner in charge of the apportionment of military lands. Next in succession were two business men of Cumberland, John Galloway Lynn and David Lynn, the latter being father of the architect, who was born November 10, 1873, in Wheeling, West Virginia, where his parents were staying temporarily while looking after business interests.

The public schools of Cumberland, and the Allegany County Academy furnished educational training for the future architect; and on July 1, 1901, he entered the office of the Architect of the Capitol during Edward Clark's tenure. Due to the illness of Mr. Clark, Elliott Woods served as Acting Architect and, following

PLATE 92. Elliott Woods, Architect of the Capitol (1902-1923). Photograph by Harris & Ewing

Clark's death, Woods was appointed his successor, on February 1, 1902, with David Lynn as his understudy. Lynn retained this position until the death of Woods when, on August 22, 1923, he was appointed seventh Architect of the Capitol.

Since then the duties of this office have increased immeasurably and the responsibilities have been more arduous than at any time in its long history, due to the extensive volume of public works that has been placed under the Architect's supervision by direction of Congress.

During the period, from 1923 to 1939, the following public works have been carried forward under Mr. Lynn's direction at an approximate cost of $45,000,000:

Library of Congress (Old Building): Construction of northeast bookstacks, and alterations and additions to east and southeast bookstacks.

Capitol Buildings: Air conditioning of Senate and House Chambers.

United States Botanic Gardens: Relocation of the gardens, including purchase of new site, construction of new exhibition conservatory, Director's residence, and development of an outdoor garden site.

House Office Building (New): Construction of additional office building for the House of Representatives, including purchase of site, construction, furnishing, and equipping of the building.

Senate Office Building: Completion of the Senate Office Building by the erection of the First Street Wing, alterations to the C Street Façade, and construction of terraces, balustrades, and approaches.

United States Supreme Court Building: Construction of United States Supreme Court Building, together with necessary furnishings and equipment.

Capitol Grounds: Enlarging the Capitol Grounds, including the purchase and development of 61.8 additional acres as a park area, and construction within the area of a large underground garage.

Library of Congress: Construction of the Annex and Addition

PLATE 93. David Lynn, Architect of the Capitol (1923-   ). Photograph
copyright by Harris & Ewing

PLATE 94. The Capitol as seen from the southwest, dominated by new House wing. The wings and dome designed by Walter; landscaping by Olmsted. Photograph by the author

to the Library of Congress, including purchase of site, construction, furnishing, and equipping of the buildings.

Capitol, Senate, and House Office Buildings: Air conditioning the Capitol, Senate, and House Office Buildings, including construction and equipping of a central refrigeration plant at the Capital Power Plant.

In addition to the $45,000,000 appropriated by Congress for expenditure on Public Works, the following amounts have also been appropriated for expenditure by the present Architect during the period, 1923-1939:

For care, maintenance, repairs, alterations, and improvements in connection with the Capitol, Senate and House Office Buildings, Capitol Power Plant, Library of Congress, Legislative Garage, and Capitol Grounds—$24,000,000.

For care, maintenance, repairs, alterations, and improvements in connection with the United States Supreme Court Building, Building of the District Court of the United States for the District of Columbia, United States Court of Appeals Building, District of Columbia, United States Court of Claims Building, and Columbia Hospital—$793,000.

During the period, July 3, 1934 to 1939, the Architect of the Capitol has been serving as Acting Director of the United States Botanic Garden, in addition to his office as Architect of the Capitol, and has had charge of the appropriations for the care, maintenance, and improvement of the gardens, totaling $557,000.

Grand total appropriations placed under the present Architect of the Capitol during the period, 1923-1939, for construction and maintenance of buildings and grounds—$70,350,000.

The Architect of the Capitol is a member of the Zoning Commission of the District of Columbia and Alley Dwelling Authority, District of Columbia.

In connection with construction projects, the Architect of the Capitol has served in the following capacities: Member of Commission for Enlarging the Capitol Grounds, United States Supreme Court Building Commission, Joint Commission to Acquire a Site and Additional Buildings for the Library of Congress.

This recital presents a vivid contrast to the early history of the

Capitol when a single architect, with perhaps one assistant, worked under direct supervision of the President of the United States to solve the problems of housing a new government, in a new environment of woodland and swamp.

MUCH REMAINS UNSAID

It is impossible to mention here the innumerable art works of pigment, marble, and bronze that are to be found in the Capitol. Space restricts us to such as may be regarded as integral features of the structure.

The Capitol has passed through the control of men variously endowed and with conflicting ideals, yet, curiously enough, it has retained as a whole a consistent character. It has its faults, and critics at various times have suggested changes that might bring it nearer to perfection. However, in spite of possible slips from absolute flawlessness, it is generally regarded as one of the beautiful buildings of the world.

We have a sentimental attachment for the Capitol that is amply justified. The north and south wings of the old building stand today as they appeared, and as they were, in 1814, when British vandals sought their destruction. The east portico and steps have provided a setting through many generations for presidential inaugurations. The great Dome has been the dominating feature of the city since midway in that regrettable struggle between North and South.

The Capitol has been a symbol of our Nation's greatness and growth through all the years that have elapsed since the day when President Washington laid its corner stone. As such we cherish it.

STATISTICS
THE OLD BUILDING

Area covered .... 67,220 sq. ft.
Length .... 351' 4"
Depth of wings .... 131' 6"
Height of wings to top of balustrade .... 70'
Height to top of Dome, in center .... 145'
Exterior walls and porticoes .... Aquia Creek sandstone.
Roofs of wood, covered with copper.
Senate Chamber (later Supreme Court Room):
   Diameter .... 75'

Greatest width .... 45'
Height .... 45'
Hall of Representatives (now Statuary Hall):
Diameter of semicircle .... 96'
Rectangular space on south .... 73 x 35'
Height to top of cornice .... 35'
Height of domed ceiling .... 57'
Original Library of Congress (in west projection):
Length .... 92'
Width .... 34'
Height .... 36'
Present Building:
Length, north to south, over all .... 849' 7½"
Length, north to south, building proper .... 725' 7½"
Width, east to west, over all in center .... 480' 4"
Width, east to west, building proper .... 184' 6½"
North and South Wings:
Length, east and west .... 239' 7"
Width, north and south .... 142' 10"
Dome and Rotunda:
Old Dome, height .... 145' 0"
Old Rotunda, height .... 96' 0"
Rotunda, diameter, inside .... 94' 9"
New Dome, height from ground, east side .... 287' 6"
New Dome, height from ground, west side .... 307' 6"
Lantern, diameter .... 24' 4"
Lantern, height .... 50' 0"
Statue of Freedom, height .... 19' 6"
New Hall of Representatives:
Length .... 139' 0"
Width .... 93' 0"
Height .... 36' 0"
New Senate Chamber:
Length .... 84' 0"
Width .... 51' 0"
Height .... 36' 0"

COSTS

Old Building:
Senate and House Wings ....$ 788,077.98
Central portion 957,647.36
Rebuilding after destruction by British 687,126.00
                                                   _____
          TOTAL $2,432,851.34
Extension:
New Senate and House Wings ....$ 8,075,299.04
New Dome 1,047,291.89
Marble terraces and landscaping 3,626,579.93
Heating and ventilating 493,015.26
Lighting (approximately) 250,000.00
                                                   _____
          TOTAL ORIGINAL COST $15,925,037.36

PLATE 95. West approach and terraces of Capitol; designed by Frederick Law
Olmsted. Photograph by the author

PLATE 96. A glimpse of the Capitol from west lawn. Landscaping by Olmsted. Photograph by the author

PLATE 97. After nightfall; from the Library of Congress. Photograph by the author

CHRONOLOGY

In preparing this chronology the aim has been to provide a skeleton history of the Capitol, as well as a check list of dates and events. The condensed notes will, it is hoped, make it possible to follow the story in outline.

Many disagreements in dates have been encountered among the authorities consulted, and where it has been impossible to determine with assurance which is correct, each has been given.

The author acknowledges frankly that he is not infallible, and it is quite possible that among the great number of references that have been hunted, copied, checked, and rechecked, a few errors may have crept in to torment him. For these he humbly craves charity and pardon.

KEY TO REFERENCES

A.I.A. The Genealogy of L'Enfant's Washington, by Elbert Peets. The Journal of The American Institute of Architects, Volume XV.

A.R.   The Origin of the Plan of Washington, D. C., by Fiske Kimball. The Architectural Review, Volume VII.

B.   History of the United States Capitol, by Glenn Brown.

Br.   History of the National Capital, by Wilhelmus Bogart Bryan.

C.B.   Life and Letters of Charles Bulfinch, by Charles A. Place.

D.   History of the Arts of Design, by William Dunlap.

D.B.   Dictionary of American Biography.

D.H.   Documentary History of the United States Capitol Building and Grounds.

E.   Andrew and Joseph Ellicott, by Dr. G. Hunter Bartlett.

E.A.   Encyclopedia Americana.

E.B.   Encyclopedia Britannica.

E.K.   L'Enfant and Washington, 1791-1792, by Elizabeth Kite.

F.   Art and Artists of the Capitol, by Charles E. Fairman.

F.W.P. Washington, City and Capital, Federal Writers' Project.

H.   The National Capitol, by George C. Hazelton, Jr.

J.F.   The Writings of Thomas Jefferson, edited by Paul Leicester Ford.

J.J.J. With Americans of Past and Present Days, by J. J. Jusserand.

K.   Thomas Jefferson, Architect, by Fiske Kimball.

K.B.   William Thornton and the Design of the United States Capitol, by Fiske Kimball and Wells Bennett, Art Studies, Volume I.

L.   The Journal of Latrobe, by B. H. Latrobe, edited by J. H. B. Latrobe.

L.B. The Writings of Thomas Jefferson, by Lipscomb and Bergh.
L.L. Latrobe-Lenthal Letters, Unpublished Manuscripts.
M. Robert Mills, Architect of the Washington Monument, by H. M. Pierce Gallagher.
R.M. Guide to the Capitol of the United States, by Robert Mills.
W.B. Stephen Hallet and His Designs for the National Capitol, by Wells Bennett.
W.N.C. Washington, the National Capital, by H. P. Caemmerer.

THE UNITED STATES CAPITOL

MEETING PLACES OF CONTINENTAL CONGRESS

Philadelphia	September 5, 1774	to	December 12, 1776
Baltimore	December 20, 1776	"	February 27, 1777
Philadelphia	March 4, 1777	"	September 18, 1777
Lancaster, Penna.	September 27, 1777		
York, Penna.	September 30, 1777	"	June 27, 1778
Philadelphia	July 2, 1778	"	June 21, 1783
Princeton, N. J.	June 26, 1783	"	November 4, 1783
Annapolis, Md.	November 26, 1783	"	June 3, 1784
Trenton, N. J.	November —, 1784	"	December 24, 1784
New York	January 11, 1785	"	March 4, 1789

MEETING PLACES OF CONGRESS AFTER ADOPTION OF CONSTITUTION

New York	March 4, 1789	to	August 12, 1790
Philadelphia	December 6, 1790	"	May 14, 1800
Washington	November 17, 1800		

(W.N.C. 3.) (E.A. 7; 508.) (Br. 107; 341.)

1779. (November.) Members of Congress suggested that a few square miles of land, near Princeton, New Jersey, be purchased as permanent home for Congress. (W.N.C. 4.)

1783. (January 29.) Trustees of Kingston, N. Y., memorialized State Legislature for authority to erect one square mile of their "estate * * * into a separate district for the Honorable Congress of the United States." (W.N.C. 4.)

(March 14.) State Legislature granted above request. (W.N.C. 4.) (Br. 4-5, 15.)

(May 25 [May 12?]) Maryland House of Delegates authorized city of Annapolis to tender 300 acres of land to Congress for a "fixed place of residence." Also offered State-house and public circle, and to erect "thirteen dwellings for the residence of the delegates * * * and that a sum not to exceed 30,000 pounds be applied for that purpose." (Br. 5-6, 15.) (W.N.C. 4.)

(June 19.) New Jersey legislature offered district twenty miles square, with 30,000 pounds "for the purpose of procuring lands and erecting buildings thereon." (Br. 5-6, 15.) (W.N.C. 4.)

(June 28.) Virginia legislature offered town of Williamsburg with "the palace, the capital, and all the public buildings, and 300 acres of land * * * together with * * * 100,000 pounds this state's currency, to be expended in erecting thirteen hotels for the use of the delegates in Congress." (Br. 7, 15.) (W.N.C. 4.)

(September 18.) Report made by committee (James Madison, chairman) on permanent seat of government, including (1) extent of district; and (2) powers to be exercised by Congress. (W.N.C. 5.) (Br. 14.)

(October 7.) Congress decided to locate seat of government on Delaware River, near falls, above Trenton. (W.N.C. 5.) (Br. 16.)

(October 17.) Congress decided to have a second capital near lower falls of the Potomac. Pending erection of buildings, meetings to be held at Trenton and Annapolis. (W.N.C. 6.) (Br. 17.)

1784. (December 23.) Plan to have two capitals repealed by act adopted at Trenton. (W.N.C. 6.) (Br. 18.)

(————.) Commission appointed by Congress to select site on the Delaware River for a national capital. No action taken. (Br. 19.) (E.B. 23, 395.)

1787. (————.) Provision made in the Constitution, Article I, Section 8, clause 17, for the acceptance by Congress of a District to become the seat of government of the United States of America. (Br. 20-22.) (D.H. 5.) (H. 2.) (E.B. 23, 395.)

1788. (December 23.) Maryland legislature passed act to cede tract ten miles square to the United States. (E.B. 23, 395.) (D.H. 5.) (H. 2.) (W.N.C. 8.) (A.I.A. XV, 151.)

1789. (April 30.) George Washington inaugurated President in Federal Hall, at New York. Building designed by L'Enfant as meeting place for Congress. Previously had met in old City Hall, which had been used as a prison by the British. Federal Hall was hastily and poorly constructed, and was demolished a few years afterwards. (W.N.C. 7.)

(————.) Locations favored for new capital city were: (1) Wright's Ferry, Pennsylvania, on the Susquehanna, and (2) Georgetown, Maryland, on the Potomac. (W.N.C. 8.) (Br. 29.)

(September 11.) L'Enfant wrote President Washington asking appointment to design "the capital of this vast Empire." (W.N.C. 28.) (F.W.P. 43.) (J.J.J. 163.) (E.K. 14.) (E. 4.)

(September 27.) Both Houses of Congress voted to locate Capital at Germantown, Pennsylvania. Adjourned before further action could be taken, and opposition defeated move at next session. (F.W.P. 42.) (Br. 33-34.)

(December 3.) Virginia legislature passed act to cede tract ten miles square to the United States. (D.H. 5.) (H. 2.) (E.B. 23; 395.) (W.N.C. 8.)

1790. (————.) House of Representatives proposed bill naming Baltimore as capital. (Br. 36-37.)

(July 16.) Location of Federal City near Georgetown, and appointment of three Commissioners authorized by Congress and approved by President Washington. Also provided that seat of government be established at Philadelphia from the first Monday in December, 1790, until the first Monday in December, 1800, when it "shall be transferred to the district and place aforesaid." (B. 1.) (D.H. 6.) (F.W.P. 42.) (K. 48.) (Br. 38-39, 105.) (E.B. 23; 395.) (W.N.C. 9.) (E.A. 28; 791.) (H. 2.) (A.I.A., XV, 151.) (E.K. 2.)

(July.) First map of city authorized by Congress. (B. 1.)

(November.) Maryland offered $72,000 to be "advanced toward the expense of erecting the public buildings."

(November 29.) Jefferson wrote an "Opinion on proceedings to be had under the Residence act," covering size of District; qualifications of Commissioners; site for Capitol and President's House; plan of lots; width of streets; authority of President over purchase and development of town; building restrictions; etc. (J.F.V. 252-253.) (K. 48-49.)

(December 10.) Virginia legislature appropriated $120,000 for erection of public buildings. (Br. 37-38.) (F.W.P. 42.)

(December.) Government removed from New York to Philadelphia. (H. 2.)

1791. (January 22.) Commission of three appointed by President to supervise planning and building of capital city. (D.H. 7.) (B. 4.) (H. 2-3.) (F.W.P. 42-43.) (J.J.J. 177.) (E.K. 21, 32.)

(January 24.) Proclamation by President announced above appointment, and ordered experimental survey of district. (W.N.C. 10, 17.)

(February [1790?]) Ellicott employed to survey District. (E. 3.) (F.W.P. 43.) (J.J.J. 177.) (E.K. 32.) (E.A. 10, 253.)

(March.) Area considered for city, embracing about 6,000 acres. 3,606 acres taken in laying out streets. 540 acres bought for public buildings and grounds. 20,272 lots laid out. United States took half, returning balance to property owners. (W.N.C. 23.)

(March 2.) President Washington wrote Colonel Dickens of

Georgetown, "An eminent French military engineer starts for Georgetown to examine and survey the site for the Federal city." (E.K. 15.)

(March 3.) Amendment to bill establishing Federal City, restricted public buildings to Maryland side of Potomac. Boundary lines extended south to include Alexandria. (D.H. 9.) (H. 4.) (W.N.C. 39.)

(March 3 [March 9?].) L'Enfant commissioned to plan Federal City. (B. 1.) (E.A. 17; 249, 28; 791.) (E.B. 13; 911, 23; 395.) (Br. 127.) (D., I; 339-340.) (E. 4, 13.) (D.B., XI; 167.) (F.W.P. 43.) (A.I.A., XV; 151.) (E.K. 33.)

(March 22.) L'Enfant made first report to President. (A.I.A., XV; 151.)

(March 26.) Site for Capitol endorsed by L'Enfant in report handed personally to President Washington. (H. 7.) (J.J.J. 169.)

(March 30.) Washington rode over the site of future city with L'Enfant, Ellicott, and the three Commissioners. (W.N.C. 24-25.)

(March 30.) Nineteen of principal landholders in District signed agreement to sell property to Government. (Br. 134.) (H. 4.) (W.N.C. 19.)

(March.) Jefferson prepared a rough sketch plan for proposed city. (K. 49.) (Br. 130-131, 142.) (W.N.C. 19.) (E.K. 20, 48.)

(April 4.) Washington transmitted Jefferson's plan to L'Enfant. (K. 50.) (Br. 141.) (J.J.J. 176.) (A.I.A., XV; 152.) (A.R., VII; 42.)

(April 4.) L'Enfant requested Jefferson to furnish him with maps of various European cities. (K. 50.) (L.B., VIII; 165.) (A.I.A., XV; 152.) (B. 1.) (D.B., XI; 167.)

(April 10.) Jefferson sent plans to L'Enfant, and suggested types of design suitable for proposed public buildings. (K. 52.) (L.B., VIII; 163.) (H. 7.) (A.I.A., XV; 152.) (A.R., VII, 41.) (W.B. 291.)

(April 10.) Jefferson wrote Washington that he had engravings of handsome European residence fronts, and suggested that these be copied and "distributed gratis among the inhabitants of Georgetown" in hopes that they "might decide the taste of the new town." (K. 52.) (L.B., VIII; 166.)

(April 12.) Agreement with landholders accepted by Commissioners. (H. 4.)

(April 15.) Corner stone of Federal District laid at Hunter's Point, south of Alexandria. (H. 7.) (Br. 142.)

(June 20.) A letter from Jefferson to James Madison outlined the difficulties in Congress over proposed funding of public debt, and location of federal city. He expressed fear that "our credit will burst and vanish, and the States separate, to take care every one of itself." (L.B., VIII; 42-44.)

(June 22.) L'Enfant sent sketch plan of city to President Washington. (W.N.C. 25.) (Br. 147-153.) (D.B., XI; 167.) (J.J.J. 170.) (K. 51.)

(August 7.) First map of city submitted by L'Enfant. (B. 1.) (J.J.J. 170.) (E.A. 5; 565.) (W.N.C. 11.) (F.W.P. 91.) (D.B., XI; 167.) (K. 51.)

(September 8.) At meeting of Jefferson, Madison, and Commissioners, the latter concurred in building regulations suggested and agreed upon in Philadelphia. These were evidently originated by Jefferson. (K. 51.)

(September.) Jefferson advocated a competition for designs for Capitol and President's Palace, and sketched an advertisement for plans. (K. 52.) (Br. 165.) (W.B. 291.)

(September 9.) Commissioners, in letter to L'Enfant, agree to system of numbering and lettering streets. Adopted names: "Territory of Columbia" and "The City of Washington." (H. 9.) (Br. 154-155.) (W.N.C. 25.) (F.W.P. 92.) (E.K. 21.) (J.J.J. 177.)

(October.) L'Enfant refused to furnish plan of city for use at sale of lots, claiming it would be misused by speculators. (E.A. 17; 249.) (E. 6.) (D.B., XI; 167.) (H. 9.) (E.A. 17; 285.) (J.J.J. 179.) (Br. 157.) (E.K. 22.)

(October 17.) After meeting of President and Commissioners, building regulations (agreed upon September 8), were promulgated. (K. 51-52.) (Br. 162-163.)

(October 17-19.) First sale of city lots; 35 lots sold for $8,756, all in vicinity of the President's House. (Br. 159-161.) (E.A. 17; 285.)

(October 21.) Commissioners reported to President that they had requested L'Enfant "to prepare a draft of the public buildings." (B. 4.) (Br. 165.) (K. 52.)

(October 27.) Jefferson wrote Washington that Madison and he had urged the (Virginia) "assembly * * * to build two good private dwelling houses a year, for ten years in the new city. * * * Should they do this, and Maryland as much, it will be one means of ensuring the removal of government hither." (L.B., VIII; 105.)

(November 17-22.) L'Enfant demolished brick house belonging

to Daniel Carroll, because it obstructed a vista. (F.W.P. 44-45.) (Br. 166.) (H. 9.) (J.J.J. 181.) (E.K. 23.)

(November 20.) Washington wrote Commissioners expressing disapproval at actions of L'Enfant. (Br. 166-167.)

(December 8.) Commissioners, in a letter to Jefferson, complain of L'Enfant's arbitrary actions. (H. 9.) (F.W.P. 45.)

(December 13.) President Washington transmitted plan of city to Congress. (Br. 168.) (W.N.C. 29.) (D.H. 10.) (H. 11.) (E. 6, 9.)

(————.) L'Enfant refused to make changes suggested by the President. (E. 6.)

(December 19.) Maryland Assembly voted to transfer "all that part of territory called Columbia, which lies within the limits of this state, for permanent seat of government of the United States." (D.H. 10.) (Br. 169-170.)

1792. (February 14.) Commissioners wrote L'Enfant that they had been notified of his discharge. (H. 10.) (L. 133.) (E. 5.) (E.B. 13; 911.) (E.A. 28; 791.)

(February 26.) Dr. Stuart wrote to Washington, re. L'Enfant "all conciliatory treatment only tended to heighten the ideas of his own importance and to increase his natural perversity." (Br. 176.)

(February 27 [January ?]) L'Enfant ordered discharged. (B. 4.) (D.B., XI; 168.) (E.A. 17; 285.) (Br. 175.) (F.W.P. 45.)

(February 28.) Washington wrote to L'Enfant, "Every mode has been tried to accommodate your wishes on this principle, except changing the Commissioners." (Br. 174.)

(February.) Andrew Ellicott appointed successor to L'Enfant. (D.B., VI; 89.) (H. 10, 11.) (E.A. 17; 249, 28; 791.) (E. 8, 13.)

(March 6.) Jefferson wrote the Commissioners, that it "having been found impracticable to employ Major L'Enfant in that degree of subordination which was lawful and proper, he has been notified that his services were at an end." (E.K. 24.) (L.B., VIII; 307.)

(————.) Washington and Jefferson decide on competition for designs for Capitol and President's House. (B. 5.) (E.A. 5; 565.)

(March 6.) Jefferson wrote Commissioners advising immediate action in securing plans for Capitol and President's House. (B. 5.) (D.H. 14.) (J.J.J. 182.) (L.B., VIII; 308.) (W.B. 291.)

(March —.) Competitions advertised in newspapers. Advertisements dated March 14. (B. 5-6.) (D.H. 15.) (H. 14.) (Br. 187.) (F.W.P. 210.) (W.B. 292.)

(March 8.) Jefferson wrote to Commissioners, "there never was a moment's doubt about the parting with Major L'Enfant rather than with a single commissioner." Also "Major L'Enfant had no plans prepared for the Capitol or Government House. He said he had them in his head. I do not believe he will produce them for concurrence." (L.B., XIX; 88, 90.) (K. 52.)

(June 2.) Commissioners wrote Jefferson regarding desirability of importing Scotch and German mechanics. (D.H. 16.)

(June 3.) Jefferson sent Commissioners letters of introduction to Van Staphorts and Hubbard of Amsterdam, re. German mechanics. (D.H. 16.)

(July [June?]) James Hoban arrived in Philadelphia and Washington. (H. 21.) (D.B., IX; 91.) (Br. 194.)

(July 12 [October?]) Dr. William Thornton wrote asking permission to submit drawings for Capitol. (B. 7.) (D.B., XVIII; 505.) (Br. 196-197.) (K.B. 78.)

(July 15.) Competitions for Capitol and President's House closed. (B. 6.)

(July 17.) Commissioners retained Hallet to make further study of plans for Capitol. None submitted were satisfactory. (E.A. 5; 565.) (B. 6.) (D.B., VIII; 152-154.) (H. 15.) (Br. 196.) (W.B. 324.)

(July 17 or 18.) Hoban's design for President's House accepted; employed at 300 guineas per annum to superintend construction. (D.B., IX; 91.) (K. 54.) (Br. 195.) (E.A. 5; 565.) (D.H. 18.) (B. 6.) (H. 21.)

(July 23.) Washington wrote the Commissioners expressing satisfaction with Judge Turner's plan, but suggesting the desirability of surrounding it by columns, as suggested on Hallet's design. (D.H. 18.) (W.B. 293.)

(July-October.) Ellicott's first map engraved by S. Hill, of Boston. (Br. 176, 184-185.) (E. 7, 8, 11.) (W.N.C. 33.) (F.W.P., XIV.)

(August 29.) Competitive drawings received from Samuel Blodget, Hallet, and Harbaugh, though competition was closed. (B. 7.) (D.H. 19.)

(August 29.) Commissioners wrote Samuel Blodget that they had held a meeting to consider plans of Judge Turner, Hallet, Harbaugh, and Blodget. None were deemed satisfactory. (B. 7.) (D.H. 19.) (W.B. 293.)

(October-December.) Second engraved map of Washington published in Philadelphia, by Thackera & Vallance. (B. 2.) (H. 11, 48.) (E. 8, 9, 10, 11, 12.) (Br., I; 184-185.)

(November.) Thornton arrived in the United States. (D.B.,
XVIII; 505.)

(November 9.) Dr. Thornton wrote to the Commissioners, from
Philadelphia, that he was ready to send drawings or to take them
in person to Washington. (K.B. 78.) (D.B., XVIII; 505.) (B.
7.) (Br. 196-197.)

(November 15.) Commissioners wrote Thornton agreeing to consider his plans. (B. 7.)

(November 17.) President Washington wrote Commissioners
warning them against land speculators. (H. 8.)

(December 4.) Commissioners wrote Thornton to, "Lodge your
plan with the Secretary of State for the President's inspection."
(W. B. 293.) (B. 7.) (D.H. 19.) (W.B. 325.) (H. 250.) (Br.
197.)

(December 18.) President Washington wrote Commissioners
urging importation of European mechanics; delay on Capitol
might mean serious trouble from enemies. (D.H. 20.)

1793.   (January 4.) Commissioners wrote Municipality of Bordeaux,
asking that Mr. Fenwick be permitted to engage mechanics to
work on the Capitol. (D.H. 21.)

(January 5.) Hallet requested three weeks more to complete
drawings for Capitol. (B. 7.) (W.B. 325.)

(January 5.) Samuel Blodget appointed Supervisor of Buildings
by Commissioners. . . . Hoban "to endeavor to get a good Brick-
maker from Philadelphia." (D.H. 22.)

(January 8.) Ellicott threatened to resign. (Br. 209.)

(January 31.) Washington wrote the Commissioners praising
Thornton's design, asking time for him to complete drawings,
and suggesting that Hallet's feelings be spared. (D.H. 22-23.)
(W.B. 293.)

(January 31-February 1.) Jefferson wrote Carroll, praising Thornton's plan. (D.H. 23.) (Br. 199, 202.)

(February 7.) Commissioners expressed satisfaction with Thornton's drawings; also sympathy for Hallet. (B. 8.) (D.H. 23.)
(H. 15.)

(March 3—Date of Letter.) Thornton came to Washington with
letter from President. (D.B. XVIII; 505.) (Br. 202.) (B. 8.)
(D.H. 24.) (H. 250.)

(March 11.) Thornton submitted to Commissioners a new design,
made since arriving at Philadelphia. (K.B. 79.) (B. 8) (W.B.
293.) (D.H. 24.)

(March 12.) Ellicott discharged. (Br. 209.)

(March 13.) Commissioners wrote Hallet stating decision on com-

petition. (W.B. 293.) (Br. 202.) (B. 8.) (D.H. 25.) (H. 15.)
(April 3.) Ellicott reinstated. (Br. 209.)
(April 5.) Commissioners awarded Thornton first prize in competition for Capitol. (D., I; 336.) (B. 8, 9.) (D.H. 25.) (H. 15.)
(F.W.P. 210.) (E.A. 5; 565.) (Br. 197, 202.) (K. 55.) (D.B., XVIII; 505.) (R.M. 58.)
(April 10.) Hallet appointed to estimate costs and study Thornton's plans. (K. 55.) (D.B., XVIII; 505.) (B. 9.) (R.M. 58.)
(Br. 203.) (W.B. 294.)
(April 15.) Ellicott commissioned to survey road in Pennsylvania.
(Br. 209.)
(June 30.) President ordered investigation of Hallet's criticisms of Thornton's plans. (B. 10-11.) (K. 55.) (Br. 203.)
(July 17.) Jefferson reported findings of investigation to President. (D.H. 26-27.) (K. 55-56.) (Br. 203.) (D.B., XVIII; 505.)
(K.B. 85, 86, 87.) (W. B. 294.)
(July 25.) President wrote Commissioners giving above report.
(B. 12.) (Br. 203.) (D.H. 27.) (H. 16.) (W.B. 294.)
(July.) Hallet submitted new plan for Capitol. (B. 12-13.) (D.B., XVIII; 505.) (W.B. 294.)
(September 18.) Corner stone of Capitol laid, with Masonic rites, by Washington. (R.M. 58.) (B. 14-17.) (D.H. 29.) (H. 22-24.)
(W.B. 295.) (F.W.P. 210.) (W.N.C. 315.) (E.A. 5; 565, 28; 788.) (Br. 213-214.) (E.B. 23; 392.)
(September 23.) Commissioners decide on hard brick for inner walls, freestone for facings. (B. 17.) (D.H. 29.)
(September 23.) Drawing begun of Blodgett Hotel lottery, in name of Capitol Commissioners. (Br. 205-208.)
(September 22-25 [November?]) Hoban appointed Superintendent on Capitol; Hallet to be assistant with salary of £400 per year. (D.B., IX; 91.) (B. 14, 17.) (D.H. 29.) (E.A. 5; 565.)
(W.B. 327.)
(————.) Colin or Collin Williamson, Superintendent of Stonecutters, at same salary, appointed about this time. (B. 17.)
(October.) Hallet submitted another plan. (B. 13.)
(December 23.) Commissioners wrote President complaining of Ellicott. (H. 12.)
(Summer (?) or latter part of year.) Ellicott dismissed. (D.B., VI, 90.) (Br. I, 210.) (H. 12.)
1794. (January.) Hallet submitted still another plan. (B. 13.)
(January 28.) Commissioners report discharge of Ellicott. (H. 12.)

(———.) George Blagden appointed Superintendent of stone-work and quarries. (B. 97.)

(May 19.) Commissioners wrote Collin Williamson, stating had closed with Dermott Roe to do work by piece; had ordered Hoban "to set him to work"; and desired Williamson to "super-intend it, or employ some one for that purpose." (D.H. 29.)

(June.) President agreed to changes recommended September 23, 1793. Work delayed by wait. (B. 17.)

(June 7.) Threats by masons against Hoban and Roe, referred to in letter from commissioners to Williamson. Warrants issued. Williamson empowered to accept wage offer of men. (D.H. 30.)

(June 24.) Hallet requested by commissioners to furnish com-plete plans for Capitol. Told that Williamson, not he, is to superintend work. Letter hints at change in personnel of both architect and commissioners. (D.H. 30-31.)

(June 26.) Commissioners reprimanded Hallet for changing Thornton's plans. (W.B. 295.) (E.A. 5; 565.) (B. 17.) (D.H. 31.) (H. 251.)

(June.) Hallet resigned. Resignation not accepted. (B. 18.)

(June 28.) Commissioners ordered Hallet's discharge and a re-plevin for plans, etc., in Hallet's possession. (D.B., XVIII; 505, VIII; 153.) (D.H. 32.) (W.B. 327.)

(June 28.) Hallet claimed "original invention of plan." (W.B. 327.)

(September 12.) Thornton appointed, by President, one of the three Commissioners in charge of the district of Columbia. (B. 18, 84.) (H. 17.) (D.B., VIII; 77, XVIII; 505.) (K. 61.) (Br. 237-239.) (K.B. 89.) (W.B. 295.)

(———.) Work on Capitol still below ground. (B. 19.)

(———.) Thornton made drawings embodying certain altera-tions, restoring the Dome, and removing the square foundations laid by Hallet in center of building. (B. 19, 30.) (K.B. 89.)

(September 13.) John Trumbull, Minister to England, recom-mended George Hadfield as successor to Hallet. (B. 21.) (Br. 241-242.) (D., I; 336.)

(November 15.) Hallet officially discharged. (B. 18.) (K. 61.) Br. 241.) (W.B. 295.) (E.A. 5; 565.)

(December.) Contract made with James Reid, James Smith, and George Walker to furnish stone; and with James Dobson to lay stone. (B. 20.)

1795. (January 2.) Commissioners, including Thornton, offer Hadfield position "as superintendent of the Capitol." (B. 21.) (E.A. 5; 565.) (D.B., VIII; 77.) (D., I; 336.)

(March 9.) Trumbull gave Hadfield letter of introduction to Thornton. (B. 21.) (D.B., VIII; 77.)

(April 30.) Commissioners made new agreement with Hoban to take superintendence of Capitol for the building season. (B. 21.) (D.B., VIII; 77.)

(June 3.) Colin Williamson discharged for inefficiency. (B. 21.)

(June 26.) Commissioners reported to Edmund Randolph, Secretary of State, that "bad work has been put into the Walls; and in some parts prudence requires that they should be taken down." Guilty contractors were discharged. (D.H. 35.)

(September 27.) Commissioners wrote President Washington of danger that "our operations must cease for want of a few thousand dollars," even though "every material is collected and the season is most favorable for the rapid progressions of the work." (D.H. 36.)

(October 15.) Hadfield appointed Superintendent. Hoban's services ceased except when called. (H. 18.) (D.B., XVIII; 505.) (B. 21.) (K.B. 89.) (D.B., VIII; 77.) (R.M. 58.) (K. 61.) (Br. 242, 259.)

(November 9.) President Washington, in a letter to the commissioners, referred to Hadfield's aim to omit the basement and add an attic story. Washington declined to give a "final opinion thereon." He left the decision to commissioners. Also referred to the plan as "nobody's, but a compound of everybody's." (D.H. 36-37.)

(November 18.) Thornton and Hoban opposed, as impractical, suggestions by Hadfield for changes in Thornton's plans. (B. 21.) (D.H. 37-38.) (D.B., VIII; 77.)

(————.) After consulting President, Hadfield resigned, but withdrew resignation. (B. 21.) (Br. 260.)

1796. (January 8.) President Washington submitted to Congress a memorial from the Commissioners asking that money be borrowed to complete Capitol. (D.H. 38-40.)

(March 11.) Alexander White reported for Commissioners that "the grand vestibule may or may not be covered with a dome." (D.H. 62.) (K.B. 90.)

(May 6.) Bill approved by Congress to borrow, not exceeding $300,000 to complete the Capitol. (D.H. 40-76.)

(May 31.) Commissioners wrote Hadfield that they depended on him to guard against imposition. (B. 22.)

(June 29.) Hadfield stated would quit in three months. Commissioners accepted. Resignation again withdrawn. (B. 22.) (E.A. 5; 565.) (H. 18.)

1797. (January.) Contracts made with five men to furnish brick; with another to do all brickwork for season. (B. 22.)

(February 15.) President Washington urged the Commissioners to complete the Capitol, even if President's House and other buildings were delayed; considered this necessary because of criticism and jealousies. (D.H. 77-78.)

(March.) John Adams succeeded Washington as President. [1797-1801.] Adams did not continue same personal interest in Capitol.

(June 30.) Thornton protested omission of ventilating flues from Senate galleries. (B. 22.)

1798. (January.) Thornton protested against workmanship on cornice, north front. (B. 22.)

(March 8.) Alexander White reported for Commissioners that Capitol was to consist of a main body and two wings; the former with a "grand circular vestibule to the east * * * and a conference room to the west." (D.H. 80.) (K.B. 90.)

(May 10.) Commissioners gave Hadfield three months' notice of discharge. (B. 23.) (E.A. 5; 565.)

(May 21.) Hadfield reported: (D.H. 84.)

Free stone work of outside walls raised to upper part of frieze; within nine feet of total height. Cornice and balustrade only required to complete elevation.

Interior walls carried to full height.

"Naked flooring" completed except over Senate Room.

Roof entirely framed, and mostly set.

"The shingles to cover the roof are dressing."

Interior trim being prepared.

(May 28.) Hoban ordered to take superintendency of Capitol as well as President's House. (Br. 318-319.) (B. 23.) (R.M. 58.) (E.A. 5; 565.)

(May 28 or June.) Hadfield officially discharged. (B. 23.) (H. 18.) (D.B., VIII; 77.) (Br. 314.) (K. 61.) (L. 133.) (D., I; 336.)

(Latter part.) Smaller rooms in north wing ready for plastering. Principal rooms progressing rapidly. (B. 23.)

(December 11.) Hoban reported: (D.H. 84-85.)

Roof completed. Floor above Senate chamber being put up. Ceiling joists put up for plastering in Representatives' chamber, committee rooms, etc. Doors and windows and frames under way.

"The covering to eliptic staircase, to lobby and back staircase is finished and ready for plastering."

Stone Work: "Part of cornice has been worked * * * balustrade finished to the east front * * * tops prepared for six chimneys. * * *"

Large quantities of material on hand.

1799. (January 12.) Wilson Bryan made Superintendent of Carpenters. (B. 24.)

(January 23.) George Blagden contracted to finish stonework. Lewis Clephane contracted for painting. Plastering to be done by John Kearney. (B. 24.)

(April 17.) Commissioners Scott and White wrote Thornton asking if he would supply drawings called for by Hoban. (Br. 316-317.) (B. 23.) (D.H. 85.)

(April 18.) Another letter, to Hoban, referred him to Thornton's reply, and asked Hoban to make drawings and submit them to Commissioners. (D.H. 85.)

(May.) Peter Lenox, Wilson Bryan, and Harbaugh requested to examine and report on roofs of Capitol (north wing), and President's House, "because they leak." Roofs were of shingles. (B. 24.)

(September.) Clephane ordered to give additional coat of sand paint to roof. (B. 24.)

(September 25.) Commissioners reported to President that Capitol will doubtless be ready for occupancy by end of year, "except the glazing, which cannot be so soon completed, owing to the Glass imported for that purpose arriving in a state unfit for use." (D.H. 86.)

1800. (February.) Hoban ordered to make details of the Capitol to "conform with drawings given John Kearney by Dr. Thornton." (B. 24.)

(April 24.) Congress passed bill authorizing President to order removal of government offices to city of Washington.

Section 3. Secretaries of four executive departments authorized to purchase furniture for offices and committee rooms, to defray expenses of moving books, papers, and records; all to be done for not to exceed $9,000.

Section 4. Secretaries to order footways made "in the said city, in suitable places and directions" for the "greater facility of communication between the various departments and offices of the government." $10,000 appropriated for this purpose.

Section 5. To purchase books for use of Congress, and provide suitable apartment for them; appropriation of $5,000. (D.H. 90-91.)

(May 15.) Commissioners reported population of about 3,000,

with 109 brick and 263 wood houses in Washington. (Br. 355.) (H. 25.) (W.N.C. 39.)

(June.) Departments of State, War, Navy, and General Post Office moved from Philadelphia to city of Washington. (B. 24.) (Br. 341-342, 350.)

(July 9.) Serious damage to plaster, due to faulty lead-work, reported by Commissioners to contractor, John Emory. (D.H. 91.)

(November 17.) Second session of Sixth Congress met in north wing. No quorum; adjourned. (B. 28.) (H. 26.) (Br. 369, 377.) (W.N.C. 315.) (E.A. 5; 565.)

(November 22.) Congress took possession formally of building. (North wing): Senate met in Chamber; House met in large room in west side of building. (D.H. 91.) (H. 26, 140.) (Br. 377.) (E.B. 23; 395.) (W.N.C. 315.) (E.A. 28; 791.)

North wing complete, except for minor details.

South wing: walls of basement above ground.

Central portion (Dome): portions of foundations in. (E.B. 23; 395.) (E.A. 5; 565.)

Senate Chamber: floor on ground-floor level, extended up two stories. (Br. 377-378.)

1801. (February 17.) Thomas Jefferson elected President. (B. 29.) (H. 26.)

(February 27.) Special investigating committee reported to House that Commissioners had expended more than $1,000,000; chiefly on "the Capitol, the President's House, and the two buildings erected for the accommodation of the Executive Departments." Committee deemed it unnecessary for it to decide "Whether these expenditures have been made with economy or not * * * as the House will possess the same information." (D.H. 95.)

(March 4.) Thomas Jefferson inaugurated President. [1801-1809.]

(May 28.) Hoban directed to estimate cost of temporary quarters for House, within walls of South wing. (B. 28.) (Br. 420.)

(June 2.) President Jefferson wrote Commissioners advocating that this "temporary building" be oval, one story high. (D.H. 96-97.)

(June 10.) Bids asked for above: to be of brick, and oval. To be completed December 1, 1801. (B. 28.) (Br. 420.) (F. 1.)

(June 20.) Contract for above awarded to Lovering & Dwyer, for $4,780, to be completed before November 1st. (B.28.) (Br. 420.)

(———.) Temporary building connected with north wing by a covered passageway 145 feet long. (B. 28-29.)

(June 24.) Hoban appointed Inspector of Government works. Salary, 300 guineas per annum "as long as his services were needed." Position abolished following year, together with Board of Commissioners. (B. 29.)

(————.) Supreme Court first met in Capitol. (B. 28.) (H. 186-187.) (Br. 370.)

(December 14.) Hoban reported temporary building for House completed. (B. 28.) (Br. 420.)

(December 18.) Congress ordered large west room used for library. (B. 26.)

1802. (April 8.) House Committee recommended printing of Commissioner's map of District of Columbia. (H. 11.)

(May 1.) Commission of three abolished by act of Congress. With it Thornton's supervision ended as did that of Hoban. (Br. 417.) (D.B., XVIII; 505.) (B. 29, 85.) (D.H. 101.) (H. 17, 21.) (E.A. 5; 565.) (D.B., IX; 91.) (K. 62.)

(June 4.) Thomas Munroe appointed Superintendent of Public buildings. (B. 29, 85.) (Br. 417.) (K. 62.)

1803. (March 6.) Latrobe offered position of Surveyor of Public Buildings, by President Jefferson; salary, $1,700 per year. (F. 2.) (B. 32.) (H. 27.) (L., XXI; 115.) (Br. 450.) (W.N.C. 254.) (E.A. 17; 97, 5; 565.) (K. 63.) (D., II; 99.) (D.B., XI; 21.) (B. 33.) (D.B., XVIII, 505.) (R.M. 58.)

Latrobe accepted appointment. (D.B., IX; 91.) (Br. 450-451.) (F.W.P. 211.)

(April 7.) Latrobe appointed John Lenthal, Clerk of Works. (B. 33.) (L. 134.) (Br. 452.) (LL.) (D., I; 336.) (D., II; 476.)

(September 5.) President Jefferson expressed surprise that Latrobe had not commenced roofing Capitol and President's House with sheet iron. (B. 40.)

1804. (February 27.) Latrobe reported, to President Jefferson, unpleasant interview with Thornton. (B. 33.) (L. 115-116, 119-120.)

(February 28.) Latrobe, in report, proposed many changes in Thornton's design. Claimed had received no drawings except a floor plan. (B. 34.) (D.B., XI; 22.)

(March 29.) Latrobe submitted to President plan to change design for Hall of Representatives. (B. 34.) (L. 122.) (K. 64.) (E.A. 5; 565.)

(July 31.) Exterior of South wing completed to height of main floor; foundations ready for interior walls; temporary ellipitical room removed; the House held sessions again, in the fall, in the North wing. (B. 40.) (Br. 453.)

1805. (January 1.) Thornton replied to Latrobe's criticisms, in a letter
to Congress, making last public defense of his plan. (B. 35-38.)
(H. 252.) (D.B., XVIII, 505.)

(————.) Latrobe criticized by Congress and newspapers for
delays, quality of work, and frequent absences from city. Thornton prodded him in letters. (B. 38.) (L., XXIII.) (E.A. 5; 565.)

(January 16.) President Jefferson authorized Latrobe to order
hexagonal floor tiles from Bordeaux, France. (B. 40.)

(March 6.) Latrobe wrote Philip Mazzei, in Italy, for help in
securing sculptors to execute work in Hall of Representatives;
also for estimate from Canova on figure of Liberty. (F. 2-5.)
(L. 123-127.) (W.N.C. 254-255.)

(August.) President Jefferson and Latrobe differed regarding skylights in roof of Hall of Representatives. (K. 64.) (B. 41-42.)
(L. 138.)

(August 31.) Exterior walls of South wing completed to cornice.
Walls completed to carry columns around Hall of Representatives. Serious decay in timbers of North wing. (B. 40, 43.)

(December 22.) Latrobe reported: "The interference and competition of several large public and private buildings, which have
been carried on in the district and at Baltimore, rendered it difficult to procure any considerable body of workmen; and the
quarries of freestone, at Acquia, have proved more than usually
precarious, in the supply of the larger and finer blocks required
for the interior of the capitol." (D.H. 115.)

1806. (February.) Giuseppe Franzoni and Giovanni Andrei arrived
from Italy. (F. 5, 72.) (B. 74.) (H. 29.) (D.B., XI; 22.) (D.,
I; 337.) (K. 65.) (Br. 454.) (Br., II; 32.)

(April 12.) Latrobe wrote Mazzei that Franzoni and Andrei had
arrived with wives; Franzoni had begun modeling eagle for
frieze in Hall of Representatives; had given up plans for figure of
Liberty by Canova or Thorwaldensen; thought Franzoni might
execute figure. (F. 7.) (Br. 454.)

(April 18.) Latrobe wrote Charles Wilson Peale for drawings
of head and claws of bald eagle, as guide for Franzoni. (F. 9-
11.) (F.W.P. 238.)

(August 27.) Latrobe wrote Jefferson that Franzoni's eagle was
finest he had ever seen. (F. 11.) (B. 40.) (D.B., XI; 22.)

(September 27.) Office story ready for plastering, walls ready
for roof. (B. 40.)

(October 21.) President Jefferson wrote Lenthal a sharp note
regarding skylights in Hall of Representatives. (L.L.) (B. 42.)

(November 25.) Latrobe, in report to President, recommended

that floor of Senate Chamber be raised to principal floor level; space beneath to be used as Supreme Court Room. (D.H. 122-123.) (K. 65.) (B. 44.)

(November 28.) Latrobe issued pamphlet criticizing Thornton's design. (B. 138.)

(December 19.) Latrobe wrote Mazzei that Franzoni had completed eagle for Hall of Representatives; and was working on one for Navy Yard gate; asked for estimate from Franzoni's father on fifty Corinthian capitals 3'-6" high. (F. 11-12.)

(December 31.) Latrobe wrote Lenthal of difficulty in getting Franzoni to grasp his idea of Goddess of Liberty. (F. 12.)

(Close of year.) Columns set in Hall of Representatives, and most of cornice in place. (B. 40.)

Latrobe framed roof of Hall for skylights; and for lantern, if needed. (B. 40.)

(December 31.) In letter to Lenthal, Latrobe acknowledged difficulties with collapse of arches. (L.L.)

1807. (August 13.) Report by Latrobe; making drawings for alterations in North Wing; approved by President Jefferson and Congress. Had removed portions of roof and replaced decayed timbers.

Franzoni's model of Statue of Liberty placed in position. (B. 41, 74.)

(October 26.) House met for first time in new Hall. (F. 14.) (B. 41.) (Br. 453.) (W.N.C. 254.) (H. 27, 29, 218.)

1808. (January 28.) Latrobe reported purchase of curtains to hang back of colonnade in House. (B. 43.)

(March 23.) Latrobe reported: (B. 41.) (D.H. 131-137.) (F. 14.) (H. 261.)

Woodwork of South wing ready for painting; sculpture over entrance incomplete; ten "chimney pieces of principal story wanting."

Of 24 Corinthian capitals in Hall of Representatives, only two finished.

Heating and acoustics in South wing discussed.

Old wooden skylight and cove over great staircase in North wing, replaced by brick cupolas.

(July 16.) Latrobe wrote Lenthal expressing horror at threatened collapse of great arch in staircase hall. (B. 43.) (L.L.)

(July 25.) Jefferson wrote Latrobe ordering floor of Senate Chamber raised to level of gallery. Existing floor was about ground level. (B. 25.)

(September 11.) Latrobe reported: (F. 16.) (D., II; 274.) (D.H. 146.)

Progress in Hall; sculpture on frieze completed by Franzoni; ceiling being painted by Bridport; carving of capitals, dentils, rosettes, etc., finished or progressing rapidly; fireplaces being moved from rear of Speaker's chair to right and left of same.

(————.) Latrobe designed, at Jefferson's suggestion, a straight colonnade instead of a circular, open vestibule for west front of the central building. (K. 65.) (B. 46.) (E.A. 5; 565.)

(September 19.) Lenthal killed by collapse of masonry vaults, over Supreme Court room, that carried Senate floor. (D.H. 147.) (B. 43.) (D.B., XI; 173.) (Br. 453.) (D., I; 336.)

(December 10.) Franzoni's models for figures, in Hall of Representatives, shipped by Latrobe to Academy of Arts, Philadelphia. (F. 17-18.)

1809. (March 4.) Madison succeeded Jefferson as President. [1809-1817.]

(May 22 to January, 1, 1810.) Senate occupied room in west part of North wing, formerly used by House. (Br. 454.) (B. 44.)

(August 28.) Letter from Latrobe to Jefferson is evidence that Latrobe, not Jefferson, designed "corn-stalk" columns; model of Capitol shipped to Monticello; this was modeled by Giuseppe Franzoni. (F. 19.) (B. 45.) (F.W.P. 233.) (D., II; 99.) (H. 185.) (D.B., XI; 22.)

(September 14.) Latrobe wrote Thomas Munroe complaining of Andrei's slowness, and of cost of his models; had placed both Andrei and Franzoni on piece-work basis, on certain jobs, to be done on own time. Also stated that they could not finish work by next season. (F. 19.)

(December 11.) Latrobe reported: "Raising floor of Senate Chamber to main floor level, making room for Supreme Court below; vaulting these rooms with brick, and replacing wood construction of Chamber, staircase, hall, and lobby. Wood construction retained in west side of wing." (Br. 454.) (B. 44.)

1810. (December 28.) Senate Chamber practically completed; in Hall only two out of twenty-four capitals remain untouched. (Br. 454.) (D.H. 163-164.)

1811. (————.) Suggested carving capitals for Hall in Italy as measure of economy. (F. 25-26.)

(February 8.) Chairman, Committee on Buildings and Grounds, wrote Latrobe suggesting that area 60 feet wide be leveled in front of Capitol for carriages. (B. 46-47.)

(July 1.) Latrobe retired from office as Surveyor of Public Buildings. (L., XXIV.) (F. 21.) (D.H. 169.) (D., II; 99.)

Appropriations for Capitol stopped, due to imminence of war with England. (F. 21.) (B. 46.) (L., XXIV.)

1812. (July 5.) Congress authorized payment of $2,500 to the "late surveyor of public buildings" (Latrobe), and not to exceed $1,000 to return Andrei and Franzoni to Italy. In the same bill $4,000, appropriated to complete sculpture in South wing, made it possible for them to remain. (F. 21.) (D.H. 169-170.)

1814. (August 24.) Capitol and White House burned by British. (E.B. 23; 392, 395.) (D.B., XI; 23.) (F.W.P. 49, 211, 265.) (E.A. 5; 565, 28; 791.) (Br. 618-626.) (B. 47-48.) (F. 22.) (D.H. 171-173.) (H. 33-37, 135.) (W.N.C. 45, 315.)

(September 19.) Thirteenth Congress met in "Blodget's Hotel," corner of 8th and E Street, site of Old Post Office Building. (Br. 631.) (B. 48.) (F. 23.) (F. 44.) (H. 38.)

(November 21.) Congressional Committee reported in favor of repairing buildings rather than moving capital city. (B. 49.) (Br. 634-635.) (D.H. 174-176.) (E.A. 5; 565.)

1815. (February 13.) Congress authorized President Madison to borrow $500,000 to rebuild public buildings. (E.B. 23; 395.) (B. 49.) (D.H. 185.) (R.M. 59.)

President appointed three Commissioners to superintend restoration. (B. 49.) (Br. 636.)

(February 15.) Robert Mills applied for position as Architect of Public Buildings. (B. 72.) (M. 57.)

(March 14.) Latrobe requested to resume position as architect. (D., II; 100.) (D.B., XI; 23.) (B. 49.) (H. 41.) (L., XXXI.)

(April 6.) Guiseppe Franzoni died in Washington, (F. 25, 72.)

(April 20.) Latrobe arrived in Washington. (B. 49.) (L., XXXI.)

(April 26.) Mills memorialized Congress on heating of Capitol. (B. 72.) (M. 57.)

(May 16.) Commissioners reported that Latrobe had been employed. (B. 49.)

Latrobe estimated that Capitol could be restored before 1816; recommended changing plan of Hall to a semicircle. (B. 49.)

(July 4.) Work begun on building for temporary use of Congress. Financed and built by Capitol Hotel Company. (B. 48.) (E.A. 5; 566.) (H. 39.)

(August 8.) Andrei sent to Italy to purchase capitals, and to engage sculptor to model figures. (F. 27, 73.) (B. 50, 74.) (H. 46.)

(August 26.) Variegated marble from Frederick County, Maryland, suggested for columns in Hall. (B. 50.)

(————.) Capellano arrived in Baltimore. (F. 29-30, 39.) (Br., II; 32.)

(November.) From this time on Latrobe received many protests at delays, and his absences from the city. (B. 50.)

(December.) Congress met in new building erected by Capitol Hotel Company. (Continued there until 1819.) (E.A. 5; 565.) (B. 48.) (F. 44.) (H. 39.) (Br. 636-637.)

(December.) Landscaping of Capitol grounds suggested on plat laid out by Latrobe. (B. 50.)

(December.) Architectural assistant requested by Latrobe. Refused, but salary raised from $2,000 to $2,500. (B. 50.)

1816. (February 26.) Delay in getting marble columns from Potomac quarries caused Latrobe to suggest substituting sandstone. Commissioners refused. (B. 50.)

(April 29.) Congress abolished Commission of three, replacing with single Commissioner. Samuel Lane given appointment, with salary of $2,000. (B. 50.) (D.H. 1033-4.) (Br., II; 34.)

(April 29.) Appropriation of $30,000 made for "enclosing and improving the public square, east of the Capitol." (Br., II; 37.) (D.H. 1033.)

(April 29.) President Madison given authority to make any changes, deemed proper by him, in government buildings. (B. 51.)

(————.) Hoban and Latrobe were asked opinion as to best type of roofing. Copper chosen by Hoban and approved by Madison. (B. 51.)

(August 29.) Latrobe's plan for brick dome over Senate Chamber, opposed by President Madison.

All interior work in Senate wing ordered replaced by solid masonry, except roof and ceiling of Chamber. (B. 50, 51-52.)

(September 19.) Lane ordered Latrobe to enlarge Senate Chamber. (B. 51.)

(November 5.) Latrobe wrote Jefferson that "corn stalk" columns were so little injured by British that he proposed to leave them without restoration. (F. 29.)

(November 28.) Latrobe's report showed: (D.H. 190-192.) (H. 41-42.)

Little progress in interior of South wing, due to difficulty in getting stone; exterior restored.

Walls of Senate Chamber up ten feet from floor.

Committee rooms on that floor vaulted.

"Inexhaustible" supply of marble discovered in Potomac region, in Loudoun County, Virginia, and Montgomery County, Maryland. (Br., II; 36-37.)

(————.) Valaperti carved eagle on frieze of south wall in Hall of Representatives. (F. 30-32, 80, 452.) (H. 219.) (R.M. 34.) (Br., II; 32.) (F.W.P. 238.)

(————.) Andrei returned from Italy with Carlo Franzoni and Francisco Iardella. (F. 5, 27, 73.) (B. 74.) (Br., II; 32.)

(————.) "Tobacco leaf" capitals designed by Latrobe and modeled by Iardella. (D.B., XI; 23.) (F. 29.) (L. 150.) (F.W.P. 226.)

1817. (January 4.) Lane reported following schedule of salaries: (D.H. 194.)

B. Henry Latrobe, architect	$2,500.00	per annum
Shadrach Davis, clerk of the works	4.00	per day
Henry Hillman, foreman of the stone-cutters	3.75	do
John Queen, foreman of the bricklayers*	3.00	do
Leonard Harbaugh, foreman of the carpenters	2.50	do
Thomas Howard, overseer	2.12½	do

*When the bricklayers are discharged, the compensation of their foreman stops, of course.

In a later report, Lane gave the following schedule of wages for this period: (D.H. 232.)

Stone-cutters, per day	$2.50	to $2.75
Bricklayers, " "	2.00	to 2.25
Carpenters, " "	1.62	to 1.88
Laborers, " "	1.00	

(February 15.) Increased costs and delay were due to changes ordered by President and Senate, according to Latrobe and Lane. (B. 52.) (D.H. 196.)

(March.) Valaperti disappeared; supposed to have committed suicide. (B. 75.) (F. 31.) (H. 219.) (R.M. 34.) (Br., II, 32.) (F.W.P. 238.)

(March 4.) Monroe succeeded Madison as President. [1817-1825.]

(March 17.) President Monroe requested General Swift and Colonel Bomford to report on strength of foundations and marble columns to carry vaulting and roof of House and Senate chambers. (D.H. 220-221.)

(March 19.) Swift and Bomford reported foundations "are of sufficient strength to support the superstructure." Also the columns. (D.H. 221-222.)

(March 31.) Swift and Bomford recommended that architect employ two good draftsmen and furnish promptly plans for Capitol; Commissioners procure material and tools, and employ "one hundred good men and a leader" from New York or Boston; also, in addition to local men employ "from Philadelphia, thirty or forty quarry men, and twenty stone cutters—from New York the same numbers." They recommended "that domes over House and Senate chambers be of wood * * * the base of both domes to be encircled with three iron bands." (D.H. 222-223.) (B. 52.)

(April 4.) President Monroe authorized Latrobe to employ two skilled draftsmen to expedite work. (D.H. 199.) (B. 52.)

Also ordered construction of brick dome over Senate Chamber; wood dome over Hall of Representatives. (B. 52.) (D.H. 198.) (H. 43.)

(April 11.) Additional appropriation made for improving grounds. (D.H. 1035.)

(April to Fall.) Latrobe made weekly reports to President. (B. 52.) (D.H. 199.)

(September 14.) William Lee wrote Charles Bulfinch intimating that Latrobe might resign, and suggesting that he apply for position. Bulfinch refused to apply for place held by another. (F. 40.) (B. 54.) (H. 44.) (C.B. 242-243.)

(September 24.) North wing without roof; entablature in Hall incomplete; columns in Senate Chamber not set up; doors and windows not ordered. (B. 52.)

(October 31.) Captain Peter Lenox appointed Clerk of Works on Capitol, being transferred from President's House to take place of Shadrach Davis, who was transferred to President's House. (B. 52-53, 96.) (D., I; 337.)

(November 20.) Latrobe sent resignation to President Madison. (E.A. 5; 566, 17; 97.) (Br., II; 36.) (D., II; 100.) (D.B., XI; 23.) (R.M. 59.) (F. 40.) (B. 53.) (H. 43.) (L. 150-151.)

(November 24.) Resignation accepted, by letter from Lane. (B. 53.) (C.B. 243.)

(December 4.) John Quincy Adams wrote Bulfinch offering him office of Architect of the public buildings. (D.B., III; 247.) (F. 41.) (C.B. 243.)

1818. (January 8.) Bulfinch officially appointed. Salary, $2,500; travelling expenses extra; $500 for draftsman. (E.A. 5; 566.) (Br., II; 36.) (D., II; 467.) (R.M. 59.) (F. 41.) (B. 55.) (H. 45.) (C.B. 243.) (E.B. 4; 355.)

Wooden model of Capitol to show President and Congress, made for Bulfinch by a Mr. Willard, of Boston. (B. 56.) (C.B. 248-249, 256.)

Bulfinch found on hand a large amount of stone; three columns and two pilasters for Hall of Representatives, with others under way; fifty mantels; marble doorways, window frames, sash, and parts of doors. (B. 56-57.)

(January 18.) Lane reported necessity for taking over marble quarries of the Potomac due to inability of contractors to continue contract. (D.H. 219.)

(April 20.) First appropriation made for central (Rotunda) section. Amount, $100,000. (B. 58.) (D.H. 226.) (C.B. 250.) (W.N.C. 315.)

(May 1.) Causes of accident to brick arch, planned by Latrobe to carry cupola above flat dome of Senate wing, reported on by Bulfinch. (D.H. 209-210.) (B. 57.) (H. 45.) (C.B. 260.)

(November 21.) Report by Bulfinch: (D.H. 207-209.) (H. 46-47.) (C.B. 250.) (B. 58.)

> North wing: Stone cupola completed; stone balustrade over cornice, on east and west sides completed; attic on north completed; roof covered with copper. Interior: Marble staircase installed to main floor; colonnade in small rotunda, and part of east gallery in Chamber completed. Rooms of attic and main stories plastered and paved. Court room to be finished in December. Chambers delayed by marble.
>
> South wing: Balustrade on roof nearly completed; columns of Hall complete and in place; also entablature and enclosure for gallery; ribs of domed ceiling in position; exterior roof complete.
>
> Central (Rotunda) section: Excavation completed; foundations laid, and walls up to level of ground floor arches; external walls of basement begun.

(December 8.) Latrobe wrote a lengthy reply to Bulfinch's report, defending himself. (B. 57.) (D.H. 210.)

1819.   (February-March.) Supreme Court met for first time in its room in Capitol. Additional appropriation of $136,644 made for Dome. (Br., II; 39.) (D.H. 226.)

Car of History completed by Carlo Franzoni. (F. 41, 80.) (B. 74-75.) (R.M. 35.) (H. 228.)

(May 12.) Carlo Franzoni died at Washington. (F. 43.) (R.M. 35.)

C. A. Busby, an English architect, made drawings of building; engraved, and published in 1822. (B. 56.)

(December.) First sessions held in new Hall of Representatives. (B. 58.) (E.A. 5; 566.) (Br., II; 39.)

(December.) Senate met in new Chamber. (Tablet in room.)

(December 20.) Samuel Lane reported dissapointment in quality of Potomac marble. An apparently perfect block would be full of dry veins, and "in working would fall to pieces." (D.H. 220.)

1820. (February 16.) North and South wings complete, except painting and a few changes in temporary building, for committee rooms. Wall and iron railing around Capitol Square completed. Walls of the center building "have been raised as high as was contemplated." (D.H. 226.) (B. 58.)

(April 13.) Questionnaire regarding acoustics sent to Bulfinch. (B. 58.)

(———.) Thornton called on for advice regarding acoustics. (B. 59.)

(August 28.) Ellicott died at West Point. (E.A. 10, 253.) (D.B., VI; 89.)

(September 3.) Latrobe died of yellow fever at New Orleans. (E.A. 17; 97.) (F. 41.) (D.B., XI; 24.)

(November 19.) Bulfinch reported progress on center of Capitol; walls of Rotunda commenced. (D.H. 234.)

1821. (January 10.) Bulfinch submitted report suggesting three possible ways of correcting acoustics in Hall. (B. 70.) (D.H. 236-237, 307-308.)

(January 19.) Committee, appointed on December 19, 1820, to investigate possibilities of correcting acoustics, presented its report. (B. 70.) (D.H. 235.)

(March 5.) Monroe inaugurated second time; on 5th, as 4th was on Sunday.

1822. (January 4.) Bulfinch reported illness among workmen; stonework of western projection complete, except chimneys; roofs covered with copper. (D.H. 242.)

(———.) Another committee appointed to investigate acoustics. (B. 70.)

(———.) Joseph Elgar appointed Commissioner of Public Buildings. (B. 59.)

(March 25.) Committee on Public Buildings recommended that dome be built of wood. (D.H. 243.)

(October 1 or September 30.) Commissioner Elgar announced cut in salaries. (B. 59.) (D.H. 255.)

Bulfinch protested cut, to John Quincy Adams. (See 1823, January 31.) (B. 59.)

(October 22.) Mills memorialized Congress on acoustics of Capitol. (B. 72.) (M. 57.)

(December 9.) Bulfinch reported progress for year. (B. 60-61.) (D.H. 251.)

Dome nearly ready for copper sheathing.

Projection west of Rotunda; copper covering completed; walls painted; window frames and sash in place; scaffolding removed from west front, which was nearly complete except for iron railings between columns of loggia.

Two principal stories of committee rooms with corridors, plastered, and most of carpenter work finished.

Interior walls of Rotunda "raised to full height and covered with entablature and blocking course."

Exterior walls "carried up with stone * * * and crowned with a cornice and four receding gradines."

"About two-thirds of the interior dome is built of stone and brick and the summit of wood. The whole is covered with a wooden dome * * * serving as a roof. * * * a few days of favorable weather will enable the workmen to sheath it * * * in readiness for the copper covering." (C.B. 252.)

Bulfinch requested appointment of a guard, and guides for the building. (B. 61.)

1823. (January 31.) President Monroe referred Bulfinch salary cut to Attorney General Wirth. (B. 59.)

(January 31.) Wirth reported to President, upholding Bulfinch. (B. 60.)

(————.) Enrico Causici and Antonio Capellano arrived from Italy, Nicholas Gevelot from France. (F. 47.) (B. 75, 100.) (Br., II; 32.) (D., II; 468.)

(March 21.) Causici contracted to design and model clock for Senate; $2,000 appropriated. (F. 48-52.) (D.H. 262.)

1824. (February 16.) Model for Senate clock completed by Causici. Project dropped because of expense. (F. 50.)

(March 24.) $3,000 appropriated "for improving the Capitol square and painting the railing around same." (D.H. 1036.)

(October 21.) Andrei died at Washington. (F. 47, 73.)

(December 10.) Interior of Capitol reported complete, except for some painting and stonework. Colonnade of east portico still unfinished. (D.H. 265-6.) (B. 61.) (E.A. 5; 566.)

1825. (February.) Hallet died at New Rochelle, N. Y.

(March 4.) John Quincy Adams succeeded Monroe as President. [1825-1829.]

(April 25.) Iardella succeeded Andrei; salary $1,250; from January, 1825 to December 31, 1827. (B. 63.) (F. 73, 84.)

(May.) Competition authorized for figures on pediment of east portico. (B. 76.) (E.A. 5; 566.)

(June 14.) L'Enfant died near Bladensburg, Maryland. (H. 10.)

(E. 14.) (E.B. 13; 911.) (E.A. 17; 285.) (F.W.P. 45.) (J.J.J. 190.) (Br. 183.) (E.K. 27.)

(June 22.) Bulfinch wrote a letter describing details of sculpture on east pediment as specified for Persico. (B. 76.) (F. 48.)

1826. (January 26.) Elgar reported Capitol grounds "so encumbered with materials and shops" and with no plan provided, not possible to estimate cost of improving same. (D.H. 1036.)

(February 5.) Hadfield died at Washington. (D.B., VIII; 76.)

(March.) Bulfinch recommended a wall, and terrace of earth to mask west basement; vaults to store wood; two porters' lodges; four iron gates with stone piers; stone steps to west front; and grading of ground. (D.H. 272-274.)

(May 19.) House authorized employment of Strickland on acoustics. (D.H. 284-285.) (F. 63.)

(June 3.) George Blagden killed by caving of embankment. (B. 61, 97.) (D., I; 336.)

(August 28.) William Strickland asked to advise with Bulfinch on acoustics of Hall of Representatives, reporting to committee composed of Secretaries of War and State, and the Attorney General. Bulfinch reported November 1st; Strickland on October 31.) (D.H. 285-287-288.) (B. 70-71.)

(October 22.) Mills memorialized Congress on acoustics. (Presented during session of January 14, 1830.) (D.H. 304-7.) (B. 71.) (M. 75.)

1826-1827. Bulfinch devoted time to new work, and to landscaping grounds, principally the west approach. (B. 61.) (E.A. 5; 566.) (C.B. 260-261.)

1827. (February 7.) Gates, piers, and four lodges struck from architect's estimate, by Congress. (D.H. 283.)

(February 8.) Reports of Strickland and Bulfinch submitted to House. (D.H. 284-285.) (H. 264-268.)

(December 27.) Carved panels above doors in Rotunda completed; severely criticized in Congress. (D.H. 277-8, 293.) (F. 53, 63.) (D.H. 295.) (R.M. 25-29.)

Progress made on Capellano's sculptured panel over east door of Rotunda, and on Persico's tympanum of portico pediment. (D.H. 295.) (H. 90.)

1828. (February 7.) Guard-houses and lodges again deducted from architect's estimate. (D.H. 297.)

(March 28.) William Thornton died. (H. 21.) (D.B., XVIII; 504.)

Gallery on east side of Senate Chamber removed because obstructed light. Circular gallery erected on west wall. (B. 61.)

(May 2 [March 2?]) Congress abolished office of Architect of the Capitol. (B. 61.) (H. 49.) (C.B. 274.) (E.A. 5; 566.)

(June 30.) Persico's figures for east pediment nearly completed. (H. 87.)

(December 9.) Trumbull submitted report on preservation of Rotunda paintings. (D.H. 302-4.)

1829. (January 21.) Bulfinch recommended railing to keep cattle out of Capitol grounds; stone gutters for roadways; stable for messengers' horses; grading Maryland Avenue, near Capitol, "and to plant the whole avenue with four ranges of forest trees." (D.H. 1038-9.)

(March 3.) Statues of War and Peace ordered from Luigi Persico. Completed March 2, 1833. Installed about 1837. (F. 76-77, 78.) (B. 73, 76.) (H. 89.)

(March 4.) Andrew Jackson succeeded John Quincy Adams as President. [1829-1837.]

(June 25.) Bulfinch notified by Elgar that office had been abolished. (B. 61.) (F. 84.) (D.H. 1038.)

(June 27.) Bulfinch wrote President Jackson, asking that he be retained until work should be completed. (B. 61-62.) (F. 84.)

(———.) Negative reply from President. (B. 62.) (E.A. 5; 566.)

(June 30.) Bulfinch retired. From then until July 4, 1836 there was no official government architect.

Repairs to Capitol were made under William Noland, Commissioner of Public Buildings, and Pringle Slight, Assistant Superintendent. (B. 72.) (E.A. 5; 566.)

1829-1836. Many discussions on subject of water supply for Capitol Hill, resulting in purchase of springs and installation of water pipes and reservoir. (D.H. 311-317, 325-331.) (D.H. 1038-1040-51.)

1830. (January 14.) Mills' memorial on acoustics and ventilation, dated October 22, 1826, presented to Congress. (M. 75.) (B. 71.) (D.H. 304-7.)

(January 24.) Bulfinch reported to Congress on acoustics and ventilation of House. (B. 71.) (D.H. 307-308, 236-237.) (H. 262-263.)

(March 30.) Mills submitted long letter on possible sources of water supply for Capitol. (D.H. 1045-1047.)

(June 3.) Bulfinch returned to Boston. (B. 62.) (C.B. 241.) (F. 84.) (E.B. 4; 355.)

(———.) Mills moved from Charleston to Washington. (D.B., XIII; 12.)

1830 or 1831. (January 23.) Iardella died in Washington. (F. 73, 84.)
(————.) Tripoli naval monument placed on terrace before west portico. (B. 77, 181.) (F. 98.) (Br., II; 328.)

1831. (December 8.) Hoban died in Washington. (D.B., IX; 91.) (B. 95.)

1832. (January 13.) Mills reported on water supply for public buildings. (D.H. 316.)
(February 4.) Mills reported to select committee of the House, repeating former recommendations on acoustics. (D.H. 320-324.) (H. 268-272.) (B. 71.)
(June 30.) Committee recommended changes in accordance with report. (B. 71-72.) (D.H. 319-320.) (H. 268.)
(July 14.) Congress appropriated $5,000 for statue of Washington. Commission given to Horatio Greenough. This was first award to an American sculptor. (B. 76-77.) (D.H. 325.) (F. 65.) (H. 75.)
(————.) Water piped into Capitol from near-by springs. (B. 72.)

1833. (March 2.) Persico's figures for east pediment reported completed. Not placed in position until 1837. (B. 73, 76.) (E.B. 23; 392.)
(October 11.) Mills memorialized Congress on distribution of water in Capitol. (B. 72.) (M. 57.)

1834. (January.) Old copper roof on dome replaced by new. (B. 72.) (D.H. 327.)
(November 24.) Persico's figures, "Peace and War," arrived at Norfolk. (F. 69.)

1835. (November 9.) Roofs of both wings re-coppered. Roof timbers badly decayed. (Report by Slight.) (D.H. 332.)

1836. (May 28.) Mills reported on plan for proposed new Hall of Representatives "upon the site of the library room." (D.H. 334.)
(July 6 [June 6?]) President Jackson appointed Robert Mills "Architect of New Buildings, (Treasury and Patent Office) Salary $1,800." (B. 72.) (M. 57.) (D.B., XIII; 12.) (A.E., 5; 566.)
(October 26.) Mills' salary raised to $2,300. (B. 72.)

1836-1851. Mills in charge of maintenance and changes in Capitol. Raised floor of Hall of Representatives, and placed partition in rear of and concentric with colonnade. (B. 59, 72.)

1837. (March 3.) Two groups of figures ordered from Persico for blockings on east approach. One was transferred subsequently to Greenough. Persico's group was installed in 1844 (1846?) (B. 78, 176.) (F. 75, 78, 139-140.) (H. 89.) (E.B. 23; 392.)

(March 4.) Martin Van Buren succeeded Jackson as President. [1837-1841.]

1838. (April 26.) Public buildings placed under jurisdiction of Secretaries of State, Treasury, and War. (John Forsyth, Levi Woodbury, and J. R. Poinsett then in office.) (B. 72.)

1839. (May 17.) Post Office Building authorized, Mills' salary raised to $2,400. (B. 72.) (M. 57.)

(October.) Mills allowed $500 for assistant in drawing and copying. (B. 72.) (M. 57.)

1840. (March 5.) Report and estimate, on installing Greenough's statue of Washington, presented to House of Representatives by Mills. (Report dated February 10 and 26.) (F. 99-102.)

(April 5.) Mills reported favorably on use of gas instead of oil for lighting public grounds. (B. 72.)

(————.) Exterior views of Capitol made by Bartlett, English painter. Engraved on steel for book of American scenery by N. P. Willis. (B. 73.) (C.B. 262.)

(May 8.) House authorized Clerk to order "glass chandelier, with lamps and plain shades," for Hall of Representatives. (D.H. 337.)

(December.) Committee appointed to investigate fall of chandelier in Hall of Representatives, reported it was not fault of contractor; who was paid for same, less $400 for material salvaged. (D.H. 336.)

1841. (January 13.) Mills reported strengthening of rotunda foundations to carry Greenough's statue of Washington. Statue placed in Rotunda. (Report dated December 15.) (D.H. 338-339.) (Br., II; 328-329.)

(March 4.) William Henry Harrison succeeded Van Buren as President. [1841-1845.]

(————.) Experiments with gas lighting made by Robert Grant. (B. 72.)

1843. (March 3.) Congress ordered removal of Greenough's statue from Rotunda. (B. 77.) (F. 103.) (D.H. 339.) (H. 76.) (Br., II; 329.)

1844. (April 15.) Bulfinch died. (B. 93.) (E.B. 4; 355.) (E.A. 4; 716.) (C.B. 284.)

(————.) Greenough's statue of Washington removed from Rotunda to pedestal in front of east entrance. (F. 103.)

1844 - (1846?) "Discovery Group," by Persico, installed at east portico. (F. 109.) (B. 176.)

1845. (March 4.) James Knox Polk succeeded Harrison as President. [1845-1849.]

1846-1847. Andrew Beaumont, appointed Commissioner of Public Buildings. (B. 72.)

(July 9.) Congress retroceded to Virginia the area ceded to the Government, December 3, 1789, as part of the District of Columbia. (E.B. 23; 395.) (D.H. 11.) (H. 12.) (Br. 262.) (E.A. 28, 791.) (W.N.C. 49.)

1847. Lantern, six feet in diameter, containing 30,000 candle power solar gaslight, placed on 100-foot mast, above Dome. Planned to install similar type of light in Senate, House, and Rotunda. (B. 72-73.)

(————.) Charles Douglas appointed Commissioner of Public Buildings. (B. 72.)

1847-1851. Ignatius Mudd held position of Commissioner of Public Buildings. (B. 72.)

(————.) Hall of Representatives heated by furnaces, with brass registers in floor over mixing chamber. (B. 73.)

1849. (March 4.) Zachary Taylor succeeded Polk as President.

1850. (May 28.) Senate considered memorial by Robert Mills (dated May 1, 1850) with plans and estimates for addition to the Capitol. (H. 52.) (D.H. 430-437.) (B. 115-116.)

(May 28.) Committee on Public Buildings recommended extension of Capitol in accordance with drawings and report of Mills. (B. 115.) (H. 52.) (D.B., XIII; 13.) (D.H. 430-431.)

(July 9.) Millard Fillmore succeeded Taylor as President. [1849-1853.]

(September 25.) Senate did not approve report by Mills, and authorized a competition for the Capitol extension. (D.H. 443.) (F. 111.) (D.B., XIII; 13.) (B. 116.) (H. 52.) (M. 71.)

(September 30.) Congress appropriated $100,000 for extension of the Capitol. (B. 119.) (D.H. 445.) (F. 113.) (H. 52.)

(October 2 to 21.) Competition advertised in Washington papers. (B. 116-117.) (D.H. 445.) (D.B., XIII; 13.)

(December 1.) Competition closed. Four designs selected from which final design was to be studied. (B. 117.)

(————.) Mills wrote F. Stanton, Chairman of Senate Committee on plans and designs, outlining suggestion for extension of east front; with House in east, and Senate in west wings. (M. 71-73.)

1851. (February 8.) Jefferson Davis presented report on competition to Senate. Robert Mills ordered to draw plan combining features of the four premiated designs. (B. 117.) (D.H. 446.) (D.B., XIII; 13.)

(March 4 to July 1, 1853.) William Easby held position of Commissioner of Public Buildings. (B. 72.)

President Millard Fillmore appointed Thomas U. Walter, "Architect of the United States Capitol Extension." (Walter had entered several plans in the competition.) (B. 117, 119, 193.) (H. 53.) (M. 73.) (D.B., XIII; 13, XIX; 397.) (F.W.P. 211-212.) (E.A. 5; 566.)

(June 10.) The President approved, in general, Walter's plan. (B. 119.)

(————.) Mills retired from office. (D.B., XIII; 13.) (A.E. 5; 566.) (B. 98.)

(June 11.) Walter took oath of office. (F. 113.) (B. 119.)

(July 4.) Corner stone of "Capitol Extension" laid. Daniel Webster delivered oration. (B. 120.) (D.H. 448.) (F. 129.) (H. 53-56.) (F.W.P. 212.) (W.N.C. 11, 49, 315.) (E.A. 5; 566.) (E.B. 23; 392.) (D.B., XIX; 397.)

(July 29 and September 13.) Walter submitted reports on advisability of doing work on Capitol by contract system. (D.H. 449-451.)

(December 22.) Commission appointed, November 3, 1851, by Alex. A. A. Stuart, Secretary of the Interior, to test samples of marble; submitted lengthy report. Recommended marble from quarries at Lee, Massachusetts. (D.H. 554-558.) (B. 123.) (E.B. 23; 392.)

(December 24.) Library of Congress, in west part of Capitol, destroyed by fire. (B. 124, 178.) (D.H. 342, 347.) (H. 60, 137.) (Br., II; 305.)

1852. (January 13.) Samuel Strong resigned as Superintendent, following charges that he had taken over brick contract from Adams, the original contractor. (B. 125.)

(January 27.) Walter submitted plans for restoring Library of Congress. (B. 124.) (D.H. 342-346.)

(March 11.) House of Representatives received report of special committee on tests of stone used in foundations; submitted by Walter R. Johnson. (D.H. 559-566.) (B. 123.)

(March 16.) Senate considered resolution directing Committee on Public Buildings to examine work on Extension, especially the stonework. (B. 122.) (D.H. 505.)

(March 19.) Congress appropriated $72,500 for reconstruction of Library. (B. 124.) (D.H. 344.)

(March 24.) Senate called on President for information regarding plans for Extension, especially in connection with lighting, heating, and ventilating. (D.H. 509.) (B. 122.)

(March 25.) Report made by officers of Engineer Corps, on stone and masonry. (D.H. 506-508.) (B. 125.)

(March 29.) Senate answered by President's message. (D.H. 515.) (B. 122.)

(March 30.) Report made by Topographical Engineers, on stone and masonry; extension of Capitol grounds, and cost of same, taken up by resolution of Senate. (D.H. 508-509.) (B. 125.)

(August 26.) Senate asked for further information. (B. 122.)

(————.) While control of the Capitol had been invested in Commissioner of Building and Grounds, the Extension was placed in charge of the Secretary of the Interior. (B. 124.)

(August 28.) Commissioner William Easby felt slighted, and brought charges of fraud, etc. (B. 124, 125.)

(December 1.) Walter reported: "Cellar walls completed, marble, in places, twelve feet above granite sub-basement." Quoted reports on foundation material (March 11), and marble tests (December 22, 1851). (B. 122-123.) (D.H. 554-558, 559-566.)

(December 4.) Stuart reported: "Foundations complete for sub-basement; brick floor arches turned, and pavements ready for tiling; much of cut granite finished; portion of basement marble work under way; refitting of Library nearly completed." (B. 124.) (D.H. 347, 566.)

(December 18.) Horatio Greenough died at Somerville, Massachusetts. (F. 140.) (D.B., VII; 586.)

1853. (March 4.) Franklin Pierce succeeded Millard Fillmore as President. [1853-1857.]

(March 22.) House Committee reported on Easby investigation. (B. 125.)

(March 23.) Control of Capitol transferred, by President, from Department of Interior to War Department. (D.H. 585.) (F. 139.) (B. 126, 200.)

(April 4.) Secretary of War Jefferson Davis appointed Captain M. C. Meigs, Superintendent of Extension. (D.B., XII; 507.) (H. 53.) (B. 126.) (D.H. 585, 586.) (F. 139.)

(May 6.) Attorney General sustained validity of contracts, made by Walter for supplying, cutting, and laying marble. This decision, and reports by Meigs, disposed of charges against Walter's work. (B. 128.) (D.H. 591.)

(May 19.) Meigs, in report, advised various changes in interior of Capitol. (D.H. 594.)

(May 20.) Prof. A. D. Bache and Prof. Joseph Henry commissioned to study heating, ventilating, and acoustics of Capitol. Reported June 24. (D.H. 587-588.) (B. 126.)

(May 28.) Meigs reported investigation of foundations for Extension. (B. 128.) (D.H. 592-594.)

(June 27.) President approved changes in new South wing. (D.H. 588.) (B. 126.)

(July 5.) President approved changes in new North wing. (D.H. 588.) (B. 126.)

(August.) Meigs invited estimates and designs for east doors, and for sculpture for east pediment. (F. 140-143.)

(September 22.) Hiram Powers declined to enter competition for pediment sculpture. (F. 144.)

(October 13.) Thomas Crawford accepted invitation to submit designs for pediment. (F. 143.) (B. 176.) (D.B., IV; 526.)

(October 22.) Meigs reported to Jefferson Davis: "had accompanied committee on trip to northern cities to study rooms in public buildings in relation to acoustics; described plans of extension, as worked out by Walter, with great minuteness; explained that failure of contractor to supply brick necessitated purchasing same elsewhere at higher rates." (B. 126.) (D.H. 586-592.)

(November 30.) Meigs notified Crawford of acceptance of his design for pediment sculpture. Price, $20,000. (E.B. 6; 649.) (B. 173.) (F. 145.) (D.H. 613, 653.) (D.B., IV; 526.)

(————.) "Rescue" group by Greenough, installed on east portico. (F. 139-140.) (B. 176.) (E.B. 23; 392.)

(————.) Contracts made with Cornelius Wendell to supply brick at $5.85 per thousand; with Frederick A. Burch to lay brick for $2.49 per thousand. Both threw up contracts, as prices were too low. Work then done by day labor. (D.H. 590-591.) (B. 128.)

1854. (————.) Marble facing carried to top of main story; interior walls to ceilings of halls. (B. 129.) (H. 56.)

(June 14.) The House debated with warmth and wit, the water supply, fire hazard, price of brick, system of ventilation, and extravagance due to military control of Capitol Extension. (F. 152.) (D.H. 609-616.) (B. 151.)

1855. (February 22.) An amendment to a pending bill was introduced by Mr. Stanton of Kentucky "For removing the present dome over the central portion of the Capitol, and the construction of one upon the plan designed by T. U. Walter, architect of the Capitol extension, $100,000." Adopted by the House, March 3, 1855. (D.H. 990, 993.) (B. 129.)

(March 3.) Robert Mills died at Washington. (D.B. XIII; 9.) (E.A. 19; 129.) (M. 37, 215.) (B. 98.)

(March 3.) Congress appropriated $100,000 to replace old dome with a larger one, of cast-iron construction. (D.H. 993.) (B. 129.) (H. 60.) (E.A. 5; 566.) (F.W.P. 218.)

[1853 or 1854?]. (May 25.) Randolph Rogers given commission for bronze doors. Originally intended for opening between south corridor and Statuary Hall; eventually installed in east entrance of Rotunda. (F. 153-157.) (D.H. 654-655.) (B. 178.) (H. 90.) (D.B., XVI; 107.) (E.B. 23, 392.) (F.W.P. 219.)

(October 11.) Crawford engaged to design bronze doors for east entrance. (D.B., IV; 526.) (H. 215.) (F. 213.)

(October 14.) Annual report by Meigs. (D.H. 627-631.) (B. 129-176.) (F. 159.)

Marble facing on east front up, so setting of pilaster caps was begun; about half of columns and three-quarters of pilasters in grand corridor of south wing in place; brick vaulting for floors leveled for tiling; roof trusses completed for Hall of Representatives, and some in position; Senate Chamber roof ready for erection; both rooms full of scaffolding. Several of Crawford's models for pediment received and being carved in American marble. One of basement rooms being painted in fresco.

Several of Crawford's models for Senate pediment arrived. Men at work carving figure of Mechanic, and groups of Commerce and Instruction. Crawford modeling other figures.

Bronze decorations for doors to gallery of House being cast.

Capitals of columns in principal corridor of South wing "of very elaborate design, introducing in a Corinthian capital details selected from the foliage of native plants."

Tennessee variegated marble procured for three of "the great stairways"; green serpentine from Vermont for the fourth; "A very beautiful marble has been discovered in Frederick County, Maryland"; specimens of colored marbles also received from Vermont.

(November 16.) Plans for new Dome given in detail, in report by Meigs. (D.H. 993-997.)

(————.) Constantini Brumidi employed to execute mural decorations. Continued work more than twenty-five years. (F. 160-161.) (B. 173, 187, 199.) (H. 95-98.)

(————.) First real fresco in America done by Brumidi in committee room on Agriculture. (F. 159.)

1856. (March 5.) Commissioner of Public Buildings instructed by Senate to secure definite prices on land required for extension of Capitol grounds. (D.H. 1054.)

(March 18.) Crawford wrote that he had changed the liberty cap on his "Freedom" to "a helmet, the crest of which is composed of an eagle's head and bold arrangement of feathers." This was done because of objections of Secretary of War, Jefferson Davis, to the liberty cap and Roman fasces. (H. 64-65.) (B. 177.) (F. 226-228.) (F.W.P. 216.)

(May 26.) Edward Ball, of Ohio, spoke at length in House, criticizing transfer of direction of Capitol Extension from Department of Interior to War Department; of results secured by Meigs; and quoted costs to show gross extravagance. (D.H. 633-641.) (F. 165.)

(July 3.) Committee on Public Buildings and Grounds requested Secretary of War, Jefferson Davis, to furnish costs of various items. (D.H. 644.)

(July 5.) Secretary Davis refused to give above information except on order from President, as previous inquiries had been sent to the President. (D.H. 645.)

(July 9.) House discussed alleged frauds in connection with work on Capitol. (D.H. 643-649.)

(July 28.) Lengthy, itemized report from Meigs gave costs as requested. (F. 165.) (D.H. 651-656.)

(August 4.) President Pierce laid before the House a letter, dated August 2, from Jefferson Davis, who transmitted a report, dated July 28, from Meigs. (D.H. 650-651.)

(November 13.) Report by Meigs. (D.H. 660-663, 1006-1009.) (B. 130.)

Exterior marble-work up to top of architrave; much of cornice finished. Marble columns of basement corridor, south wing, all set; corridors in north wing progressing rapidly; granite stairways to cellar and attic finished; floor tiling progressing; copper roofing and glass all in place; iron ceilings of both Halls completed; cast-iron door and window frames in basement set; many of committee rooms and corridors painted.

Part of foundation laid for corridors between wings and old building. Vaulting completed under pavements for boilers, coal, etc.

"Stonework of old dome removed down to exterior cornice, 64 feet above Rotunda floor; iron-work being received, including 36 columns for peristyle; the 2½ ton brackets, on which the wall and columns of the Dome will rest, were about to be cast in Baltimore."

Work on Dome limited to completing derricks and hoisting machinery, and casting columns for peristyle, as Congress wished changes made in design. Old masonry being tested and reset.

1857. (March 4.) James Buchanan succeeded Franklin Pierce as President. [1857-1861.]

(March 7.) John B. Floyd appointed Secretary of War.

(September 10, October 10 or 16.) Thomas Crawford died in London. (F. 174.) (D.B., IV; 524.) (W.N.C. 320.) (E.B. 6; 649.) (B. 176.)

(November 30.) Annual report by Meigs. (D.H. 665-669.) (B. 131, 176.)

Boiler vaults, under outside terraces, arched over; boilers being installed.

Foundations of corridors, between wings and old building, completed, and walls of principal story under way; vestibules practically completed.

Floors laid throughout basement, and in part of principal story. Ornamental glass for skylights in Hall of Representatives not arrived.

Men working day and night on heating system for south wing; boilers were delivered one month late; this system regarded as "one of the most extensive and complete in the world" and as "of great interest to all persons engaged in the construction of public buildings in our variable climate."

Crawford's models for pediment sculpture received; mostly cut. Most of mantels completed.

Roofs closed, but had much trouble during year with leakage at eaves because cast-iron gutters had not been installed. Cast-iron door frames and window casings throughout building nearly all set.

Wood window sash and frames, completed, and set where masonry was prepared.

Storm water and sanitary drainage provided for by brick sewer, about one-half mile in length, emptying into canal southwest of Capitol.

Work progressing on the Dome; iron brackets embedded in masonry of walls to carry superstructure; ironwork being received and placed. Structure referred to as "one of the most complicated and difficult works of engineering and architecture ever attempted."

(December 13.) First meeting held in Hall of Representatives was a religious service. (B. 130.) (E.A. 5; 566.) (D.H. 704.)

(December 16.) House held first session in new Hall. (D.H. 704.) (F. 176.) (W.N.C. 315.) (B. 130.) (H. 59, 204, 218.)

(————.) Dissensions developed between Walter and Meigs. (B. 132.)

1858. (January.) Above quarrel centered on possession of drawings for Capitol. Question submitted to Secretary of War, Floyd. (B. 132-133.)

(January.) Meigs rented house on A Street for office, and ordered Walter to move with him.

Walter moved into attic rooms in old Capitol building.

Meigs accused Walter of abstracting drawings from his office. (B. 133.)

(April 17.) Meigs ordered "Columbus" bronze doors cast in Munich. (W.N.C. 320.) (F. 184.)

(April 19.) Crawford's model for statue of Freedom shipped from Leghorn, Italy. After various disasters it arrived at Bermuda, July 29, and was shipped later to New York. (F. 183.) (W.N.C. 320.)

(July 31-December 8.) Models for Rogers' "Columbus" doors shipped from Rome to Munich for casting. (B. 178.) (H. 90.)

(October 4.) Meigs obtained order from Secretary Floyd, that Walter give him "all drawings necessary to carry on the building." (B. 132.)

In reply, Walter wrote Secretary questioning intent of order, claiming that Architect's office should be place of deposit for drawings. Offered to resign if Meigs was to be in control. (B. 132-133.)

(November 15.) Meigs' annual report. (D.H. 702-709, 1011-1012.)

Heating and ventilating systems satisfactory. Acoustics excellent. Gives himself due credit for this.

Arcades of portico basements erected.

Interior decorating at a standstill because of action by Congress in prohibiting use of appropriation for that purpose until passed on by committee of artists. (B. 131.) (F. 179.)

Discusses problem of securing designs and artists for decorations of Dome; skeleton of "principal story in two stages, as high as the top of the cornice of the circular colonnade, has been finished, and the columns have all been set in their places. * * * The shell which covers this skeleton, with forms of architectural decoration, is now being prepared." He regrets that more progress has not been made, but attributes delay to "want of cordial cooperation on the part of the architect."

1859. (January 4.) Senate held first session in new Chamber. (D.H. 736.) (F.W.P. 212.) (W.N.C. 315.) (E.A. 5; 566.) (B. 131.) (H. 59, 140.)

(March 3.) A select committee reported on petition presented by the artists of the United States, asking that American artists be employed on decorations of Capitol. Petition headed by signature of Rembrandt Peale. (D.H. 729, 733-734.) (F. 185-186.) (H. 94.) (B. 173.)

(May 18.) Committee of three artists appointed by President to pass upon designs for sculpture and paintings for Capitol. Authorized by House, June 12, 1858. (D.H. 736.) (F. 179,185; 186, 187.) (B. 173.)

(August 23.) Meigs wrote to Acting Secretary of War, William R. Drinkard, regarding controversy with Walter, referring to the latter as a "Disobedient and rebellious assistant." (B. 133.)

(August 30.) Walter replied to above. (B. 134.)

(August 30.) Meigs asked Department for order to obtain drawings. (B. 134.)

Drinkard replied, did not intend to give Meigs permanent possession of drawings. (B. 134.)

(September 23.) Meigs replied, repeating charges against Walter, and objecting to Acting Secretary of War speaking for Secretary. (B. 134.)

Secretary Floyd, on returning, upheld Drinkard. (B. 134-135.)

(September 27.) Crawford's models for Senate pediment sent to West Point by Meigs. Have since disappeared, probably destroyed. (F. 199.)

(October 27.) Report by Meigs. (D.H. 736-740.) (B. 131.)

Interior nearly completed.

All stairways ready for use.

Crawford's pediment sculptures completed; set up in old Hall of Representatives, except statue of America, which was on a pedestal in eastern park.

Mrs. Crawford asked authority to complete models for bronze doors.

Coal consumed in heating and ventilating north wing twelve months preceding October 1st, 1859, was 688 tons of anthracite. Same period in south wing, 439 tons.

Rogers' bronze doors partly cast and chased in Munich. (H. 90.)

(November 1.) Meigs wrote to President Buchanan, over head of Secretary of War, asking that his letters to War Department be read by President before deciding case. (B. 135.)

(November 1.) Meigs relieved from duty in connection with public buildings. Captain W. B. Franklin, of Topographical Engineers, detailed to fill place. (D.B., XII; 507.) (B. 135.) (F. 139.)

(December 1.) Work on Capitol suspended; appropriations were withheld. (F. 190.) (B. 136.) (D.H. 781.)

1860. (February 22.) Committee on art of Capitol submitted voluminous report. (D.H. 744-749.) (B. 173.)

(February 29.) Report by Franklin. (D.H. 740-743.)

Contract cancelled for 100 monolithic marble columns from quarries at Lee, Massachusetts.

Meigs had visited many other quarries in search of source from which could be secured promptly.

(March 9.) Bill to enlarge Capitol grounds introduced in Senate. (D.H. 1067.)

(May 24.) Statue of Freedom to be cast in foundry of Clark Mills, in Bladensburg. (F. 201.) (B. 177.) (D.B., IV; 526.) (W.N.C. 320.) (F.W.P. 218.)

(June 20.) Committee on art for the Capitol abolished. (D.H. 780.) (F. 189.)

(June 25.) Senate authorized conversion of old Senate Chamber into a courtroom; the old courtroom into a law library. (H. 185-186.) (F.W.P. 226.) (D.H. 356.)

(July 1.) Work on Capitol resumed. (D.H. 781.)

(August 18.) Contract closed for 34 monolithic columns for porticoes, from Conoly's quarry, in Baltimore County, Maryland. (B. 136.) (D.H. 781.)

(November 6.) Captain Franklin reported. (D.H. 781-784, 1019-1020.) (B. 136.) (D.B., IV; 526.) (F. 190.)

Platforms of porticoes completed, ready for columns; floors and other interior work completed, excepting decorations.

Foundations for all steps laid; steps on north and south fronts set.

Mrs. Thomas Crawford to complete husband's two bronze doors.

Rogers' doors three-quarters finished.

Dome raised to height of thirty feet above colonnade; contract made for base of Dome and all above the colonnade, at a fixed price of seven cents per pound.

Data regarding Crawford's statue of Freedom.

Crawford's marble figures of Justice and History received.

(November 16.) John B. Blake, Commissioner of Buildings and Grounds, reported old Senate Chamber converted into Supreme Court Room; old Supreme Court Room into Law Library. (B. 148.)

(December.) Supreme Court first occupied old Senate Chamber. (H. 140.)

(———.) Tripoli Naval Monument removed from west approach to Naval Academy, Annapolis. (F. 15.) (B. 181.)

1861. (February 27.) Meigs ordered to resume charge of the Capitol Extension, by Secretary of War, Joseph Holt. (D.H. 785.) (B. 136.)

(March 4.) Abraham Lincoln succeeded Buchanan as President. [1861-1865.]

(April.) Meigs transferred to Gulf of Mexico; detailed J. N. Macomb to act in his place during absence. (D.H. 785.) (B. 136).

(May 15.) Work ordered suspended. Little done on Dome during year because of the Civil War. (F. 201.) (H. 60.) (W.N.C. 320.)

(————.) Contractors continued to erect ironwork a. own risk. (H. 60.)

(June 20.) Meigs advised contract with Emanuel Leutze for painting picture of "Emigration" on wall of western stairway in House wing. Felt action would give people increased confidence in Government. (F. 202.)

(July 2.) Above action approved by Simon Cameron, Secretary of War. (F. 202.)

(Summer.) Western portion of old building used as a military bakery. Capitol commandeered as a military hospital; 1,500 beds installed. (B. 137.) (D.H. 786-790.) (H. 241-243.)

(October 15.) President Lincoln ordered Army to vacate Capitol. (B. 137.)

(December 17.) Senate ordered Commissioner of Public Buildings to ascertain "by whose direction, and under what authority, a portion of the national Capitol has been converted into a baking establishment for the Army * * * also * * * the nature and extent of the injury, if any, to the Capitol building and grounds." (D.H. 787.)

(December 21.) Commissioner of Public Buildings, B. B. French, reported that it would cost $7,800 to repair the damage. He transmitted a report from the military, and denies some of the statements made. Stated that an old gas house directly west of the Capitol could be substituted at slight expense. Quoted Librarian of Congress that "continuance of the bakeries will very much injure, if not ruin, the vast and valuable collection of books." (D.H. 787-788.)

1862. (March 5.) Senate discussed a joint resolution, reported by Committee on Public Buildings and Grounds, proposing that superintendency of Capitol Extension and erection of the new Dome be transferred from War Department to Department of the Interior. (D.H. 790-808.)

(April 16.) Above transfer ordered by Congress. (D.H. 808.) (F. 208.) (B. 137.)

(April 30.) Work on Capitol resumed. (B. 137.)

Walter again placed in charge, as both Architect and Superintendent. (B. 137.)

(May 8.) Report by Walter. (D.H. 809-811, 1021-1022.)

Doors by Randolph Rogers completed, and at Munich awaiting orders from the Government.

Model for one of Crawford's doors completed; other still under way.

All porticoes and steps, of exterior, still to be constructed.

Of the 100 columns for the exterior, eleven completed, twenty-one on the ground in various stages of completion.

Interior of Extensions practically completed.

Much damage being done to both exterior and interior because of wash from unfinished walls.

Urged appropriation for completion of wings in order to save from damage finished marble, on which $115,000 in labor has been expended.

After work was ordered stopped a year before, contractors on Dome decided to go ahead, at their own risk, putting up castings that were on hand, thus handling about 1,300,000 pounds. (H. 60.)

Top of iron-work of Dome 207 feet above basement floor; 97 feet still to go.

(October 29.) Commissioner of Public Buildings, B. B. French, urged extension of Capitol grounds. (D.H. 1071-1072.)

(November 1.) Walter's report. (D.H. 815-820, 1022-1023.) (H. 64.)

Steps and cheek blocks and carriage ways on eastern porticoes set and more than half completed; all columns of connecting corridors in place; cleaning of exterior marble work begun.

Principal framework of Dome erected; ribs of cupola in place; statue of Freedom completed, and set up in grounds east of Capitol.

1863. (March.) Brumidi contracted to fresco canopy over "eye of the Dome." (F. 216.)

(November 1.) Walter's report. (D.H. 822-826, 1025-1027.) (H. 88, 90, 164.) (D.B., IV; 526.) (B. 137-138.) (E.A. 5; 566.)

Difficulty in obtaining sufficient marble, because of war conditions; copper covering of roof and cast-iron gutters unsatisfactory due to joints opening caused by expansion.

Crawford's figures for pediment of north wing in place. Models made in Italy; carving done in shops of Capitol. His figures of Justice and History, carved in Italy, in place over east door of north wing.

Plaster models for doors of north wing, completed by Rinehart, from Crawford's designs. Shipped from Rome to New York.

Bronze doors by Randolph Rogers being installed between old Hall of Representatives and south corridor.

Exterior of Dome completed, including frame of lantern; castings for inner Dome mostly on hand and partly erected.

Equipment installed for lighting the gas by Gardiner's electromagnetic gas lighting apparatus.

(December 2.) Statue of Freedom placed in position above Dome. Salutes fired from cannon at all surrounding forts. (F.W.P. 212.) (W.N.C. 320.) (E.A. 5; 566.) (D.B., IV; 526.) (H. 64.) (B. 138.) (D.H. 1025-1026.) (F. 219-222.)

1864. (March 29.) Charles F. Anderson, a competitor in 1850, claimed compensation for features of his design, used in Extension. (B. 127.) (D.B., XIX; 397.) (D.H. 833, 834-835.)

(June 29.) Question of "ventilation and acoustics of the Hall of Congress" discussed by House. (D.H. 833-838.)

(July 2.) Old Hall of Representatives ordered restored, as Statuary Hall, by act of Congress. (D.H. 361.) (F. 222-226.) (H. 228.) (W.N.C. 317.)

(November 1.) Walter reported. (D. H. 838-841, 1072-1073.) (D.B., IV; 526.) (B. 138, 166, 177.)

Eastern portico of north wing completed, with steps and stairways; plaster casts of Crawford's door for north wing arrived and being cast in bronze at Chicopee, Massachusetts. Marblework delayed by lack of workmen and of vessels to transport material.

Walter made study and plan of landscaping for Capitol grounds; urged their extension.

Experiments in progress on ventilating, heating and lighting.

1865. (February 20.) Complaint regarding ventilating system made by joint committee of the two Houses; referred to plans prepared in 1864, by Charles F. Anderson. (B. 151.)

(April 15.) Andrew Johnson succeeded Lincoln as President. [1865-1869.]

(May 26.) Walter submitted resignation, to James Harlan, Secretary of the Interior, because of cancellation by him of contracts, and of orders to Commissioner of Public Buildings to take charge of construction of public buildings in District of Columbia. (F. 243.) (B. 139-141.) (H. 60.) (W.N.C. 315.) (D.B., XIX; 397.)

(August 30.) Edward Clark appointed successor to Walter. (F. 243.) (D.H. 12.) (W.N.C. 315.) (B. 139, 143, 194.)

(November 1.) Report by Edward Clark. (D.H. 366-367, 841, 1027-1028.) (B. 143, 148.) (F. 241.)

East portico of south wing practically completed; work commenced on enlargement of Congressional Library, to include whole of west extension, old building; iron and brick substituted for wood, steam heat for hot air.

Decorations in "eye" of the Dome, completed by Brumidi. (H. 96.)

1866. (May 4 or 6.) Walter, after resignation, made report on heating. (B. 151.) (D.H. 842.)

(July 10.) Senate discussed extension of Capitol grounds. (D.H. 1074-1079.) (B. 166.)

(July 23.) A long, spirited debate in Senate on ventilation and lighting of the two halls of Congress. (D.H. 842-850.)

(November 19.) Northern and western porticoes of north wing completed. (B. 143.) (D.H. 855.)

(———.) Apparatus for lighting, by electricity, the 1,083 gas-burners in Dome, "proved a complete success." (B. 159.) (D.H. 1028.)

1867. (March 14.) Senate passed bill appropriating $20,000 "to be expended * * * in grading, filling up, removing buildings and improving the public grounds and streets around the Capitol." (D.H. 1080.)

(March 30.) Old building and all repair work placed in charge of Architect of Capitol. (Previously had been under Commissioner of Buildings and Grounds. (B. 143.)

(November 1.) Reported by Clark. (D.H. 859.) (B. 143, 147.)

Last of porticoes completed; hot-air furnaces removed from basement of old building; steam heat substituted.

Proposed that air of Halls be cooled by taking it through ducts from fountain basins in eastern grounds. Crawford's bronze doors nearly completed.

1868. (June 20.) Chairman, Committee on Buildings and Grounds recommended investigation of means for obtaining a "sufficient supply of pure air." (B. 152.)

(———.) Report by Clark. (B. 143.)

Balustrades and exterior marble-work completed; toilets installed in upper story of north wing; chimneys capped; grading done on grounds and terraces.

Recommended that one comprehensive plan be adopted for grounds of Capitol, Mall, and President's House.

(1864?) Crawford's bronze doors for Senate wing were cast at Chicopee, Massachusetts, by James T. Ames. (W.N.C. 322.) (H. 164.) (B. 177.)

1869. (March 3.) All repairs, improvements, and extensions to the Capitol building placed in charge of Architect of the Capitol extensions. (B. 143, 200.) (D.H. 865.)

(March 4.) Ulysses S. Grant succeeded Johnson as President. [1869-1877.]

All stables and temporary buildings removed from grounds, and grading continued. (B. 143.)

1870. (January 13.) Congress ordered Rogers' "Columbus" bronze doors removed to a more suitable location. (F. 230.) (H. 90.)

(January 14.) Architect of the Capitol, Edward Clark, decided on east entrance of Rotunda as suitable location for "Columbus" doors. (F. 230.) (B. 178.)

(————.) Cleaning and pointing of stonework finished, and exteriors of extensions completed; stone stairway that led from Supreme Court room removed; painting and interior decorations carried on by Brumidi; a few hot-air furnaces removed (each year) and steam heat substituted. (B. 143, 147, 148.)

1871. (March 3.) Chairman of select committee made exhaustive report on heating and ventilating. (B. 153.)

(————.) Depressed floor between Rotunda and Statuary Hall raised to level of other floors; steps of west portico relaid because of settlement of made ground. (B. 144, 148.)

(————.) "Columbus" bronze doors installed in east entrance to Rotunda. (B. 178.) (H. 90.)

1873. (1872?) (March 3.) Congress authorized purchase of two squares, north and south of Capitol, for extension of grounds; and removal of existing buildings. (D.H. 1153.) (B. 144, 166.)

(November 1.) Clark again recommended employment of landscape architect to plan grounds. (B. 144, 166.) (D.H. 1153.)

Also recommended fireproofing whole of old building. (B. 148.)

1874. (March 21-June 23.) Frederick Law Olmsted placed, by Congress, in charge of planning Capitol grounds. $200,000 appropriated for purpose. (D.H. 1156-1157, 1159.) (D.B., XIV; 26.) (B. 144, 166.) (F.W.P. 213.)

(November 1.) Clark reported. (D.H. 1159-1160.)

Greater part of eastern grounds cut down to grade of surrounding streets; worthless trees cut down, healthy ones let down and placed to suit new plan; fire-engine house removed.

Planned to replace earth embankment, which concealed basement of building on west, with a fifty-foot terrace of same material and character as structure.

(————.) Screw elevator installed in Senate wing changed to cable type because of noise. (B. 145, 159.)

1875. (September 17.) Olmsted reported. (D.H. 1162-1163.)

One hundred fifty-seven trees transplanted; parapet wall, seats, lamp posts, flower vases, etc., around east carriage court, completed.

Grading, graveling, and paving done.

Stables and workshops removed.

1876. (August 15.) Congress placed supervision and direction of Capitol building and grounds in hands of Architect of the Capitol. (F. 244.)

Hydraulic elevator substituted for cable type. (B. 159.)

Two large flues installed to conduct air into Hall of Representatives. (B. 155.)

(November 1.) Report by Clark. (D.H. 1166-1167.)

Grading of north, south, and west grounds complete.

Walks graveled or paved with concrete.

Main drives paved with macadam.

Granite curbing all set, and bluestone edging partially done.

Trees transplanted last year, in thrifty condition; sod becoming firm.

1877. (February 21.) Report on heating and ventilating Hall of Representatives submitted by special committee of government officials. Dated February 2, 1877. (B. 155.) (D.H. 892-893.)

(March 3.) Rutherford B. Hayes succeeded Grant as President. [1877-1881.]

(October 1.) Clark reported that Brumidi had under way fresco frieze of Rotunda. (F. 287.) (D.H. 369.)

(October 1.) Report by Clark. (D.H. 1170-1172.)

Intense heat of 1876 summer parched some of grass, but only two large and twenty-two small trees lost.

Thirty-three large and fifty small trees moved; one hundred Oriental plane-trees, 186 choice plants imported; 7,837 plants and trees set out. Numerous plants and shrubs removed by vandals, and some damage done by stray cattle.

1877-1879. Heating and ventilating systems reconstructed. (B. 155-156.)

1878. North portion of east park completed.

Committee appointed to investigate electricity as a substitute for gas light. (B. 145.)

1879. Three "dynamo-electric machines" installed for lighting gas jets. (D.H. 924-925.)

1880. (February 4?-February 19.) Constantino Brumidi died in Washington. (F. 288.) (B. 187, 199.) (H. 98.)
Expert reported electric arc light too insteady for legislative halls. (B. 145, 159-160.)
Costaggini continued work on frescoes begun by Brumidi. (F. 288.) (D.H. 372. (H. 99.)
Air duct and shaft completed, opened "some distance from the building on the west front." (D.H. 929.)
Summer-house and drinking fountain recommended for grounds. (D.H. 1180.)
Most of stone boundary walls completed; work progressing on walks of west front.

1881. (March 3.) Congress authorized fireproofing gallery of old House of Representatives by replacing wood construction with wood and iron. (B. 149.) (D.H. 372.)
(March 4.) James A. Garfield succeeded Hayes as President.
Space under House gallery, and north part of old building reconstructed as document rooms. (B. 149.)
(September 20.) Chester A. Arthur succeeded Garfield as President. [1881-1885.]
(October 1.) Report by Clark. (D.H. 933, 1181.) (B. 156.)
Elevator being installed in south wing.
Cold of last winter damaged trees, shrubs and pavements.
Citizens objected to use of water for sprinkling during day.
Changes in heating and ventilating systems proved satisfactory.
(October.) Olmsted wrote Clark recommending marble terraces on west, and portions of north and south fronts of Capitol to replace earth terraces. Claimed it would add effect of "stability, endurance, and repose"; also afford storage space. (B. 166.) (D.H. 1209-1211.)

1882. (January 7.) Letter from Olmsted stated "that the air of the Capitol is always, during the larger part of the year, charged with poisonous miasma" rising from "low ground lying from half a mile to a mile south."
He advised that "movement of the poison may be arrested by planting * * * the strip of land now held by the United States along the base of the Capitol Hill on the south." (D.H. 1182-1183.)
Attached was copy of a letter, dated May 23, 1879, in which he went into detail regarding protection from malarial poison. (D.H. 1183-1184.)
(June 30.) Olmsted reported. (D.H. 1184-1185.) (B. 144-145.)
All entrances completed, with walls and coping; foundations

for parapet finished; 24,000 feet of plain and 10,000 feet of mosaic artificial stone flagging laid.

Protested lack of appropriations for marble terraces.

Terraces, stairways, and other architectural features of landscaping, designed by Thomas Wisedell, under supervision of Mr. Olmsted. (B. 145, 166, 197.)

(June 30.) Olmsted urged reconstruction of terraces and western stairways. (D.H. 1217-1218.)

(August 7.) Rebuilding passenger elevator, and installing freight elevator in Senate wing, approved by Senate. (D.H. 938.) (B. 159.)

1883. (March 1.) Senate discussed appropriation for above. (D.H. 1218-1227.)

(July 1.) Clark reported that north approach had been built, and southern approach approved by Congress. (D.H. 1227.)

(September 27.) Estimates on terraces, approaches, and improvement of grounds, submitted by Clark and Olmsted. (D.H. 1228-1230.)

1884. (February 6.) During one of the numerous discussions on the terraces and stairways, an interview with Olmsted (from the *Evening Star*) was read into the Record. This gave much data regarding proposed improvements to grounds, including terraces and stairs. (D.H. 1230-1236.)

1885. (March 4.) Grover Cleveland succeeded Arthur as President. [1885-1889.]

Incandescent lights installed in cloak rooms, lobbies, and stairways. (B. 145, 160.)

Arc lights on the exterior deemed undesirable, as attracted insects. (B. 145, 160.)

(July 1.) Olmsted resigned. (B. 166.)

1886. North approach and terrace completed. (B. 145.)

(July 24.) Senate considered appropriation of $5,000 for gilding statue of Freedom. Rejected. (D.H. 1030-1031.)

(August 4.) Incandescent lights ordered installed in Senate extension wing. (B. 145.) (D.H. 939.)

1887. (March 3.) Appropriation made for completion of terraces and west stairways. Amount $330,000. (D.H. 1262.)

(October 30.) Thomas U. Walter died. (B. 193.) (D.B. XIX; 397.) (E.A. 28; 249.)

1888. 200 incandescent lights installed in House wing. (B. 145, 160.)

An additional elevator placed in each wing. (B. 145, 159.) (D.H. 954-955.)

1889. (March 4.) Benjamin Harrison succeeded Cleveland as President. [1889-1893.]
A tower built 200 feet west of Senate wing for fresh air inlet. (B. 155.) (H. 245.) (D.H. 955, 957.)

1889-1891. Lighting installations extended. (B. 146, 160.)

1890. (July 1.) Stonework and committee rooms of principal terrace mostly finished. (B. 145, 166-167.)

1891. Electric bells installed in committee rooms and offices. (B. 146.)
(July 5.) Exhaustive report on sanitary condition of Capitol received from Col. George E. Waring, Dr. A. C. Abbot, and Col. John S. Billings. (D.H. 965-970.) (B. 146.)
Senate kitchen extended under pavement of court; coal vaults built under pavement east of building. (B. 149.) (D.H. 970.)

1892. (January 2.) Meigs died in Washington. (B. 198.) (D.B., XII; 507.)
(January 15.) Rogers died in Rome. (F. 153.) (D.B., XVI; 107.)

1892-1893. (———.) Modern plumbing installed. (B. 146.)

1893. (March 4.) Grover Cleveland again became President. [1893-1897.]
(September 18.) Centennial celebration of original corner-stone laying. (B. 149.)

1895. (———.) Electric bells installed to summon pages. (B. 146.) (D.H. 971-989.)

1896. (———.) Installation of electric lighting plant (authorized in 1895), completed. (D.H. 971.) (B. 146, 160.)
(———.) House restaurant enlarged. (B. 149.)

1897. (March 4.) William McKinley succeeded Cleveland as President. [1897-1901.]
(July 1.) Report by Clark. (D.H. 972.) (B. 150, 156-158.)
Heating and ventilating system of Senate wing, including Supreme Court room, remodeled in accordance with plans prepared by Prof. S. H. Woodbridge of Institute of Technology, Boston. Woodwork of floor and gallery replaced by light iron framework, covered with air-tight wood floor. Space beneath used as plenum chamber. Outlets for air provided near desks, and through legs of gallery chairs. Similar changes recommended for Hall of Representatives.
(November 16.) Report of Cornelius N. Bliss, Secretary of the Interior. (D.H. 972-973.)
Changes in Senate ventilating and heating system of Hall of Representatives made, as reported July 1, including also Senate restaurant.
Similar changes in House again recommended.

Electric lighting system of Capitol extended.

Library of Congress moved to new building. (H. 134.) (F.W.P. 266.)

(————.) Electric lights substituted for gas over glass ceilings of both chambers. (D.H. 973, 1200.) (B. 146, 160.)

100 arc lights substituted for gas in Capitol grounds. (D.H. 1200.) (B. 160.)

1898. (November 6.) Explosion and fire damaged portions of Senate wing. (B. 171.) (D.H. 376-377.)

1899. (December.) or 1900. (June 6.) Space formerly occupied by Library ordered remodeled. (D.H. 377-396.)

1900. (July 1.) Report by Clark. (D.H. 973-974.)

Recommended that heating and ventilating system of Hall of Representatives be reconstructed on same principles as Senate Chamber. Special attention to be given House kitchen and restaurant. Gallery benches to be replaced by chairs. This will also prevent crowding.

1901. (March 3.) Act passed, providing for "improving the ventilation of the Hall of Representatives and the corridors adjacent thereto, including new floor for the Hall * * * ventilation of the House restaurant and kitchen * * * refurnishing the Hall * * * the Speaker's rooms, and the office of the Sergeant-at-Arms" and metal furniture for new committee rooms in old library section; also refitting file room of House with metal fire-proof cases. (D.H. 974-975, 987-989.)

(July 1.) Clark reported; space formerly occupied by Library of Congress remodeled into three stories; first and second divided into rooms as directed by House and Senate; marble vestibule built from west Rotunda entrance to new corridor; third floor to be Reference library. (D.H. 396-402.)

(Early in year.) Committee authorized by Congress to study "development and improvement of the park system of the District of Columbia." Action secured by Senator James McMillan, of Michigan. (F.W.P. 95.)

(September 14.) Theodore Roosevelt became President at death of McKinley. [1901-1909.]

(December 3.) Lengthy report by Elliot Woods, acting Architect on work done in improving ventilation in Hall of Representatives; refurnishing same with 400 mahogany desks and chairs, and other necessary features. Desks built segmental in plan to save space. (D.H. 981-987.)

1902. (January.) Report submitted on development of park system. Usually referred to as "The McMillan Plan." (F.W.P. 95.)

(January 6 [February 6?]) Edward Clark died in Washington after fifty-one years of employment on architectural work for the Government. (F. 243.) (B. 194.)

(February 19.) Elliott Woods appointed Architect of the Capitol. (F. 243.)

(July 1.) Woods reported: Roof of old building reconstructed and fireproofed; also ceilings of Supreme Court and Statuary Hall. Echoes preserved in latter by accurately reproducing original contour of ceiling. (D.H. 405-406.)

(July 1.) Report by Woods. (D.H. 981-987.)

Lengthy, detailed report on ventilating, heating, refurnishing, and refitting various rooms in House wing.

1903. (August 28.) Frederick Law Olmsted died. (B. 196.) (D.B., XIV; 24.)

1905. (Autumn.) Bronze doors of south wing installed. (W.N.C. 324.)

1907. (April 13.) Filippo Costaggini died at Upper Falls, Baltimore County, Maryland. (F. 290.)

1908. (November.) Greenough's statue of Washington removed from the Capitol to the Smithsonian Institution. (F. 103.) (Br., II; 329.)

1909. Paul W. Bartlett awarded commission for modeling figures for pediment of south wing. (F. 480.) (D.B., II; 12.)

(February 11.) Charles E. Fairman entered office of Architect of the Capitol.

(March 4.) William Howard Taft succeeded Roosevelt as President. [1909-1913.]

1916. (August 2.) Sculptures of pediment on south wing unveiled. (F. 480.) (D.B., II; 12.)

1923. (May 22.) Elliott Woods died. (F. 244.)

(August 22.) David Lynn appointed Architect of the Capitol. (F. 244.)

Duties of Architect of the Capitol expanded widely; and great amount of construction and supervision done under direction of David Lynn.

1930. (June 6.) Charles E. Fairman continued in service as Art Curator, after reaching age of retirement, by special act of Congress.

1923-1939. Work executed under direction of David Lynn: See pages 254, 257.

BIBLIOGRAPHY

Bartlett, Dr. G. Hunter "Andrew and Joseph Ellicott." Publication of the Buffalo Historical Society. 1922.

Bennett, Wells "Stephen Hallet and His Designs for the National Capitol, 1791-94." The Journal of the American Institute of Architects. 1916.

Brown, Glenn "Dr. William Thornton, Architect." The Architectural Record, New York. (July, 1896.)

Brown, Glenn *History of the United States Capitol.* Two volumes. Government Printing Office. 1900.

Bryan, Wilhelmus Bogart *History of the National Capitol from its Foundation through the Period of the Adoption of the Organic Act.* In two volumes. New York. 1914-16.

Bulfinch, Miss Ellen S. *The Life and Letters of Charles Bulfinch.* Houghton, Mifflin and Company. 1896.

Caemmerer, H. P. *Washington, the National Capital.* Government Printing Office. 1932.

Columbian Historical Society, Records of. In thirty-two volumes. 1897-1935.

Dictionary of American Biography. Twenty volumes. Charles Scribner's Sons, New York. 1928-1937.

Dunlap, William *History of the Arts of Design in the United States.* Two volumes. George P. Scott and Company. 1834.

Encyclopedia Americana. Americana Corporation. New York and Chicago. 1926.

Encyclopedia Britannica. Fourteenth Edition. 1929.

Fairman, Charles E. *Art and Artists of the Capitol of the United States of America.* Government Printing Office. 1927.

Federal Writers' Project. *Washington, City and Capital.* Government Printing Office. 1937.

Ford, Paul Leicester *The Writings of Thomas Jefferson.* G. P. Putnam's Sons, New York and London. 1895.

Gallagher, H. M. Pierce *Robert Mills, Architect of the Washington Monument.* Columbia University Press.

Government Printing Office *Documentary History of the Construction and Development of the United States Capitol Building and Grounds.* Washington. 1904.

Hazelton, George C., Jr. *The National Capitol: Its Architecture, Art, and History.* J. J. Little and Company, New York. 1897.

Howard, James Q. "The Architects of the American Capitol." International Review, Volume I. (1874.) A. S. Barnes and Company, New York.

Jusserand, J. J. *With Americans of Past and Present Days.* Charles Scribner's Sons, New York. 1916.

Kimball, Fiske *Thomas Jefferson, Architect.* The Riverside Press, Cambridge. 1916.

Kimball, Fiske "The Origin of the Plan of Washington, D. C." The Architectural Review, Volume VII, pp. 41-45.

Kimball, Fiske and Bennett, Wells. "William Thornton and the Design of the United States Capitol." Art Studies, Volume One. The American Journal of Archaeology. Princeton University Press. 1923.

Kite, Elizabeth S. *L'Enfant and Washington, 1791-1792.* The Johns Hopkins Press, Baltimore. 1929.

Latrobe, B. Henry Correspondence with John Lenthal. Unpublished manuscript in possession of Hamilton Abert.

Latrobe, Benjamin Henry *The Journal of Latrobe.* D. Appleton and Company. 1905.

Lipscomb and Bergh *The Writings of Thomas Jefferson.* Thomas Jefferson Memorial Association, Washington, D. C. 1905.

Manuscripts and Reports in the Library of Congress, and various departments of the Government at Washington.

Mills, Robert *Guide to the Capitol of the United States.* Washington, D. C. 1834.

Mills, Robert *Guide to the National Executive Offices and Capitol of the United States.* Washington, D. C. P. Force, Printer. 1841.

Moore, Charles *Washington, Past and Present.* New York. 1929.

Peets, Elbert "The Genealogy of L'Enfant's Washington." Journal of the American Institute of Architects, Volume XV.

Place, Charles A. *Charles Bulfinch: Architect and Citizen.* Houghton, Mifflin Company. 1925.

Porter, J. A. *The City of Washington, Its Origin and Administration.* In Johns Hopkins University Studies, Volume III. Baltimore. 1885.

Proctor, John Claggett; Williams, Edwin Melvin; Black, Frank P. *Washington, Past and Present.* Five volumes. New York. 1930.

Townsend, George Alfred *Washington, Outside and Inside.* J. Betts and Company, Hartford, Connecticut. 1878.

Willard, Ashton R. "Charles Bulfinch." New England Magazine. (November, 1890.)

INDEX

Abbe Correa de Serra, 58.
Aberdeen University, 29.
Abert, Hamilton, vi.
Abert, Hamilton, 159.
Academie des Sciences et Beaux Arts, 41.
Accademia di San Luca, Rome, 210, 211.
Acoustics of Hall, 72; Strickland and Mills, advisors on; experiments in correcting, 147.
Adams, Mrs. John, comments on city, 57, 58.
Adams, John Quincy, 149.
Adams, Samuel, 136.
Agricultural Committee-room, 230.
Alexandria, in District, 5; church at, 77.
Alexandria Masonic Lodge, 37.
American Biography, Dictionary of, vi.
American Institute of Architects, 53, 203, 238.
American Institution of Architecture, The, 203.
American Philosophical Society, 17, 203.
Anas, Jefferson's, 3, 4, 5.
Andrei, Giovanni, 86; sent to Italy, 96, 112; arrived, 108; capitals for Hall; criticized by Latrobe, 110.
Antonelli, Cardinal, 210.
Antes, Ann Margaret, married Benjamin Latrobe, 61-62.
Apthorp, Hannah, married Bulfinch 136.
Arc lights installed; unpopular 238.
Arches collapsed, Lenthal killed, 72.
Architects of the Capitol appointed: Dr. William Thornton, 33; Benjamin Henry Latrobe, 61; Charles Bulfinch, 141; Thomas Ustick Walter, 175; Edward Clark, 237; Elliott Woods, 252; David Lynn, 252.
Architect of Capitol; office abolished, 153; presidential appointee, 215.
Architectural handbooks, 21.
Architecture, domestic, understood by master builders, 21; essential in a Virginian's education, 17.
Art and Artists of the Capitol, by Charles E. Fairman, vi.
Ashland, Henry Clay's house, 95.
Assumption for war debts, 4, 5.

Bacon, Senator Nathaniel, 127.
Baltimore, Cathedral at, 80; Cathedral Exchange, supervised by Latrobe, 104; St. Paul's Church, Battle Monument, Washington Monument, 123-125; Mills planned utilities, railroads, waterworks, 172.
Bank of Pennsylvania, 63-64.
Bartlett, Paul W., 232-233.
Bartolini, Lorenzo, 226.
Battle Monument, Washington Monument, 123-125.
Biddle, Nicholas, 201.
Blagden, George, 161-162.
Blodgett's Hotel, Patent Office, Post Office Department, 51; Congress met in, 95.
Blodgett, Samuel, 35.

Bonanni, Pietro, portrait by, 113.
Boneval de la Trobe, Henri, 61.
Bordeaux, letter to, 25.
Botanic Gardens, 254.
Braddock, General, 58.
Brentwood, 55.
Bridport, decorated Dome, 76.
British held L'Enfant, 8; threaten Patent Office, 51.
British minister, commented on city, 59.
British officer, admired House, 76.
Brodeau, Mrs. Ann, 29.
Brown, Glenn, *History of the United States Capitol,* v.
Brown, H. K., 228.
Brumidi, Constantino, 206, 210.
Brush-Swann Company, 238.
Buffalo, founded by Joseph Ellicott, 15.
"Builders Guides," 22.
Bulfinch, vii.
Bulfinch, Charles, built east steps, 77; letter re: sculpture on east pediment, 116; life and works, 133-137; arrived in Washington; letter to wife; ordered model of Capitol; began work on central portion; designed Dome, 141-143; varied west front, 145; salary cut, 149; report to Elgar, 149, 151; letter from Elgar, 153; services terminated, 153; left Washington; designed Unitarian Church; penitentiary; State House, Maine; deaths of Bulfinch and wife, 155; designed gate lodges, 250.
Bulfinch, Charles, Life of, vi.
Building curtailed by War of 1812, 92.
Builders, importation of; few available, 22.
Bunker Hill Monument, 172.
Burnham, Daniel H., 11.
"Burr, Little," 75.

Cabot, Mr., 22.
California State Commission, 250.
Callan, County Kilkenny, Ireland, 27.
Camden, South Carolina, 172.
Camuccini, Baron, 210.
Canova, Antonio, 108, 210.
Capellano, Antonio, 123-125.
Capitol Building, Documentary History of, vi.
Capital City, possible location on Delaware River; at Germantown; at Baltimore; at Wilmington; near Hancock Town; at New York; on Potomac; at Annapolis; near Mount Vernon; at Philadelphia, 1, 2; Commission to choose site, 1; for South, 4; on Potomac, 5; to be planned by L'Enfant, 6; Commissioners purchase land for, 6.
Capitals, ordered from Italy, 96.
Capitol, competition for, 19; drawings rejected, 25; drawings in Maryland Historical Society, 27; corner stone laid, 37; Capitol, faced west, 76; East steps built by Bulfinch, 77; semicircular colonnade

324   INDEX

Union Terminal, passenger traffic concentrated in, 12.
Unitarian Church, Washington, 155.
United States Capitol, History of, by Glenn Brown, v.
United States Lighting Company, 238.
U. S. Post Office and U. S. Patent Office designed by Mills, 173.
University of Lewisburg, Pennsylvania, 203.
University of Michigan, Rogers' models at, 227.
Upjohn, Richard, 203.

Valaperti, Giuseppe, 125-127.
Valley Forge, L'Enfant at, 8.
Van Ness mausoleum, 45.
Van Ness, John P., 95.
Versailles, 8.
Vestibule, circular, replaced Great Staircase, 81.
Vicenza, Villa Rotunda, 27.
Virginia Capitol, designed by Jefferson, 17; exterior completed by Latrobe, 64.
Virginia, offered area for District, 2.
Virginia penitentiary, designed by Latrobe, 64.

Wadsworth, Colonel, 23.
Walter, Deborah, 201.
Walter, Joseph S., 201.
Walter, Thomas, vii.
Walter, Thomas U., appointed architect of extension, 175; quarrelled with Meigs; offered resignation, 187; sustained by Floyd, 187, 189; difficulty securing marble, 194; resigned, 196, 198; life and works of, 201, 203, 206; Clark in employ of, 237; planned landscaping, 240.
War between States, 189.
"War," by Persico, 116.
War debts, 3.
War of 1812, curtailed building, 92, 111-112.
Washington, City of, planned as Capital, 1; appearance of in 1800, 55; commented on, 57-59; movement to transfer seat of government, 58-59, 95.
Washington Hall, Philadelphia, 172.
Washington Monument, Baltimore, 123, 125, 171.

Washington Monument, Richmond, 172, 216, 222.
Washington Monument, Washington, 11, 172.
Washington, President, wished Capital to be near Mount Vernon, 2; agrarian life, 4; invited Jefferson to be Secretary of State, 4; appointed commissioners, 5; chose L'Enfant, 6; portrait by L'Enfant, 8; confidence in L'Enfant, 9; alterations in L'Enfant's plan, 13; report from Ellicott, 14; as architect, 17; friend of Ellicott, 17; feared shortage of workmen, 23; commended Thornton's design, 31, 33; ordered conference, 34; letter to Jefferson, 35; Trumbull introduced Thornton to, 31; letter to commissioners, 33; Washington, laid corner stone, 37.
Washington Statue, by Greenough, 128, 130.
Washington Statue, Raleigh, North Carolina, 125.
Water supply, inadequate; Tiber creek and canal, wells, as sources; surveys to locate, 162; report on near-by springs, 163; plan to include "grand basin"; Tiber Creek, Rock Creek, 164; report by Mills, 164; appropriation 165; spring purchased, 165-166; second report from Mills, 166.
Waverley, Massachusetts, 250.
West Point, L'Enfant refused professorship, 10; Ellicott accepted professorship, 15.
White, Alexander, reported on dome above vestibule, 46, 48.
Widow's Mite, 6.
Wilcox, Miss Ruth, vii.
Willard, prepared model of Capitol, 141.
William and Mary College, Jefferson at, 17; degree to Andrew Ellicott, 17.
Wilmington considered for Capital, 2.
Wirt, Bulfinch's salary cut, 149.
Wisedell, Thomas, 249.
Woodlawn, 55.
Woolcott, Oliver, 57.
Workmen, shortage of, feared, 22; available in Connecticut, 23; sought in Bordeaux, 25.
Woods, Elliott, 252.
Wyatt, James, 44.

Yosemite Reservation, 250.
Young lady, commented on city, 57.